NETAJI

'He [Subhas Chandra Bose] would never bow to a Japanese no matter how high a dignitary he might be. He was always calm and resolute. There was determination in the straight line of his lips. There was sincerity sparkling in his eyes. And finally there was faith written in invisible letters on the furrows of his forehead.

'And what was that faith? It was his faith that India would be free. It was his faith that Indians were brave soldiers. It was his faith that from the Indians in the Far East he could raise an army which would shed their last drop of blood to free India. And finally it was his faith that a strong Indian National Army would march to this noble goal, without the help of any outside Power.

'When I saw all these things which I had been longing to see, instantaneously I decided to offer myself to Netaji – my body and my soul. I realized that there was no greater honour for an Indian than to march under the banner of a man like Netaji. And further that there was no loftier ideal in life than to rescue four hundred million from the iron heel of British Imperialism.'

From 'Shahnawaz: A Born Prince' in
Meet the Heroes *by Jag Paresh Chandra*

• FOREWORD BY PT. JAWAHARLAL NEHRU •

MY MEMORIES OF I.N.A. & ITS
NETAJI

MAJOR GENERAL SHAHNAWAZ KHAN

FOREWORD TO THE NEW EDITION PROF. SUGATA BOSE

ROLI

First published in 1946
This edition published by Roli Books in India, 2025

ISBN: 9789349474611

Roli Books Pvt. Ltd.
M-75, Greater Kailash II Market, New Delhi 110 048
Phone: +91 (011) 40682000
E-mail: info@rolibooks.com
www.rolibooks.com
Also at Chennai & Mumbai

Image Credit – Alamy (Pages 2, 3 (above left & below), 4–5)

Front Cover: Subhas Chandra Bose with A. C. Chatterjee, M. Z. Kiani and Habibur Rahman (*standing left to right*)
Cover Design: Shaikh Shahid Hussain

Typeset in Sabon LT Std by Roli Books Pvt. Ltd

Contents

FOREWORD
To the edition published in 1946
Jawaharlal Nehru

When we were in Ahmednagar prison, we had heard vaguely about the formation of an Indian National Army in Malaya. We knew very little about it. Indeed very few people in India knew much about it at the time. Soon after our release from prison in June 1945, I had some further news and particulars about the formation of this army. I was naturally interested, but the Japanese war was going on then and I did not think it proper to say anything in public about what I had heard. Soon after, the Japanese war ended and I thought the time had come to make public reference to this army.

My knowledge even then was limited and I was not quite sure in my mind as to how far the formation and activities of this army had been justified, keeping in view the wider scheme of things and the implications of the World War. But I had no doubt in my mind even then of two facts – that the men and women who had enrolled themselves in this army and worked under Shri Subhas Chandra Bose's guidance had done so because of their passionate desire to serve the cause of India's freedom; also that if, owing to some technical interpretation of military law, large numbers of them received severe sentences, it would be a tragedy for India. It would be a tragedy not only because that might involve the death or long incarceration of brave and vital sons and daughters of India, but also because that would leave a deep wound in the body of India which would take very long to heal. That would mean also an intensification of the ill-will against England which was great already. It might well be an inseparable barrier between the two countries.

So quite apart from the political background, I was convinced that everything should be done to save these young men and women. I had judged rightly, for immediately there was an amazing reaction in the whole of India and even the remote villages suddenly knew about the I.N.A. and wanted to do something which might help in effecting the release of the men being tried or imprisoned. Those men, whatever they were as individuals, became symbols of India's struggle for freedom and because of this, the people of India, with an amazing unanimity, stood by those symbols and sought to protect them. A wave of excitement passed through the land and every other question, more vital in its larger significance, became secondary for the moment. The trial of some of these men conducted with great ability by Shri Bhulabhai Desai held the stage in India and Shri Bhulabhai's final address became a classic.

Public memory is notoriously short and in any event the public mind could not function at that pitch for long. Nevertheless, the I.N.A. made history not only in Malaya and Burma and elsewhere but also in people's minds all over India, and that fact will endure. When the passions of the day have cooled down, a very objective estimate of the I.N.A. and its leaders and the work it did will be made. Many books have already come out on this subject reflecting the excitement of the moment. Perhaps it is too early to survey the work of the I.N.A. dispassionately. Opinions will differ about the political aspects of much that was done. But, however that may be, it is desirable to know the facts at least. My friend and colleague, Major General Shahnawaz Khan of the I.N.A., has presented these facts in sober fashion, and has thus provided an important record of an important undertaking.

I must confess that I have not been able, through lack of time, to read through this record, but I have read parts of it and it seems to me that this account is by far the best we have at present. I commend it, therefore, to others and I hope that a reading of it will bring enlightenment about many aspects of this brave adventure. JAI HIND.

New Delhi
10 October 1946

FOREWORD
To the edition published in 2025
Prof. Sugata Bose

'When Netaji arrived in Singapore [in July 1943],' Shahnawaz Khan narrated at the Red Fort trial in November 1945, 'I watched him very keenly. I heard a number of his public speeches, which had a profound effect on me. It will not be wrong to say that I was hypnotized by his personality and his speeches. He placed the true picture of India before us, and for the first time in my life I saw India through the eyes of an Indian.' Until that transformative moment Shahnawaz had been interested only in soldiering and sport. Many in his clan of Janjua Rajputs from Rawalpindi in Punjab had served in the British Indian Army. Netaji challenged him to choose whether to owe allegiance to 'the King or the country'. 'I decided to be loyal to my country,' Shahnawaz testified at his court-martial, 'and I gave my word of honour to my Netaji that I would sacrifice myself for her sake.'*

---

*   Quoted in Sugata Bose, *His Majesty's Opponent: Subhas Chandra Bose and India's Struggle against Empire* (The Belknap Press of Harvard University Press, 2011, 2022), pp. 8-9.

For taking this decision Shahnawaz was put on trial along with Prem Kumar Sahgal and Gurbaksh Singh Dhillon on the charge of waging war against the King-Emperor. During the trial in November and December 1945, the story of the saga of Netaji and his Indian National Army reached every corner of India. The Indian people expressed themselves forcefully on the side of Netaji's soldiers. The slogan 'Lal Qile se aayee awaz, Sahgal, Dhillon, Shahnawaz' reverberated across the length and breadth of the country. On 31 December 1945 at the Red Fort, the three were found guilty and sentenced to deportation for life, the same punishment that had been handed to Bahadur Shah Zafar in 1858. Within three days, on 3 January 1946, the British Commander-in-Chief Claude Auchinleck was forced to release Sahgal, Dhillon, and Shahnawaz to a heroes' welcome from the Indian public. Netaji and his I.N.A. had successfully undermined the loyalty of Indian soldiers to their British colonial masters and replaced it with a new devotion to the cause of free India.

Shahnawaz wrote his book *My Memories of I.N.A. and its Netaji* during the tumultuous days of 1946. He did so 'in the method and language of a soldier.' Yet this soldier of freedom opened with an evocative chapter on Netaji and 'a strange influence' that his leader exercised over him. He revered his Netaji as a man, a soldier, and a statesman. 'His was a personality,' Shahnawaz writes, 'which captivated everyone who met him, even foreigners. It was he and he alone who welded all Indians in East Asia into one unit and created a feeling of friendship and harmony among the nations of the East and its people. He was greatly loved and esteemed not as a sacred deity but as a man, as a hero, as a friend, and as a comrade.'

Netaji named three regiments or brigades of the first division of the I.N.A. commanded by Mohammad Zaman

Kiani after Gandhi, Nehru, and Azad. Once a guerrilla regiment was formed drawing on some of the finest soldiers of the three brigades, its members decided to call it the Subhas Brigade despite being forbidden by Netaji to do so. It is this brigade of the I.N.A. of which Shahnawaz Khan was put in command. In this book the author gives a factual account of the training of this brigade in Taiping, Malaya, from September 1943 onwards and its advance to Burma (present-day Myanmar) in late November 1943. He describes the brave actions of the Subhas Brigade on the Haka Falam front in the spring of 1944, especially the excellent service of a young major Mehboob Ahmed, before moving the main body of this brigade towards Ukhrul and hoisting the Indian tricolour on the mountain tops around Kohima in May 1944. The attack on Mowdok by Major Raturi, the touching scene of I.N.A. soldiers kissing the soil of their motherland and singing the national anthem '*Subh Sukh chain ki*' with great gusto are all described in vivid detail.

In addition to military facts, Shahnawaz supplies fine insights into the forging of national unity by Netaji and his I.N.A. He notes that 'the most ardent supporters and admirers of Netaji were found among Muslims.' The leader 'respected every man for what he was worth' and not based on his religious or provincial identity. The Nagas, Shahnawaz records, 'were most helpful to our troops.' They bitterly recalled the humiliation heaped by the British on their queen. 'All that we would like to have,' they assured Shahnawaz, 'is our own Raja, Netaji Subhas Chandra Bose.' Describing a battle of the Gandhi Brigade against the Seaforth Highlanders on the outskirts of Imphal, Shahnawaz notes that most of the I.N.A. troops taking part in that action were 'raw Tamil recruits from Malaya' who 'acquitted themselves most creditably and smashed the British theory of martial and non-martial classes.'

After the INA's march towards Delhi was halted in Imphal and Kohima, Shahnawaz recounts the remarkable fortitude shown by I.N.A. soldiers and their leader during battles in Burma until the spring of 1945. Perhaps most moving is his telling of the breakout from being trapped in Meiktila towards Pyinmina on 26 February 1945:

> Everyone looked cheerful. One thing was certain, the enemy would never capture us alive. When we entered the car and started off, Netaji was sitting with a loaded Tommy gun in his lap. Raju had two hand grenades ready. The Japanese officer was holding on to another Tommy gun and I had a loaded Bren gun in my hand. We were all ready to open fire instantaneously.

On reaching Pyinmina, Netaji expressed his desire to 'fight his last battle against the British there'. Shahnawaz was eventually captured by the British near Pegu on 18 May 1945, after Netaji had made his epic retreat from Burma to Thailand on foot with some of his officers, soldiers, and women of the Rani of Jhansi Regiment. The Red Fort trial would turn their military defeat into a spectacular political victory.

Shahnawaz's 1946 book that has been out of print deserves to be brought before the public eye in this new edition. It served as a valuable source for the writing of my chapter 'Roads to Delhi' in my book *His Majesty's Opponent: Subhas Chandra Bose and India's Struggle against Empire*. Shahnawaz's memoir can be read with profit alongside S. A. Ayer's *Unto Him A Witness*, Mohammad Zaman Kiani's *India's Freedom Struggle and the Great INA*, 'Abid Hasan's Eye-Witness Account' in Krishna Bose's *Netaji: Subhas Chandra Bose's Life, Politics and Struggle*, and other memoirs of men and women of the I.N.A. meticulously curated by Dr. Sisir Kumar Bose over the decades at Netaji Research Bureau. Ten years after writing this book Shahnawaz Khan performed another signal service in 1956 by chairing the committee that collected relevant evidence and reached the correct conclusion about the tragic mortal end of Netaji on 18 August 1945.

To conclude on a personal note, I had the privilege of meeting Shahnawaz Khan in the 1960s and early '70s during his visits to Netaji Bhawan in Kolkata. At that time, he was working with my father Dr. Sisir Kumar Bose to ensure the welfare of surviving veterans of the Indian National Army and give due recognition to their sterling contribution to India's freedom. As Shahnawaz Khan writes poignantly: 'In those streams of blood of the soldiers of the Indian National Army, the blood of Hindus, Muslims, Sikhs and Christians intermingled and flowed freely for one cause – a great, free and united India.'

Gardiner Professor of History
Harvard University
2024

PREFACE

An authentic account of the Indian National Army (I.N.A.) will constitute a glorious chapter in the history of the struggle for the liberation of India from foreign domination. It is abundantly clear that no trial in India either by court martial or in the civil courts attracted so much attention as the first I.N.A. trial. After my release, I had an opportunity to travel a good deal throughout India and everywhere I went I found the Indian people anxious to know more about the I.N.A. and its Netaji. Impelled, therefore, by a burning desire to put down what I knew, I have undertaken to narrate the entire and an absolutely uncoloured story of I.N.A. in the method and language of a soldier.

I felt the urgency for this all the more when I saw that some authors in their eagerness to be first in the market, both in vernacular and in English, have written books on the I.N.A. without having any real knowledge of it, with the result that the narrative remained incomplete and unconvincing. In addition to this, there were certain very other important aspects of the I.N.A. which were either never touched upon, or were only brought out very inadequately during the court martial. These were the brilliant achievements of our so many thousand brothers who lived, moved and had their being in the movement during the most fateful and eventful period of three years and eight months, under the inspiring guidance and dynamic leadership of Netaji Subhas Chandra Bose. The history of these achievements is as fascinating as soul-lifting.

This book would enable people to view the Movement in proper perspective. It will dispel many a doubts and many a mistrust which they entertained in their minds. This book would also reveal that from time to time it was made clear by people in authority that the plan and the programme of the Independence Movement was directed to be in line with the aims and intentions of Indian National Congress.

In the pages of this book I have also endeavoured to give my readers an idea of my leader as a man, a statesman and a General.

My grateful thanks are to Sjt. Pandit Jawahar Lal Nehru, Vice-President of the Interim Government who has written a foreword for this book. I am also thankful to Sjt. Kalyan Sen, and other nephews and nieces of Netaji for their encouragement given to write this book.

I trust the public would read this book with interest.

Shahnawaz Khan
2, Windsor Place
New Delhi

CHAPTER ONE

'NETAJI'

It is indeed a very difficult task, nay almost an impossible one for a humble person like me, to attempt to depict a true picture of Netaji, who would certainly go down in history as one of the greatest men India has ever produced.

I have been asked by several friends to give a true picture of Netaji as I saw him. The attempt I am making would probably be unworthy of the glory of my great leader. Nevertheless, I would request my readers to forgive me for this failing for Netaji was such a great man and I, a humble soldier. How can I then describe him adequately?

I must frankly confess that from the moment I came into personal contact with him he exercised a strange influence over me. Even now I do not know in what proportion the man, the soldier and the statesman in him were blended. At home, the man in him seemed to dominate, at the front and in the midst of his troops, the soldier in him shone in splendid glory, and in the councils and conferences and at his desk, as Head of the State of the Provisional Government of Azad Hind, his brilliant statesmanship made a profound impression on one and all of us.

As I have described elsewhere, I was one of those officers who were brought up in a military atmosphere with a loyalty to the British Crown. Ever since the start of the first I.N.A., I had been fighting against it, as I felt all along that the Japanese were exploiting us, and at heart I was an admirer of the British people. Therefore, when Netaji arrived, I watched him very keenly. What impressed me most about him was his absolute devotion to his country. To secure the independence of India, he was prepared to make any sacrifice. He held the independence of his motherland above everything else in the world.

It is essential to know a man in order to understand his work and I have known Netaji for the entire period he was in East Asia. I was with him in Singapore; then I moved with him to Burma, where we stayed together for nearly a year and a half. It is beyond my power and ability to describe one who was so unique in his qualities. All his qualities are abundantly clear from the respect he received from Indians in East Asia. His was a personality which captivated everyone who met him, even foreigners. It was he and he alone who welded all Indians in East Asia into one unit and created a feeling of friendship and harmony among the nations of the East and its people. He was greatly loved and esteemed not as a sacred deity but as a man, as a hero, as a friend, and as a comrade. What was the secret of this abounding love and profound respect which the masses had for him? Why was he acclaimed as the undisputed leader of Indians in East Asia? It was because he was a man of courage, character and generous impulses.

As a man, he was a good friend and kind companion. He was the leader of Indians in East Asia and yet he was unassuming. He lived a very austere life; he worked very hard and shared with his comrades their sufferings. He took great care of them and saw to it that they were looked after. He went into the details of every matter, big or small, and took pleasure in helping the needy. He despised pomp and grandeur.

At first we were sceptical about Netaji's relations with the Japanese. We had seen how they had behaved with the people of Malaya and Burma, and quite frankly, we did not trust them. They also behaved in an unbecoming and rather a treacherous manner with General Mohan Singh. We were anxious to see how they would behave towards Netaji and how he would react to their behaviour. Very soon we found out that Netaji was not the person who would ever bow down before anyone or sell the honour of his country for any price.

His frankness was another quality which won the hearts of his officers and men alike. One day, some officers asked Netaji to explain to us exactly where we stood with the Japanese. He told us that the Japanese realized that as long as the British held India, and could use it as a base of supply and operation against them, they would never be safe; and that, in their own interests, the Japanese must drive the British out of India, otherwise they themselves would be driven out of East Asia. He said that the Japanese by assisting Indians were doing no favour to them. We were helping them as much as they were helping us. We had a common aim in that we were both interested in driving the British out of India, the Japanese for their own safety and, we for the independence of our motherland. He said that quite frankly he trusted neither the British nor the Japanese. He went on to say that when the question of the independence of one's country arose, one could trust no one and as long as we were weak we would always be exploited. Netaji said that the surest guarantee against being betrayed by the Japanese was to build up our own strength. He said that we should ask for no safeguards from the Japanese, our surest safeguard must be our own strength; and if we found that the Japanese wished to replace the British in India, we should turn round and fight them too. In several lectures at mass meetings, Netaji repeated this. He warned his soldiers that anyone who joined the I.N.A. should come prepared, first to fight the British, and then, if necessary to fight the Japanese too. Although we had a common strategy with the Japanese Army, we had our own independent sectors on the front, where the I.N.A. sectors' units operated entirely on their own. There was no Japanese central direction within the I.N.A. Some critics of the I.N.A. said on the All India Radio that since I.N.A. was working in cooperation with the Japanese for us it was merely a 'puppet' force. Netaji's reply to this was that the British and French Armies were fighting under exactly the same conditions in France under the command of General Eisenhower. If the British could accept the strategy dictated by the Americans, then how could they themselves criticize the I.N.A.?

Netaji was absolutely selfless and he never appeared to have any personal ambition. This was very well demonstrated at a Conference of the Greater East Asia Nations, when Premier General Tojo said in a speech that Netaji would be 'all in all' in Free India, Netaji stood up and told him that he had no right to make such a statement as it was entirely up to the people of India to decide who would be who in India. He told General Tojo that he was only a humble servant of India and the people who really deserved to be 'all in all' in India, were Mahatma Gandhi, Maulana Abdul Kalam Azad, and Pandit Jawaharlal Nehru.

For him there were no religious or provincial differences. He refused to recognize them. He looked at everyone – Hindu, Muslim and Sikh – without any distinction, and his spirit animated, as his men. In the I.N.A. there was no 'communal' feeling of any sort in spite of the fact that every man had full liberty to practise his religion in any way he liked. He made his soldiers realize that they were the sons of the same motherland, and, as such, there could be no differences between them. We were all completely united and we realized that the communal differences in our country were the creation of an alien power. The success of this can be gauged from the fact that the most ardent supporters and admirers of Netaji were to be found among Muslims. Netaji respected every man for what he was worth and not for his religion or the province he came from.

It is amazing to see that when Netaji selected one officer from Germany to accompany him during his most hazardous journey to Tokyo by submarine, it was Abid Hussain, a Muslim, on whom his choice fell upon.

Again, when his troops were sent to the fighting line both Divisional Commanders were Muslims – Major General M. Z. Kiani and I. When he went on his last trip to Tokyo by plane in August 1945, it was Colonel Habibur Rehman whom he selected to accompany him. This feeling was not confined only to the members of the army. Among the civilians, too, some of the greatest supporters of Netaji were Muslims. It was one Mr Habib, a wealthy merchant of Rangoon, who gave all his property amounting to nearly one crore of rupees for one garland being presented to Netaji. It is on account of these facts that we of the Azad Hind Fauj refuse to believe that it is not possible for all Indians to unite and live together like brothers and sisters and work for the creation of a great, free, and united India.

Netaji made us realize that we were an army of the starving millions fighting for a very sacred cause. It was this elevation in the character of his soldiers that enabled them to face hardships and fight against almost impossible odds.

He had no private life as such. He used to work from the early hours of the morning till about 02:00 hours daily. At home, he was a most charming personality and a perfect host. He would invite officers to come and play badminton with him. Then he would take some of them to his room, give them his own clothes if they did not have a change, and very often he would even hold soap or towel for an officer who was having a wash.

To all the Rani of Jhansi girls, he was like a father and was always concerned about their welfare and honour. On one occasion, one young lady of the Rani of Jhansi, on hearing that her husband had been killed fighting on the front, took poison. Luckily, it was discovered in time and she was saved. Netaji detailed two elderly ladies to always accompany her everywhere she went. He too would send for her and talk to her for hours consoling her like a father.

Netaji dearly loved his soldiers and was always most concerned about their welfare. He would go and inspect their kitchens sometimes and would have frequent meals with them. He had issued strict orders that the food cooked for him should be exactly the same as was given to his soldiers. He was always a frequent visitor to hospitals where he used to send special sweets prepared for them in his own house.

All these qualities and the refusal to bow before the Japanese wishes, his sincerity and devotion to his country, his selflessness and his love for his soldiers greatly endeared him to his followers and each one of them felt that Netaji was his personal friend and a leader for whom it was a privilege to lay his life down.

Every day he would listen eagerly to the news from India, and when he knew of the terrible famine in Bengal, which was taking a heavy toll of valuable human lives, Netaji was greatly perturbed. He would perpetually think how he could come to the aid of his starving countrymen, especially the people of Bengal for whom his heart bled. Eventually, he made arrangements for buying 100,000 tons of rice from the Siamese and Burmese Governments. He then made an offer of sending this rice to Calcutta under his own arrangement and asked the British government to give a guarantee for the safe return of the boats and ships bringing rice to India. As he had expected, the British government did not reply to this offer. Netaji repeated this offer several times but the British who were not interested in the starving millions gave no reply.

On another occasion, the Japanese Chief of the General Staff came to Netaji and revealed his plan of bombing Calcutta and wanted to know Netaji's opinion on it. Netaji replied that as far as he was concerned he would never like to see his beautiful city with ugly scars of bombing. 'Encouragement and hope is what I wish to give to my people and not devastation and sufferings.' He advised the Japanese to withhold the bombing. 'After Imphal is captured, we will send over Calcutta large formations of Bombers, which will drop not bombs but thousands of Tricolours to the people of Bengal. That,' Netaji continued, 'would destroy the British Imperialism more effectively than bombs.'

Netaji was an astute student of international politics. He always played the right card at the right moment, and thus scored over his opponents. Sometimes we were stunned by his masterly discourse on the international situation. In most cases his analysis of the situation turned out just as he had predicted it to us. He was not only the leader of Indians in East Asia but he was acclaimed as the leader of all people in East Asia. His was the most impressive personality during the Greater East Asia Conference, and he was requested by the Japanese government to speak to the Japanese people at Habiya Park in Tokyo. It was a real honour, an honour which very few foreigners were accorded, especially at the time when the Japanese were at the height of their success and glory. I was told by a few high ranking Japanese officers that Netaji was a mastermind. He was far more experienced than any other statesman in East Asia. I accompanied him to several meetings and parties and one could easily fathom his towering personality and vast experience before the other statesman.

Indian politics was at his fingertips. He knew Indians and their leaders, and thus he could visualize with ease the means and ends of all matters which took shape in this country. It was a difficult problem to cooperate with the Japanese military personnel, and especially at the time when everything was moving in their favour, but Netaji handled everything so well and so diplomatically that there was never a time when any serious breach occurred, although the lower ranking Indian Officers and the Japanese were always at loggerheads. As a matter of fact, our boat of State was almost always in rough waters, but its smooth sailing and success was mainly due to its skipper Netaji. I tried to study him and his methods and found him extraordinarily shrewd. Japanese militarists had wanted to help us but at the same time they wanted to influence our actions, which was resented all along. After the arrival of Netaji, however, the position changed, and thereafter, the Japanese militarists were influenced by Netaji to such an extent that no new move was made without consulting him and without his advice. The sudden change in the Japanese policy of domination in China to the policy of friendship was entirely due to his influence. Some of the Burmese, Chinese and Japanese statesmen approached him for advice on matters of international politics. He was the champion of all dependant people in East Asia. Greatness is inborn, it is seldom created, and thus, to utilize the inborn qualities to achieve the ultimate purpose it must nourish many other auxiliary and supplementary qualities to fit in with the course adopted. Netaji went through the whole course with flying colours. He kept above board all along and thus traversed the course of greatness without any difficulty. He advised all the leaders in the Far East and could explain with ease the mischievous propaganda of the British in those days.

Netaji's most extraordinary move was the formation of the Provisional Government of Azad Hind. It was a master move in the game of international politics. The original Indian Independence League could not freely declare war on their enemies and could not cooperate on equal terms with the League of East Asiatic Nations. It was Netaji who foresaw the necessity of equality and thus declared the inauguration of the Provisional Government of Azad Hind. The officers and workers remained the same but this switch over carried us overnight to the status of a free state and since then the Provisional Government of Azad Hind was recognized by nine sovereign states as an equal partner in the committee of those nations. We were a refugee government but our privileges and status was no less than that of any of the sovereign states there.

At one time the Japanese suggested to Netaji that since the Japanese Army was the senior one, when I.N.A. and Japanese officers of equal rank met, Indian officers should salute first. Netaji was furious at this. He said that would mean that the I.N.A. had accepted an inferior status, which he was not prepared to do. He said they both should salute at the same time. This was finally accepted by Japanese.

In addition to this, the I.N.A. was the only army in East Asia which was not under the military law of the Japanese. Several times the Japanese approached Netaji and told him that the I.N.A. should also be subject to the Japanese Military Law. But Netaji refused staunchly and told them that the I.N.A. was an independent army. This matter had to go to Tokyo ultimately where Netaji finally had his way. Whenever the occasion arose Netaji made it absolutely clear that he would fight only for the independence of India and would never allow his country to be exploited by the Japanese. There were two occasions when the Japanese approached the I.N.A. to fight for them. Once in August 1944 against the Siamese in the area of Chumpong, where a small Japanese force was besieged by the Thais (Siamese), and a second time against the Burmese army in March 1945 after the Burmese National Army had rebelled against the Japanese. On both these occasions, with Netaji's consent, the I.N.A. refused to fight on behalf of Japan.

To keep up our end, Netaji never asked any help from the Indians living in the Far East. He refused to accept any assistance other than the supply of war material. He gave the message to the Indian residents in Japan that he would not ask for any help as long as the I.N.A. could manage things on its own. It was for this sincerity of his that the Indians showered everything upon him – man-power, money and materials, wherever he went. Several Indians in the East brought into practice the slogan of total mobilization. It is seldom, if ever, that people sacrifice all that is theirs for something of the end of which is uncertain. Yet, Indians of all castes and creeds threw in their lot with Netaji and were ready to give whatever was required of them.

By organizing Indian Independence League all over East Asia Netaji's was able to instil a spirit of patriotism in the heart of every Indian, rich and poor alike, and from whom voluntary contributions flowed in freely. As I have mentioned already, a large number of Indians – from almost every community – gave their all to the Azad Hind Fauj and became *fakirs* for the sake of their country. Whole families joined the I.N.A.: fathers joined the I.N.A. Fauj, mothers joined the Rani of Jhansi Regiment and little children joined the Balsena. *Karo sab nichawar, Bano sab Fakir* was the slogan that Netaji gave them, and men like Habib Betai, Khanna and numerous others willingly gave all their fortunes amounting to several lakhs to the Azad Hind Fauj, and became *fakirs*. A total sum of 20 crore rupees was collected and deposited in the Azad Hind Bank, Rangoon.

Rich people were not the only ones who contributed to the I.N.A. In fact the greater proportion of our funds came from people who had a comparatively average income. It was mostly the poor labourers, *gwalas* and others like them that made the greatest sacrifices.

I will never forget a scene that I witnessed at one of the meetings addressed by Netaji at Singapore.

After Netaji had finished his speech, he made an appeal for funds. Thousands of people came forward to donate. They formed a queue in front of Netaji; each one coming up on his turn handed over his donation to Netaji and left. Most of the people who formed the queue were donating large amounts. All of a sudden I saw a very poor labour woman come up to the stage to hand in her donation. She was in tatters and had no cloth to cover even her head. With bated breath all of us watched her. She took out three one-rupee notes and offered them to Netaji... Netaji hesitated. She said to Netaji, 'Please accept these. This is all I possess.' Netaji still hesitated as tears rolled down his cheeks. And he extended his hand and accepted the money from her.

After the meeting was over, I asked Netaji why he had hesitated to accept the money from that poor woman and why he had cried. Netaji replied, 'It was a very hard decision for me. When I looked at the condition of that poor woman, I knew that those three rupees were all the wealth that she possessed and if I took it she would probably suffer terribly, but on the other hand, when I thought of her sentiment, her desire to give her all for Indian freedom, I felt that if I refused she would feel hurt and probably think that I accepted only large sums from the rich. In the end, in order not to hurt her feelings I accepted the money and to me those three rupees have a greater value than lakhs contributed by rich men out of their millions.'

Netaji was absolutely fearless and did not seem to care for his life, or for comfort. He seemed to lead a charmed life for I have personally seen him miss death at very close quarters several times, and it is on account of that trust that I can never believe that Netaji is dead... 'Netaji Zindabad'.

CHAPTER TWO

ORIGIN OF THE AZAD HIND FAUJ

It was in January 1944, on a beautiful moonlit night, when Netaji invited some officers to dinner. We were all sitting out in the porch and Netaji was in a particularly pleasant and conversational mood. All of a sudden one inquisitive young officer asked Netaji as to how the idea of escaping from India and raising the I.N.A. had occurred to him; and how his armed struggle outside India would be viewed by Mahatma Gandhi. Netaji replied that after 1935, it should have been quite evident to any clear-sighted person that a world-conflict was fast approaching. He said that it was known to him that in the event of England being involved in such a conflict, India would automatically be dragged into it; and that as soon as hostilities commenced all Indian political leaders would be clapped in jail, where they would stay for the whole duration of the war.

'The choice before me,' he said, 'was that of being imprisoned for the duration of the war or of escaping from

India, joining hands with the enemies of England and through their help raising an army to fight for India's liberation.' He explained that it was not easy to choose between the two alternatives, and that before he finally made up his mind, he discussed with Mahatma Gandhi the world situation and the part to be played in it by India. He pointed out to Mahatma Gandhi that it would serve no useful purpose if Indian leaders were shut up inside jails for the duration of the war. The only way in which India's liberation could be achieved would be possible if some Indian leaders escaped, raised an army outside India and then invaded India as an army of liberation. Netaji explained that in saying so, he had before him the examples of Garibaldi and General Franco.

Mahatmaji replied that he personally did not believe that it was possible to secure India's liberation by these methods. If, however, Netaji succeeded in freeing India by these means, he (Mahatmaji) would be the first one to congratulate him. Thus, Netaji felt that he had got Mahatmaji's blessings for an enterprise which he believed would prove successful in securing freedom for India.

As was expected at the outbreak of the Second World War, Netaji found himself behind prison bars. The first problem for him then was how to get out. Netaji said that he thought over it for several days and finally decided that he would go on a hunger strike as a protest against his illegal detention. He knew that having once started the fast, there would be no going back for him, and if the British persisted in detaining him he would have to starve himself to death like Jatin Das. Knowing the British as he did, he felt that there was an even chance that he may have to starve to death. 'Anyhow,' he said, 'I took the plunge and went on a hunger strike.' For the first few days, the British authorities were adamant and it looked as if they would never give in. The Jail Superintendent approached him and pointed out the futility of such a move.

But Netaji paid no heed to his warming, and after a fast which lasted twelve days his condition became very grave. This alarmed the British jailer who finally released him and Netaji returned to his ancestral home. Once back home, Netaji began to prepare for his next move – that of escaping from India to one of the axis countries.

The house in which he was residing was under the closest watch of the C.I.D. and the local police. It was unofficially learnt that there were as many as sixty-two men of various police departments detailed to keep watch over him. He shut himself up in his bedroom for several days and allowed no one except a young niece to enter it occasionally to serve his meals. It was learnt that he divided his bedroom into two parts. One was curtained off as his prayer room and the other portion was used as his bedroom and dining room. He rarely came out of his prayer room. Finally, how, unnoticed, he escaped from his house by completely deceiving the guards and reached Afghanistan must, for the time being, remain a mystery.

Finally, with the help of the German Counsel in Afghanistan, Netaji managed to reach Germany, where he met Hitler and discussed the possibility of forming an army of Indians residing in German-occupied territory and from among the Indian prisoners of war. Early in January 1942, Netaji raised the first battalion of the Free India Legion in Germany.

On the outbreak of hostilities in the Far East between Great Britain and Japan, Netaji met the Japanese Ambassador in Berlin and requested him to advise the Japanese government in Tokyo to start a similar organization in the Far East, from among the Indians residing in Japanese-occupied territory and the Indian prisoners of war who had fallen into Japanese hands. The Japanese government liked the idea and started organising an Indian Army in East Asia.

A Japanese major general (then colonel) by the name of

Yamamoto, who was an official of the Japanese Embassy in Berlin, kept Netaji informed of the progress of the formation of the I.N.A. in the Far East; and when finally at the end of May 1943, Netaji arrived at Penang in a Japanese submarine, Major General Yamamoto who had accompanied him from Berlin, became Head of a Japanese liaison organisation known as the *Hikari-Kikan*.

Thus the original idea of raising an army of free Indians to fight for India's liberation was conceived and given effect entirely by Netaji.

I will now turn to the East, and try and trace, as accurately and faithfully as possible, the events that led to the formation of the First I.N.A. under the command of General Mohan Singh, its disbandment, and the raising of a second I.N.A. under the leadership of Director of the Military Bureau Major General (then Lt. Colonel) J. K. Bhonsle – the arrival of Netaji, the part played by the I.N.A. in the operations in Burma, and its final surrender to the British forces in Rangoon.

Prelude to the formation of the I.N.A.

Before dealing with the actual formation of the I.N.A., I would like to explain very briefly the pre-disposing causes which motivated Indian officers and men to join it.

1. *Indian Commissioned Officers*

When the Indianization of the Indian army was started and the Indian Military Academy was established at Dehradun, the cadets seeking commissions were promised equality of status, pay and allowances, accommodation, etc. with the British Officers of the Indian Army. Actually, none of these promises were fulfilled. The Indian Commissioned Officers (ICO) on commission were posted as platoon commanders in the Indian Units, whereas Junior British Officers were commanding companies in non-Indianized units.

Pay: The rates of pay admissible to the ICOs were much lower than the corresponding ranks of the British officers. The excuses given for the difference in pay scale was that the British Officers were serving away from their homes.

On arrival in Malaya, the ICOs contended that they too were serving away from their homes, and should therefore draw the same pay as the British Officers. No heed was, however, paid to these grievances. The ICOs continued to receive a consolidated pay. A Lieutenant drew approximately 400 rupees, whereas his British counterpart received approximately 600 rupees a month. Even in the same unit, while holding a similar appointment, the allowances were different. For instance, a British Adjutant or Quarter Master recruited higher allowances as compared to his Indian counterpart. The British officer received 100 rupees for the same appointment, whereas an Indian officer was given only 60 rupees. Thus the British insisted on forcing an inferior status on Indian officers, which they bitterly resented.

Clubs: Indian officers were not admitted as members in a large number of clubs in Malaya. The British authorities always impressed upon the Indians that they had come to Malaya to protect the person and property of the inhabitants of Malaya, and ironically of the Europeans who refused admission to their protectors to their clubs.

Colour Bar: In Malaya there was an order by the railway authorities of Federated Malaya States that an Asiatic could not travel in the same compartment as a European, and even the fact that they both held the same rank and belonged to the same unit did not seem to matter in this respect.

2. *Indian Soldiers*

In Malaya, an Indian soldier was given only 25 rupees per month, whereas a British soldier received approximately 75 rupees.

On the fighting front, the Indian soldiers were more often than not ahead of British soldiers. Therefore, this difference in pay became a big cause of great discontentment and indignation among them. As if this was not enough, there was a vast difference in the food, accommodation and general treatment afforded to the Indian and the British soldiers. The Indian soldier often asked himself why he was being given this step-motherly treatment in spite of the fact that he was, if anything, a tougher and braver fighter than a British 'tommy'.

General

On the outbreak of the Second World War (1939–1945) Indian leaders unanimously declared that since the war was an imperialist one which Britain was fighting to protect her vested interests, India would not be a part of it. Unfortunately, they had no control over the army the British used the Indian army as, when and where they liked.

To the Indian soldier, the British propagandist said that the war was being fought to save democracy and freedom in the world from Fascist aggression. In the beginning, the Indian soldier, simple-minded as he was, believed them. But gradually he began to doubt the truth of such statements, and when on proceeding overseas, he saw with his own eyes the discriminatory treatment meted out to him, he began to ask himself if it was fair for the people for whose freedom he was fighting should treat him in that manner. It was only then that it dawned upon him that he was a slave fighting to preserve the empire of his master, and that by his actions he was strengthening the chains of imperial slavery.

Thus by the time the much boasted 'impregnable' fortress of Singapore fell, the Indian soldier had realized that if he had to fight for democracy and freedom, it was much better to fight for his own democracy and freedom. It was in this mood that the fall of Singapore found the greater number of Indian soldiers.

The debacle in Malaya, a brief account of which follows, and the sight of white soldiers fleeing for their lives before the Japanese, an Asiatic nation, further lowered the prestige of Englishmen in the eyes of Indian soldiers and removed all traces of racial inferiority from their minds.

They argued, and quite rightly too, that they were as good soldiers as the British tommies and they had as much right to be free and independent as the British.

Debacle of Malaya

Inspite of the fact that all Japanese activities prior to the War in the Far East indicated that a war was imminent, the British authorities in Malaya – both civil and military – had lulled themselves into a false sense of security. Therefore, all efforts made for the defence of Malaya were quite half-hearted. The armed forces available and their equipment were far from adequate for the task allotted to them. On the fall of Singapore, Prime Minister Winston Churchill made a speech in the Parliament in which he explained that Malaya had been starved of men and, materials – especially the air power because of the urgent need of others, and more important theatres of war. When the war did come, it came as a shock to everyone and no one had a chance to recover from it until the end of the campaign.

Air Marshal Brooks-Popham, the Commander-in-Chief of the British forces stationed in Malaya, had based the defence of Malaya on a strong air force dispersed on a series of aerodromes scattered all over Malaya. Consequently, the majority of the Military units in the country had also been scattered all over for the defence of these air bases. This enabled the Japanese to defeat these scattered units easily, and it was not even possible for the British Commander to marshal enough forces to stem the Japanese advances. The essential condition for the success of Brooke-Popham's plan – a strong air force – was conspicuous by its absence and the plan failed completely.

Most of the British air planes were put out of action in the earlier days of the war and the remainders were forced by the Japanese to remain on the ground. Throughout the Malayan campaign the R.A.F. could not give any support to the land forces. Towards the end of the campaign, about 60 Hurricane fighters arrived in Singapore to reinforce the air force stationed there but the Island surrendered before they were even assembled; and they were presented to the Japanese in their crates themselves.

The Naval squadron, after the sinking of its two capital ships – 'Prince of Wales' and 'Repulse' – was rendered completely useless and except for a minor action off the coast of Marsing, there was no naval activity anywhere off the coast of Malaya.

Owing to the inactivity of air and naval forces, throughout the campaign, the Japanese were able to land troops wherever and whenever they wanted, and were thus able to outflank the retreating British forces.

The land forces in Malaya were inadequate for meeting the Japanese attack. They had no armoured units and it was invariably the Japanese tanks that broke through the defences. Most of the units of the army had been mechanized in Malaya, but they could neither efficiently use the motor vehicles nor the new weapons provided to them. Most of their time was spent in building up their defences as they were not trained to manage large units and formations. Their training in jungle warfare had been completely neglected and they were completely 'road-bound'. The Japanese, on the other hand, were masters in jungle craft and always managed to outmanoeuvre the British forces in jungles which appeared impregnable to the British troops. The land forces in Malaya had to fight against much superior Japanese forces for days on and without any relief or rest; whereas the Japanese were able to employ their troops in 24 hours shifts.

Lack of cooperation

The British civil servants who had ruled in Malaya as tin gods resented the military intruders whom they considered to be an unmitigated nuisance. Instead of extending every cooperation to the military authorities, they became an invariable source of hindrance. Some instances of their arrogant and obstructionist attitude have already been cited before. During the Malayan Campaign, it was no uncommon sight to see important military trains held up because the civil authorities had made no arrangements for the cooling of the engines; nor could the civil authorities be ever relied upon to provide labour at any time.

There was also a complete lack of cooperation between the three services. The air force – supposed to be the kernel of the defence of Malaya – considered the army only of secondary importance, an attitude the army naturally resented. After the outbreak of hostilities, the air force disappeared from the scene and became the butt of sarcasm of the army. The naval forces were of such a small consequence that no one bothered about them. Such lack of cooperation was responsible for the tragedy which led up to the sinking of the *Prince of Wales* and the *Repulse*.

Racial differences between the Indian, Australian and British forces had become very acute before the outbreak of hostilities, and there had been some instances of armed clashes too. These differences worsened during the campaign as there was more recrimination than co-operation among these armed forces.

Poor leadership

The military leadership in Malaya was very poor indeed. As the Japanese naval convoys approached the coasts of Singapore and Kota Bharu, the brass hats of the British Army sat debating in their comfortable offices in Singapore whether the famous 'Metador' scheme should be put into operation or not. The 'Metador' scheme was a military plan which had been prepared previously and had entailed an advance of British forces into Thailand (Siam). Finally, they decided to put a new modified scheme into operation which was neither so bold nor so brilliantly conceived as the 'Metador' scheme, and like all half measures failed completely.

The poverty of the British military leadership was again demonstrated when during the first few days of the war, the British had to dismiss one general and the three Brigade Commanders under him.

The battle of the 'Slim River' was lost due to the inefficiency of the Commander of the 12th Indian Brigade and for the same reason, the Divisional Commander had to be reverted to his original command of a brigade.

Another Brigadier, who had become a mental case when his brigade was smashed by the Japanese, was given the command of another brigade. He allowed his brigade to be badly mauled by the Japanese by failing to issue orders for its withdrawal in time. Later, in Malaya, he was the cause of the 22nd Infantry Brigade cut off and annihilated by the Japanese. He too was sacked on arrival in Singapore.

Singapore surrender and Indian morale

During his stay in Malaya, the Indian soldier found that he was hated by other Asiatics for being a British watch-dog. Under the circumstances, he adopted the only course open to him – a haughty and superior attitude towards other Asiatics. After the fall of Singapore for which he was not even remotely responsible, he found himself in the unenviable position of a defeated soldier in the presence of those whom he had affected to despise. His vanity was hurt and he asked himself the obvious question – Why am I placed in such a predicament? The answer was not difficult to find. He knew that the answer lay in British incompetence. He realized that his humiliation was the result of his fighting a war on Britain's behalf. Is it any wonder, therefore, that he decided not to continue as a watch-dog of the British any longer?

Throughout the Malayan campaign the Indian troops, without any air support, fought courageously against the heavy odds. Time and again they were made victims of blunders committed by their British Commanders, but they patiently and loyally continued to fight while their British Commanders were taken safely to the Island fortress of Singapore. Tired and weary after their long and hazardous campaign on the mainland of Malaya, the Indian units arrived in Singapore. Last to arrive on the island, they were the first to be sent forward to meet the Japanese onslaughts directed against Singapore. Here again, they fought tenaciously when their Australian comrades were abandoning their positions and running away to take part in the indiscriminate looting and raping that their countrymen had started in the town.

The reward for all this loyalty and courageous fighting came when the British Commander, General Percival, surrendered unconditionally, and without any representation, handed over all the Indian troops to the Japanese.

The Indian troops were told to obey the orders of the Japanese commanders in the same way as they had been doing under the British. They were treated like mere cattle and quite naturally felt deserted by the British for whom they had shed their blood so freely.

The British had, through their clever propaganda, established a legend about the superiority and invincibility of the White people, a legend that the average Indian soldier, quite unconsciously, believed. To the Indian soldier, the White Sahib could do no wrong. During the battle of Malaya, the same White Sahibs were seen running about in panic trying to save their lives. Gone was the dignity and superiority of the White Sahibs. The officer class of the White Sahib did not do much credit to its race either. In a battle it is the duty of officers to lead their men, but they were so scared of being captured alive by the Japanese that they always stayed at the rear, behind their Indian soldiers. The British officers had sufficient reasons for dreading of being captured alive by the Japanese.

The Japanese, in order to lower the morale and shatter the nerves of British officers and men, had resorted to methods which were, by modern standards of civilization, quite brutal. They would tie captured prisoners to trees and then proceed to bayonet them one by one in the presence of their comrades. In some cases, they would ask the Indian prisoners to bayonet their British officers. Those who refused to do so were themselves bayonetted by the Japanese. The Japanese soldiers were trained in such a manner that they took pleasure in this sort of torture and treated it as a good pastime. While they were indulging in this sordid sport, the Japanese would release a few of the prisoners, who were awaiting their turn to be bayoneted, and send them back to the British lines to tell these tales of horror to their comrades, and thereby shatter the nerves of the British officers and men.

In dealing with Indians, however, the Japanese followed an entirely different technique. Whenever Indian soldiers were taken prisoners, the Japanese would either take no notice of them, or after disarming them, would give them the choice of either staying with the Japanese or going back to the British lines. To the captured Indian soldiers, the Japanese said that they regarded the Indians as brothers and not as enemies, and that, the Japanese were fighting the war to help India to win her independence from the British.

The Indian soldiers who were held prisoners by the Japanese on the front lines were generally given good treatment. This technique proved quite effective and appealed to the Indian soldiers. Therefore, they joined the Japanese forces in large numbers.

The ease and speed with which the Japanese defeated the British forces in the Far East broke the legend of the British power. The Indians became convinced that the Japanese would ultimately succeed in defeating the British quite easily. This was also true in the case of the attitude of Asiatic civilians in Malaya. The British had often boasted of their might and promised to protect them from Japanese domination, but the Malayan debacle convinced them of the British impotence.

During the campaign, Singapore became the haven of dismissed Brigadiers and Commanding Officers, who now sat idling in various headquarters, while the troops in the front line paid the price of their stupidity. The tale of the British military leadership is indeed a very sad one, and the debacle of Malaya was mainly due to their muddle-headedness.

The majority of the Military units in Malaya were encamped in rubber plantations which led to disastrous consequences. These units or troops had spent all their time in preparing defences and they had acquired a 'pill-box mentality'; a feeling that as long as they held a few strongly-built fieldworks and pillboxes, the Japanese would not be able to break through them. This led them to believe in rigid defence and they sacrificed flexibility and manoeuvrability for static defence with the result that the Japanese always managed to infiltrate through or outflank the British defensive positions.

They put all their faith in the defences which they had constructed through so much hard labour and when they saw the Japanese cutting through them, like a knife cutting through a piece of cheese, their morale was shattered. On top of this, they had the uneasy feeling of being let down by their commanders. Although the brass-hats were blissfully ignorant of the disastrous consequences of their muddle-headedness, the common soldier knew that everything was going wrong. Hundreds of men were being sacrificed in futile counter attacks which gained no tactical advantage. Time and again, well-prepared positions were abandoned without any opposition. The long trek and continuous fighting without any relief was nerve-racking. Added to all this was the constant menace of enemy air-attacks. The first to break down were the British officers who were scared of falling alive into Japanese hands. When the troops saw the officers in such a state, their own morale was completely shattered. Once the morale was gone, the army became unreliable and was incapable of putting up any organized resistance against the attacking enemy. This is the reason why one hundred thousand British troops in Singapore surrendered to a more thirty thousand Japanese.

CHAPTER THREE

THE INDIAN INDEPENDENCE MOVEMENT

Sri Rash Behari Bose, an Indian revolutionary, had been living as an exile in Japan for several years under the patronage of Mr Toyama, a well-known Japanese patriot. Soon after the commencement of hostilities in the Far East, Sri R. B. Bose called on Field Marshal Sugiyama, Chief of the Imperial General Staff of the Japanese Army, and explained to him that the war was a good opportunity for Indians to secure their independence from the British rule. He requested Field Marshal Sugiyama to help Indians in East Asia to organize themselves and launch an armed offensive against the British from the East. He also requested the Chief of the Imperial General Staff to issue orders to Japanese forces not to treat Indians as enemy subjects in the territories occupied by the Japanese army. Sugiyama did not agree with Mr R. B. Bose's proposal, as he contended that India was a part of the British Empire which was at war with Japan, and as such, all Indians were to be treated as enemy subjects.

Mr Bose then met the Deputy War Minister and managed to persuade him to agree to his suggestion. Consequently, an Indian Independence League, with the object of organizing Indians in the Far East was formed in Japan with Mr Rash Bihari Bose as its President.

After the occupation of Thailand (Siam) by the Japanese forces, Swami Satya Nand Puri, with certain other leading Indians, set up an Indian Independence League in Bangkok. Representatives of this League went with the Japanese forces as they advanced into Malaya and with the help and under the leadership of local Indians set up branches in all the states of Malaya. Later, the Indian Independence League (I.I.L.) branches were formed all over East Asia including Philippines, Thailand, Dutch East-Indies, French Indo-China, Shanghai, Burma, Korea and Manchuria. All these branches owed allegiance to India and were under the leadership of Mr R. B. Bose.

The formation of these Branch organizations was a very wise move on the part of Mr R. B. Bose. The Japanese soldiers would let loose an orgy of looting and raping in every territory they occupied. The people whom they termed as 'enemy' subjects were the ones who were especially singled out for these barbarities. Europeans, Eurasians, and Chinese suffered the most. Brutal, as the Japanese soldiers were, I will say this much for them that they never molested any Indian woman. In fact, many Eurasian and Chinese women escaped molestation by putting on *sarees* and *dupattas* and telling the Japanese that they were Indians. Apparently some instructions had been issued to the Japanese soldiers not to molest Indian civilians. Inspite of his other drawbacks and failings, the Japanese is a very fine soldier, and he obeys the orders of his superiors most implicitly. It was a very common sight to see

Japanese soldiers approaching Indian houses and trying to talk to the residents. Most of them knew no other language than Japanese. They would go up to an Indian and say 'Gandhi ka'? In the beginning, we could not understand this, but later we learnt that by this they meant are you a follower of Mahatma Gandhi? If the reply was in the affirmative they would say, 'Ha,' shake hands or bow and push off.

Captain Mohan Singh

Capt. Mohan Singh belonged to the 1st. Bn. 14th Punjab Regiment which was stationed at Jitra in North Malaya, since the beginning of 1941. On 11 December 1941, after his Battalion had been in action for a few days, he along with some officers, including Capt. Mohd. Akram Khan and his commanding officer, Lieutenant Colonel L. V. Fitzpatrick, were cut off from the rest of the battalion. The commanding officer had been wounded in action and was unable to walk. Capt. Mohan Singh and Capt. Mohd. Akram Khan carried him with them for several days through thick Malayan forests and eventually took refuge in a mosque at Alorstar. By this time the Japanese mechanized columns and men mounted on bicycles had broken through and were well on their way to Singapore.

At Alorstar, Capt. Mohan Singh came in contact with one Mr Pritam Singh, a Sikh revolutionary who had been sent by the Bangkok I.I.L. to accompany the advancing Japanese troops, and Major Fujiwara, a Japanese Officer of the Intelligence Department. Major Fujiwara tried to persuade General Mohan Singh to join the I.I.L. After a prolonged discussion, Capt. Mohan Singh agreed to join the Indian Independence Movement and to cooperate with Japanese forces.

Prior to the surrender of Capt. Mohan Singh, the Japanese had captured Capt. Pattanayak, an Indian Medical Service

Officer, and had similar discussions with him. The Japanese asked him to organize the Indian soldiers to fight for India's Independence. Capt. Pattanayak expressed his inability to do so, as he was a doctor. He was severely slapped and beaten by the Japanese for not possessing any patriotic fervour.

Capt. Mohan Singh, realizing the heavy odds against which the Indian army was fighting and the helplessness of the Indian civilians in Malaya left in the lurch by their White Masters, decided that the best course would be to cooperate with the Japanese forces and save as many Indian lives as possible, and thus provide protection to the Indian civilian population of Malaya. In pursuance of this decision, he organized a small group of officers and men from the Indian Army to work under his command. To this group he gave the name of 'Fujiwara Kikan (Department)'. These Indian volunteers advanced along with the Japanese troops and helped in gathering Indian soldiers, providing food for Indian civilians, giving aid to the sick and wounded and organizing search parties to bring back wounded and stragglers left behind in the jungles.

Collection centre for Indian soldiers was formed in Kuala Lumpur, and about 5,000 Indian soldiers gathered in a camp in the city, and arrangements were made for their feeding and accommodation. Rations and medicines were provided by the local Indian civilians. The Japanese gave no help with regard to rations, medicines, clothing, etc. The Indian troops had to fend for themselves and exist as best as they could. Parties were sent out to collect rations, medicines, clothing and whatever else they could get from abandoned British camps, and supplies and from the local civilians. The lot of the Indian prisoners at Kuala Lumpur were not happy, and for months together they lived a hand-to-mouth existence. In those dark days at Kuala Lumpur, Capt. Mahboob Ahmed of the 1/13th Frontier Force Rifles and Capt. Talibuddin I.M.S.

worked day and night and managed to collect a fair quantity of rations, clothing and medicines and opened a hospital for the Indian soldiers.

From the civilians, one Sikh gentleman by the name of Budh Singh devoted all his time and energy for the relief and assistance of Indian soldiers, and as usual, the best response to such time of misfortune came from the poorest class of labourers.

Nucleus of the I.N.A.

In the middle of January 1942, Capt. Mohan Singh explained his aims and objects to the Indian soldiers in Kuala Lumpur's main camp. He said that an 'Indian National Army' should be formed from amongst the Indian soldiers with the object of actively fighting the British in Malaya and elsewhere. He explained that the eventual object of the I.N.A. was to drive the British out of India, and that the Japanese had promised to give all possible aid to Indians to secure the liberation of their country from British domination. He, thereupon, asked for volunteers with the object of forming two groups – one group to participate actively for fighting in Malaya, and the other one to be sent for action in Burma. Eventually these two groups were raised – each one had two hundred strong soldiers and took part in the Malayan and Burma campaigns, respectively. The Malayan group was commanded by Capt. Allah Ditta Khan, 22 Mt. Regiment and was among the very first troops to land on the Island of Singapore. The Burma groups was commanded by Major Rain Sarup 4-19th Hyderabad Regiment and took part in the fighting in Burma. Major Ram Sarup proved himself to be an officer of outstanding gallantry and tact. And because of the influence he had on the Japanese he managed to save the lives of a very large number of Indian soldiers, and secured preferential treatment for Indian civilians residing in Burma.

Political lectures and plays were inaugurated in Kuala Lumpur to infuse a spirit of patriotism and nationalism among the Indian soldiers. All superficial differences of class, creed and religion were abolished, and all men lived and ate together in harmony.

Surrender of Singapore

Johore Causeway, that connected Singapore Island with the mainland, was destroyed by the British on the morning of the 31 January 1942, after all available troops had been thrust into the island. The majority of the Indian troops in Singapore had already participated in the strenuous campaign on the mainland of Malaya and were thoroughly exhausted mentally and physically. Immediately on arrival on the Island of Singapore the same troops were ordered to get prepared and man the defences of the Island. This came as a great disillusionment to all since lavish promises of rest and reinforcements had been made to them earlier. The general morale of the army and the civilians from the highest rank to the lowest was very low. There was a general feeling among all the Asiatics that they were being given a raw deal by the British, and the failure of the British to evacuate Asiatic civilians from the mainland of Malaya was also ranking in their hearts. Added to all this was the feeling that the British distrusted every Asiatic and suspected him of being in league with the Japanese forces.

The Japanese made their initial landing on 8 February 1942, and after a fierce fight the British forces surrendered unconditionally to the Imperial Japanese Army on 15 February 1942.

Surrender and concentration at the Farrer Park

On the night of the surrender 15-16 February 1942, we received orders that all Indians including the NCOs were to concentrate in the Farrer Park. All British officers and other ranks were to concentrate at Shanghai. All of us, especially the officers, were surprised to hear this order because according to the laws of warfare all captured officers, whether Indian or British, were to be kept together, separate from rank and file. We had already heard of Japanese methods and atrocities before and felt that our British brother officers were leaving us in the lurch to face it all by ourselves.

On the following morning, when we were marching off to our concentration areas our commanding officers Major Macadam, along with other British officers, came to see off the battalions. While shaking hands with me, he said, 'I suppose this is the parting of our ways.' At the time I did not understand the full significance of this, as I had no idea of Japanese intentions, whereas he must have known about it when he made the remark. Until that time, most of us did not know anything about the activities of Capt. Mohan Singh on the mainland of Malaya and his intention of raising an I.N.A. The higher British officers were, however, fully aware of it but they kept it a closely guarded secret, with the result, that when we concentrated at the Farrer Park we did not know what to expect there.

Handing over ceremony
At Farrer Park at about 14:00 hours on 17 February 1942, Lt. Colonel Hunt, a staff officer of the British Military Headquarters at Malaya, appeared on a balcony accompanied by Major Fujiwara, Colonel N. S. Gill, Capt. Mohan Singh and a few other Japanese and Indian officers.

He collected all the officers in one place and made a brief speech over the microphone in which he said, 'From today we are all prisoners of war. I now, on behalf of the British Government, hand you over to the Japanese Government, whose orders you will obey as you have been doing ours. If you don't, you will be punished.' After this, he brought the whole lot to attention and handed over some papers, nominal rolls of Indian soldiers to the Japanese representative, Major Fujiwara. Major Fujiwara then brought us to attention and said, 'I, on behalf of the Japanese Government, take you over under our command.' He went on to say, 'I, on behalf of the Japanese Government, now hand you over to G.O.C. Capt. Mohan Singh who shall have powers of life and death over you.'

We watched the representative of the British Government very carefully to see what his reactions were to the events that were taking place before his eyes. But he was apparently quite satisfied with the arrangements as he did not attempt in any way to dispute the unlawful handing over of Indian prisoners of war to a person who was as much a prisoner of war as any one of the rest. Perhaps he was not worried about the Indians any longer and was more concerned with what awaited him at the British Prison Camp at Changi. At this stage he left the balcony. Major Fujiwara then continued his speech in Japanese, which was translated into English by a Japanese officer and into Hindustani by Colonel Gill.

Major Fujiwara said, 'Japan is fighting for the liberation of the Asiatic Nations which have been for so long trodden under the cruel heels of British Imperialism. Japan is the liberator and the friend of the Asiatics. Japan wishes to inaugurate a New Order in East Asia. This new order will take the form of a Co-prosperity Sphere of East Asia, which will consist of free and equal nations, cooperating with each other for the common good. The independence of India is essential for the independence of Asia and the peace of the world; and it is the duty of Indians to free themselves. Japan is willing to give all-out aid and assistance to Indians in East Asia to achieve their aspirations.'

After this, Capt. Mohan Singh came to the microphone and delivered a speech in Hindustani. He said that the

British authorities blamed the Indian troops for not fighting well in the Malayan Campaign. But they provided no air support, nor were there armoured fighting vehicles, nor any modern weapons so necessary to wage a modern war against a formidable enemy like the Japanese Army. The British authorities were entirely to blame for the Malayan and Singapore fiasco, and the Indian soldiers had been as good fighters as ever. He then said, 'The days of British oppression in the East are numbered and their hated rule must soon come to an end. The Japanese armed forces have driven them from Malaya and Singapore and they are beating a hasty retreat in Burma. India stands on the threshold of freedom and it is incumbent on every Indian to fight and drive away those demons who have been for so many decades sucking the life-blood of Indians. The Japanese have promised us their all-out help in the realization of our coveted dreams and it is up to us now to organize ourselves and fight for the freedom of four hundred millions of our countrymen and women. For this purpose we will organize an Indian National Army from amongst the Indian soldiers and civilians in the Far East.'

This speech of Capt. Mohan Singh got a mixed reception. By some it was received with great acclamation and shouts of 'INQALAB ZINDABAD' and raising of their hands to show their willingness to join the I.N.A. Apart from the hatred of the British that existed in the mind of every self-respecting Indian, another possible reason for this acclamation might have been that we had been told numerous tales of Japanese barbarities and inhuman treatment that would be accorded to prisoners of war; and now we were being told by the Japanese themselves that we would be accorded the treatment of a brother rather than that of an enemy or a defeated soldier. Naturally there was a feeling of great relief and rejoicing.

But there was a large proportion of soldiers in the Farrer Park to whom the idea of joining hands with the Japanese and fighting against their own kith and kin did not appeal much. This feeling was more prominent in the officers' Cadre. To us these speeches came as bomb shells. The very idea of joining hands with our former enemies and fighting against our own kith and kin was unimaginable. I, as well as most other officers, had a feeling of being completely helpless at being handed over like cattle by the British to the Japanese, and then by the Japanese to Capt. Mohan Singh, whom they gave powers of life and death over us. With all due regards to Capt. Mohan Singh's sincerity and leadership that he displayed later, I, who had known him well for the last ten years, knew that he had always been an efficient but a very average officer. The mere fact of being handed over to him and his having power of life and death over us, made us feel suspicious of Japanese intentions because among the Indian prisoners of war there were some very senior and capable officers like Colonel Gill, Colonel Bhonsle, Major Mehtab Singh and Major Bhagat. All these officers had at least fifteen to twenty years of service in the army, whereas General Mohan Singh had only eight to nine years of service as an officer.

I was fully convinced, knowing Capt. Mohan Singh so well, that politically, at any rate, he would not be able to cope with Japanese intrigue and that we would be exploited by the Japanese purely for their personal ends. I, therefore, firmly made up my mind not to have anything to do with such an I.N.A., and in spite of a feeling of frustration and helplessness, the element of traditional loyalty to the King overcame these feelings and not only did I make up my own mind to keep out of the I.N.A., but as the head of a famous military tribe, I felt it was my duty to warn all others, especially the men I commanded, and those men who came from the same area as I did, to keep out of it.

Here I would like to explain that I belonged to a soldier family that had been serving in the Indian Army for the last three generations and in which loyalty to the King had become almost a tradition. At the Indian Military Academy, I was given a scholarship known as the 'King Emperor's Cadetship' – an honour that was given to a cadet who had the best military traditions and was likely to live up to it. There was a fairly large section among the prisoners of war who thought on the same lines as I did. The type of remarks we made were. 'If anyone asks you to shoot at your own brethren, turn round and shoot him first.'

There were many King's and Viceroy's Commissioned Officers, whom I had known well before the war, who got together and decided to keep out of the I.N.A. We fully realized that the Japanese were raising the I.N.A. to utilize us and fulfil their own selfish ends.

It was in this frame of mind that I marched off with 20,000 other prisoners of war to a camp in Neesoon. Even after our arrival there, I was firm in my mind and kept on telling everyone who came to me for advice to keep out of the I.N.A. After a few days I was appointed as the Commander of Neesoon Camp.

Administration and life in camps

After the meeting in Farrer Park, Capt. Mohan Singh set up his Headquarters at Mount Pleasant in Singapore, adjacent to the Headquarters of 'Fujiwara Kikan', an organization set up under Major Fujiwara to promote the Indian Independence Movement in the Far East. A Prisoner of War Headquarters was set up at Neesoon under Colonel N. S. Gill with Colonel J. K. Bhonsle as the Adjutant and Quarter Master General, and Colonel A. C. Chatterji as the Director of Medical Service, to administer all the Prisoner of War Camps. These headquarters were under the I.N.A. H.Q. at Mount Pleasant.

All prisoners of war were allocated to different camps in Singapore. These were situated at:

1. Neesoon under the command of Major M. Z. Kiani
2. Bidadari under the command of Lt. Col. I. Z. Nagar
3. Tyrsal Park under the command of Major Tehl Singh
4. Kranji under the command of Lt. Parshotam Das
5. Seletar under the command of Major Windman

In all these camps living conditions were deplorable. The accommodation was sufficiently only for about l/5th of the strength stationed there. Consequently, there was a terrible amount of over-crowding, which led to the outbreak of various epidemics. The water supply of Singapore had been cut off during the operations, with the result that all the sanitary arrangement had also broken down. With such a large number of men in these camps, it was the most difficult task to keep up the sanitation. It was only as a result of the most strenuous efforts of Camp Commandants and the Medical Officer that deadly epidemics, like cholera and dysentery were brought under control.

Another major problem that the Medical Officer had to contend with was the lack of medical supplies. There were as many as 5,000 sick and wounded soldiers in various hospitals which received no fresh supplies of medicines from the Japanese; and all the British stocks of medicines had been cleverly taken to the British Prisoner of War Camp at Changi by the Director of Medical Services, who was an Englishman. Eventually Indians, lodged a protest against the Director, and the Japanese were able to persuade him to part with some of his stocks for Indian soldiers.

In the early stages there was no supply of fresh meat or vegetables which made the diet very deficient in Vitamins. As a result, a large number of soldiers developed deficiency diseases, like Beriberi and scurvy. The Japanese had taken charge of all the ration stores in Singapore and it was the most difficult thing to explain to them why rice, atta, dal, ghee, chillies, spices and salt were all required for one and the same meal. The Japanese soldiers eat a very simple diet of boiled rice and vegetable or fish with a little salt added to it. Hence they could not understand why the Indian soldiers would require so many things. They delivered many lectures to us, rebuking us for eating such luxurious meals, and stressing on virtues of the simple Japanese meal. On some occasions they tried to force these virtues on us by refusing to issue more than one item of food a day. On some days they would issue only pepper and say go and live on this today. After a few days, however, we got to know each other better, and we had to give a practical demonstration of Indian cooking to them to convince them that so many different items were really required for one meal. After the Japanese had a few meals with us, they almost gave up their virtuous Japanese meals of which they had talked so much in the beginning.

No pay of any sort was paid to the troops for the first six months.

While all this was going on, Capt. Mohan Singh, with his original band of 200 volunteers under Capt. Alia Ditta Khan and some new and zealous workers, was busy organizing propaganda lectures and meetings with the object of infusing a nationalistic spirit in them, and to induce Indian Prisoners of War to join the I.N.A., which he promised was to be raised in the near future. His propaganda was particularly successful and he managed to convince approximately 30,000 Prisoners of War who volunteered to join the I.N.A. In a very brief space of time, Capt. Mohan Singh became very popular with the great majority of Indian soldiers. In his dealings with the Japanese he displayed extraordinary ability and firmness which endeared him to the soldiers. He was particularly fortunate in having such men as Colonels Gill and Chatterji to advise and assist him in his task.

The majority of officers, however, were still not convinced, and they felt that peeping in view the previous record of the Japanese nation, it was wrong to trust the Japanese and that the best course for them was to remain Prisoners of War. I was also one of them, and it was my intention to see that the I.N.A. was never raised. With this object, therefore, the first thing I did on reaching Neesoon was to organize a block of officers, approximately 20 in number, to resist the formation of the I.N.A.

Early in March 1942, Lt. Col. N. S. Gill and Major Mahabir Singh Dhillon went to Saigon to confer with the senior Japanese officer there. At this conference these two officers were informed that final decisions regarding the Indian Independence Movement would be discussed at the forthcoming conference of Indian delegates to be held at Tokyo.

In the last week of March 1942, a conference of Indian delegates was held at Tokyo. Malaya sent a good-will mission consisting of Capt. Mohan Singh, Lt. Colonel N. S. Gill, Capt. Mohd. Akram Khan, Mr Raghvan, Mr K. P. K. Menon and Mr S. C. Goho to attend the conference.

From Bangkok, Swami Satyanand Puri and Mr Pritam Singh also accompanied the goodwill mission from Malaya.

An unfortunate air crash on the way resulted in the death of Capt. Mohd. Akram, Swami Satyanand and Mr Pritam Singh. It was rumoured in several camps that the air crash was conveniently arranged by the Japanese, as all these three gentlemen were well known for their frankness and dislike of the Japanese.

At the Tokyo Conference, it was resolved that a conference of the delegates of all Indians residing in East Asia would be held at Bangkok in June of 1942. It was also decided there that an Indian Independence League would be found with the object, 'To secure Indian Independence, complete and free from foreign domination, interference, or control of whatever nature.' It was also decided to raise an Indian National Army to fight for India's liberation. The final and official inauguration of the Indian Independence League and the selection of the Council of Action was left to the Bangkok Conference.

Bidadari resolutions

Soon after the surrender of Singapore, Capt. Mohan Singh called a meeting of senior officers and discussed the question of raising the I.N.A. The officers were unanimously of the opinion that on such a vital question each individual should have the right to express his views. Capt. Mohan Singh agreed to this suggestion and Commanding Officers of all units were asked to seek the opinions of all officers and men under their command and to forward them to Capt. Mohan Singh's headquarters.

In April 1942, after the return of Capt. Mohan Singh from Tokyo, another meeting of senior officers was held in Bidadari Camp, Singapore. After a great deal of discussion, the following resolutions were passed:

1. We are Indians first and Indians last. We do not recognize any differences of class, creed or religion.
2. The Independence of India is our birth-right.
3. An Indian National Army will be raised to fight for the independence of India. This Army will only go into action on the invitation of the Indian National Congress and the people of India.
4. Until then we shall endeavour to make ourselves better and patriotic Indians.

It was also decided that these resolutions should be explained to all the officers and soldiers of the Indian army and a list of those who accept these resolutions be prepared. Eventually, these lists were prepared and volunteers, who accepted these resolutions were separated from the rest.

While these important events of far-reaching consequences were taking place between February-April 1942, all the troops living in various camps were aligning themselves to two different camps.

1. Volunteers: Who trusted the Japanese and were prepared to join the I.N.A.

2. Non-Volunteers: Who did not trust the Japanese and were not prepared to join the I.N.A.

Speaking very broadly, the bulk of Sikhs, Dogras and Jats were volunteers. The Punjabi Muslims, Pathans and Gurkhas, were non-volunteers. But this was a purely psychological difference. In reality, there was no difference in the treatment, rations and accommodation given volunteers as well as non-volunteers. They were all living in the same barracks, eating the same food and doing the same work. Capt. Mohan Singh's propaganda agents were, however, busy all the time assessing the feelings of soldiers in various camps and were continuously reporting the situation to Capt. Mohan Singh.

In March 1942, the Japanese asked for a number of labour parties to be sent to Thailand and Borneo. A party of approximately 1,000 men and some officers, including Capt. Dhargalkar, Capt. Hari Budhwar of the 3rd Cavalry, Capt. Tajik and Capt. Jiwan Singh were sent to Bangkok; and another party of approximately 500 men under Major N. S. Bhagat of the Indian Engineers, was sent to Borneo. Both these parties consisted of non-volunteers, and it is true that these soldiers and officers had expressed their opinion of Capt. Mohan Singh and the I.N.A. too openly.

The party that went to Bangkok got into trouble with the local Japanese Commander, who asked the Indian officers to submit lists of their men disclosing their trades and technical qualifications. The Japanese wished to employ Indian drivers and mechanics in their motor transport companies. The Indian officers refused to submit any such lists on the ground that such a thing was not permitted by the Geneva Convention of International Law, and that as prisoners they were only required to give out was their name, rank and unit. The Japanese contended that they had not been signatories to the Geneva Convention. Moreover, even the British Prisoners of War at Changi had given all such information, and the British and Australian prisoners were actually driving Japanese lorries and working in Japanese workshops. The Indian officers, however, refused to cooperate and three of them – Capt. Dhargalkar, Capt. H. Budhwar and Capt. A. A. Tajik – were taken into custody and were ill-treated. However, some statements that appeared in the press said that they were hung upside down for 88 days. Some reports stated that the news that they had been maltreated because they refused to be given to the I.N.A. in order to appease their British masters was a gross exaggeration. In fact their maltreatment had nothing to do with their joining or not joining the I.N.A. Hence when Capt. Mohan Singh went to Bangkok in June 1942 to attend a conference, he heard about this incident and intervened to secure the release of these officers from Japanese custody, and brought them back to Singapore.

Concentration camps

When the I.N.A. members were court martialled and held in the Red Fort of Delhi, all the British allegations against them centred on the so-called atrocities committed by them against the Indian Prisoners of War. Even the prosecuting officers in the trial were forced to admit that the tales regarding the concentration camps were grossly exaggerated and unfounded in reality. In this chapter, I will attempt to draw a truthful picture of the concentration camps so that the Indian people can judge the actual facts for themselves.

After the surrender, the Japanese allowed the Indian officers and men to live together in the same camps. They made Indian officers responsible for maintaining order and discipline in their units. A large number of soldiers, however, felt that by being officially handed over by the British to the Japanese, their allegiance to the King had come to an end, and that from then on they were as good prisoners as their officers whom they did not feel bound to obey any longer. As a result of this feeling, there was indiscipline in the camp. On one occasion, even a commanding officer was severely beaten by the men of his own unit. There were also instances where Indian soldiers would creep out of their camps at night and loot and rape the civilians living near those camps. Members of a particular unit made it a habit to steal and slaughter the cows belonging to civilians. There were others who specialized in stealing pigs and slaughtering them in camps. As there were both Hindus and Muslims living in the same camps, it dawned on everyone that unless some drastic steps were taken the situation would worsen and might lead to a Hindu-Muslim fight. It was with the intention of putting an end to such offences that the concentration camp came into being. Those who were sent there on account of the offences stated above fully deserved the punishment they received. The treatment in the concentration camp was rough, but not brutal. Later on, however, particularly after April 1942, a number of officers and men were taken to the concentration camp on suspicion of being British fifth columnists and for carrying on anti-I.N.A. propaganda. At any rate, never at any time was the treatment accorded to prisoners in the I.N.A. concentration camp worse than the treatment that was meted out to the officers and men of the I.N.A. in the early stages of captivity in the Red Fort of Delhi.

In October 1942, Colonel N. S. Bhagat changed the name of the camp to 'Detention Camp'. After the formation of the 2nd I.N.A., under the director of the Military Bureau, Major General Bhonsle, and the arrival of Netaji Subhas Chandra Bose, even the British authorities were not able to quote even a simple instance of harsh or unfair treatment given to anyone in the detention camp.

After May 1942, a camp known as the Officers' Separation Camp was initiated by Capt. Mohan Singh. All such officers who were suspected of having an anti-I.N.A. propaganda or were attempting to prevent others from turning volunteers were taken to this camp and kept separated from their units. This camp was abolished by Capt. Mohan Singh in October 1942.

Japanese intentions exposed

(1) Changi Guard: Early in March 1942, the Japanese approached Capt. Mohan Singh and requested him to send a Guard of Indian soldiers to go and take over guard duties on the British Prisoners of War camp at Changi. They assured him that this was only the beginning and it was necessary to impress the Japanese Headquarters of the fact that the Indians were really eager and willing to cooperate with the Japanese. By doing this, they said, he would be creating the right atmosphere in which to lay the foundations of the I.N.A.

But the real object of the Japanese in asking for Indian soldiers to be sent to do guard duties at the British Camp at Changi was to relieve Japanese troops for more active roles in the field; and secondly, by giving the Indian soldiers this duty, they hoped to remove their 'inferiority complex'. This was a part of a general policy that the Japanese followed in all newly conquered areas in East Asia. By deliberately humiliating the white races they intended to show Asiatics that they were as good, perhaps better, than the Europeans.

Capt. Mohan Singh, in view of the larger interest of raising the I.N.A., agreed to provide this Guard, and Lt. G. S. Dhillon (I.N.A. Colonel) was selected for this unpleasant task. The majority of the Indian officers were not in favour of this step, because Indians are chivalrous by temperament and they do not believe in hitting a fallen enemy. Doing guard duty over captured prisoners was not the type of service the volunteers wished to do to liberate their country. In fact, there was a general resentment against this; but Lt. Dhillon, the fine soldier that he was, having once given his word to Capt. Mohan Singh, accepted all his orders, pleasant or otherwise. The Changi Guard was hence put directly under the command of the Japanese and continued functioning till the arrival of Netaji.

Incident of Indian anti-aircraft gunners

Early in March, closely following the Changi Guard episode, the Japanese asked Capt. Mohan Singh to provide approximately 900 Indian anti-aircraft gunners to take over the defence of Singapore Island. Capt. Mohan Singh agreed to this. He collected all the gunners in one place and lectured them that there was danger of their camps being attacked by the British aircraft, and that Indian A. A Gunners would have to defend their camps in case of such air attacks. He said that before they could be entrusted with guns, it would be necessary for them to do a short training course under the Japanese. They were given an assurance that they would only be employed in defence of their own camps and inside India to protect liberated areas against enemy air raids. Consequently, approximately 600 gunners were sent to be trained under the Japanese. In fact these man had been manning A. A. guns for several years and were experts at using them. They required no further training. The Japanese, however, only wished to use them for their own benefit. On arrival in Japanese camps, Indian men were divided into different parties each approximately 100 strong and placed directly under the command of the Japanese officers and NCOs. Some of these parties were forcibly put on board ships and taken to defend various Islands in the Pacific. The first information that Mohan Singh received about them was through a Japanese newspaper which applauded the brave deeds of Indian gunners on the Island of Cebo but regretted the death of a large number of them. This was very much resented by all officers and men of the Indian Army in whose minds many grave doubts were aroused as to the real intentions of the Japanese.

Other parties that remained behind in Singapore were subjected to a very harsh and brutal treatment by the Japanese. Indian officers were even slapped by the Japanese NCOs, and when they protested they were made to starve for several days. Some were even bayonetted. Eventually some of them managed to escape from their camp and reported to Capt. Mohan Singh that the Japanese were trying to make Japanese soldiers out of them. Capt. Mohan Singh, accompanied by one Japanese officer Lt. Kunzuka, went to see their living conditions in their Japanese-controlled camp, but he was not granted permission by the sentry to enter the camp. This also created great resentment and indignation among all Indian officers and men.

This inhuman and treacherous treatment of Indian gunners continued till the arrival of Netaji Subhas Chandra Bose who was able to extricate the remaining men from the Japanese clutches and finally enrolled them in the I.N.A.

The incidents of the Changi Guard and Indian Anti-aircraft gunners further convinced me that the Japanese were merely talking of Indian Independence without any intentions of fulfilling their promises. It seemed to me that their only object was to exploit us to their own advantage.

I was, therefore, determined that I would do everything to prevent the I.N.A. from coming into existence. In this I had the full support and confidence of the block of offices who held the same opinion as me.

In April 1942, a vigorous propaganda campaign was launched by Capt. Mohan Singh, and concentration camps were started where the officers and men who did not approve the I.N.A. were taken for detention.

I, however, staunchly refused to allow anyone under my command to be sent to the concentration camp. On one occasion, I had to resign from my command of the camp when I protested to prevent some of my officers from being taken to the concentration camp. In short, during the time that I was commanding the Neesoon Camp I allowed everyone to express his opinion freely without any fear of being sent to the concentration camp, and no one was ever sent there as long as I commanded that camp.

By early May 1942, it was quite evident that with the unlimited powers given to him and with the Japanese determination Capt. Singh would succeed in forming an I.N.A. During this month we had also to finally decide whether or not we would accept the Bidadari resolutions and become volunteers. We were told that volunteers and non-volunteers would be separated and put into different camps. In view of this new situation, we held several meetings of the block of officers who were against the formation of the I.N.A. We came to the conclusion that it was useless for senior officers to stay out of the I.N.A. and be sent to the concentration camp. We decided that the best course (a) for the senior officer was to join the I.N.A., gain control of it and prevent the ill-treatment and exploitation of Prisoners of War by the Japanese. If we failed to do this, then we would try and wreck the I.N.A. from within, if and when we had an opportunity to do so. (b) The rank and file to would remain out of the I.N.A. and if need be undergo hardships and ill-treatment; but the senior officers in the I.N.A. would do their best to help them. These decisions at that time mainly concerned the Muslims.

Therefore, in accordance with this decision, in mid-May 1942, at Neesoon, in the presence of a propaganda lecture under Colonel Chatterji and approximately 400 officers from Neesoon Camp, I told them that I had decided to volunteer for the I.N.A. on the basis of the 'Bidadari Resolutions.' I also told everyone present to make up their minds and decide one way or the other. I also asked unit commanders to hand in the lists of volunteers and non-volunteers on the following day, as they had to be separated. The same afternoon I called a meeting of all Muslim officers in the Mosque and explained my reasons for joining the I.N.A. I also told them that until then I had given them all possible help and protection and the time had come when we would be separated. I, however, promised all possible help to them wherever they might be and expressed the hope that they would never love to join the I.N.A. through force or coercion. They all promised that they would never yield to any coercion and paid a 'Dua Khair' – a religious confirmation of the decision taken.

Bangkok conference

A few days later Capt. Mohan Singh called a conference of all senior officers at his bungalow at Mount Pleasant to discuss plans for the forthcoming Bangkok Conference. He revealed that a conference would be held at Bangkok in June, and that he was entitled to take 90 delegates to it on behalf of the Indian Prisoners of War. This was a third of the total number of the delegates who were expected to assemble at Bangkok, representing Indians in East Asia. He went on to say that he did not think it necessary for all 90 army representatives to go, and that he proposed to take only 30 delegates and for the remaining 60, he said, he would take their proxy votes. He concluded by saying that since everyone had full confidence in him, he himself would nominate the delegates who were to proceed to Bangkok. Everyone present agreed with this.

My own thought was that at Bangkok we would he likely to be made 'committed' too far, and I was not in favour of Indian Prisoners of War participating in such a conference. After Capt. Mohan Singh had finished his speech, I got up and told him that I did not agree with his idea of sending delegates to Bangkok. I told him that since he was taking a delegation there, which was likely to deal with very important matters concerning the future of Indian Prisoners of War, the men going there should be those who commanded the confidence of the Prisoners of War, and I suggested three alternative methods for their selection:

1. Camps should be allotted a number of seats in accordance with the number of Prisoners of War residing there, and the choice of actual member of delegates should be left to them.

2. Failing this, vacancies should be allotted to each community in proportion to its strength and the choice of delegates should be left to them.

3. And finally, if none of the two above-mentioned methods suited Capt. Mohan Singh, and since we all had full confidence in him, it was not necessary for him to take a delegation of 30 representatives with him. Only he and his personal A.D.C. would suffice for the purpose. Moreover, then it would not be called a delegation representing the Indian Prisoners of War.

Everyone present at the meeting agreed with my proposal, and Capt. Mohan Singh, in view of this unanimous demand, promised to inform us the following day which one of the three methods suggested by me was acceptable to him. The conference then dispersed and we all returned to our respective camps.

On arrival at my camp I collected all the officers and told them what had transpired at the conference. They unanimously agreed to my suggestions.

On the following day Capt. Pattanayak, one of the Adjutants of Capt. Mohan Singh, came to me in my camp office and told me that he had 35 proxy votes which he wanted me to have filled in by the officers in my camp. I reminded him of the meeting that Capt. Mohan Singh had held at his residence on the previous day and of his promise to inform us of the method to be employed for the selection of delegates. At any rate, I asked him to let me have the list of delegates that were going to Bangkok, so that we could give our proxy votes in favour of those officers whom we trusted. The exact form of the proxy was: 'I... hereby give my proxy vote to... whose decision will be legally binding on me.'

Capt. Pattanayak was, however, unwilling to part with this information and suggested that the names of officers in whose favour proxies were to be given should be left blank, and that he would fill in the names later himself. This was very objectionable, and I refused to ask any officer to sign the proxy forms. Capt. Pattanayak then departed very annoyed and told me that I would know about the final decision by the evening. I also brought this conversation to the notice of all officers of my camp, and they all unanimously endorsed my reaction. That night, however, I received orders of transfer to Kuala Lumpur as the commander of the Parties of ardent non-volunteers. Consequently, from Neesoon, the largest Prisoners of War camp, only one delegate went to attend the conference under the orders. He was the prosecution witness No. 2 in the first I.N.A. trial, Subedar Major Babu Ram. There were several others too who were nominated to go but they refused to go as 'Nominees'. Not a single proxy vote from Neesoon camp went to Bangkok.

On the day of my transfer to Kuala Lumpur, Capt. Mohan Singh held a meeting of all Prisoners of War at Seletar and declared that he had found out that there was a party within his party which was trying to wreck the movement started by him, and that he was going to take steps to put an end to such rebellion.

The delegation to Bangkok left Singapore early in June as the conference was scheduled to be held on 15 June 1924. The Indian Army sent 30 delegates, together with 60 proxy votes. Besides these, Indian delegates from all over East Asia, including Messrs. Raghvan, Menon and Goho of Malaya, also attended the conference. Mr Bose was elected the President of the conference.

The opening day of the conference was attended by the following dignitaries:

The Foreign Minister of Thailand, the Italian Minister to Thailand, the German Minister to Thailand and the Japanese Ambassador to Thailand.

These foreign dignitaries read messages of felicitation from their respective governments, The Conference adopted seventeen resolutions, and the main points of which were:

1. A 'Council of Action' consisting of the following members was elected to direct the Indian Independence Movement in East Asia: Mr R. B. Bose (President), Capt. Mohan Singh, Mr N. Raghvan, Mr K. P. K. Menon and Lt. Col. A. Q. Gilani.

2. It was decided to reorganize the Indian Independence League Branches all over East Asia. These branches were to function entirely independent of any Japanese influence and control whatsoever. They were to function under the direction of H.Q. I.I.L. at Bangkok.

3. India was to be considered as one indivisible whole and no partition of India on whatever grounds would be considered.

4. The Indian National Congress was to be taken as the only national representative body of India.
5. Independence was the birth-right of Indians, and Indians in East Asia were determined to fight to achieve this objective.
6. The Imperial Nippon Government undertook to help Indians in East Asia with arms, ammunitions and necessary military equipment to achieve this objective.
7. The Imperial Nippon Government would recognize Indians in East Asia as citizens of a free country and would exert its influence on other friendly powers to recognize Indians in their respective territories as free citizens.
8. No property belonging to Indians in East Asia was to be considered as 'enemy' property. The property of Indians who had evacuated from East Asia would be handed over to the Council of Action of the I.I.L., and this property would be kept in trust by the League.
9. After India became free, a regular treaty would be signed between the new Government in India and the Japanese Government; and that this conference of Indians in East Asia did not bind the Indians in India to any agreement or commitment with Japan.
10. All help taken by the Indians in East Asia from the Imperial Nippon Government in the form of war materials etc. would be considered as a debt and would be paid by the Free India.
11. An Army to be called the 'Indian National Army' would be raised from among the volunteers from the Indian Prisoners of War and the Indian civilians.
12. Capt. Mohan Singh was appointed General Officer Commanding the newly created I.N.A.
13. The Japanese government was requested to approach the Government of Germany to enable Mr Subhas Chandra

Bose to come to East Asia to take charge of the Indian Independence Movement.

14. The I.N.A. would be recognized by all the Axis Powers as a free and an allied army.

15. The Imperial Nippon Government would ratify these resolutions.

My transfer and stay at Kuala Lumpur (June-September 1942)
At the time of my transfer to Kuala Lumpur other officers and I of my bloc realized that Capt. Mohan Singh had seen through our real intentions and was trying to get us out of the way. But by this time we were more than convinced that the Japanese were out to exploit us for their own selfish ends and so we were determined to stick to the I.N.A. and prevent us from being exploited.

I arrived at Kuala Lumpur by goods train early in June, and I was followed there by several groups of the staunchest non-volunteers. On the arrival of all the parties, I was ordered to assemble them for the Japanese Commander's inspection. I did so. The Jap commander then addressed all of us and said, 'I welcome you all and am very pleased to have you under my command. We regard you not as the Prisoners of War but as brothers, as we are all Asiatics. It is the most ardent desire of the Japanese nation that India should achieve its independence as soon as possible, and to enable you to participate in the freedom fight we have made arrangements for rearming and training you.'

This was greatly resented by all of us as we had no intention of being rearmed and undergo military training under the Japanese. After the parade, the Prisoners of War refused to be dismissed unless their status and position as the Prisoners of War was clarified.

I took the Japanese commander to my office and in the presence of other fellow officers explained the situation. I told him that some of us who were known as volunteers were willing to take up arms and fight the British, but those who were non-volunteers wished to remain and be treated purely as the Prisoners of War. I informed him that the question of Indian Independence was an affair of the Indians and that the Japanese should not force any Indian against his wishes to participate in the fight for freedom. I assured him that, as far as the Japanese were concerned, we were all willing to help them in our own way in their war against the Anglo-Americans. I also told him that the 'volunteers' would help by actually fighting the British, and non-volunteers would help by strengthening rear bases and lines of communications, such as building aerodromes, railways and roads.

He agreed with me and said that from their point of view the latter task was even more important than the first one, and he agreed to issue necessary orders to all Japanese Commanders in Malaya under his command that 'volunteers' were to be employed in fighting, and 'non-volunteers' were to be used as labourers.

A similar trouble occurred at Seremban where, on refusal of the Prisoners of War to take up arms, the Japanese fixed machine guns all around the camp, put the Camp Commander Capt. Ghulam Mohd. 3/16 Punjab Rifles in a cell and gave the Prisoners of War 24 hours to think about it. They were warned that if at the end of 24 hours they still refused, they would all be executed. I heard about this and at once rushed to Seremban with the Jap commanders orders given at Kuala Lumpur (mentioned above), and after a great deal of persuasion I was able to make the Commander of the Seremban Camp understand our point of view.

In a similar manner I visited all the stations in Malaya, where the Indian Prisoners of War were employed, and ensured that they would not be coerced to take up arms, or pressuring to undergo military training under the Japs.

24 men selected for execution by the Japanese

On one occasion, when I was out of station on tour, the Japanese took away 24 NCOs belonging to the 42nd Field Park Coy. Royal Bombay S. & M. unit on the accusation that they were too pro-British. They decided to execute them and made them sign their last will. When I returned from the tour and learnt about it, I at once went to the Japanese General Headquarters (G.H.Q.) and requested them to hand over my soldiers to me. I told them that I was supposed to be their commander, and in principle it was wrong for the Japanese to deal directly with my subordinate officers and decide to execute the men under my command without my knowledge or concurrence. Finally, I informed them that if they insisted on doing this I would resign from my post. Then consented to give me fifteen of them, and said that the remaining nine had to be executed as they were too pro-British, the Japanese further complained that though they were their prisoners, the Indian Prisoners of war still insisted that they had taken an oath of loyalty to the King of England.

I explained the full significance of this oath to the Japanese telling them that the normal procedure for dealing with any serious offence in the Indian Army was to hold a 'Court of Enquiry'. I assured them that I would go very thoroughly into the case, and if at the end the Court of Enquiry found their offence to be of a serious nature, I would myself hand them over to the Japanese for punishment.

They agreed to this and I brought all the 24 NCOs safely back to their unit, held a Court of Enquiry and released them all.

While the Japanese in Malaya and Singapore were attempting to coerce and exploit Indian soldiers for the benefit of Japan, leaders all over the world – in Bangkok, India and Berlin – were busy preparing for a final struggle that would be fought purely and solely for the Independence of India. We, the Indian soldiers, while burning with the desire to do our utmost for the liberation of our motherland, were unwilling to allow ourselves to be exploited by the Japanese. While in this difficult predicament, I heard a broadcast by Netaji Subhas Chandra over the Berlin Radio.

The Japanese had confiscated all our radio sets, but some of us managed to keep a few sets concealed in our camps. His voice came clear and resolute and even over the radio we could feel the power of his oratory. How we all wished he could come and lead us personally in the battle for India's liberation and do away with Japanese exploitation!

Here are some portions of his speech in his own words:

Inspite of British propaganda it should be clear to all right-thinking Indians that in this wide world India has but one enemy – the enemy who has exploited her for over a hundred years, the enemy who sucks the life blood of Mother India – British Imperialism... I am not an apologist of the Tripartite Powers; that is not my job. My concern is with India... When British Imperialism is defeated, India will get her freedom. If on the other hand, British Imperialism should somehow win the war, then India's slavery would be perpetuated for ever. India is, therefore, presented with the choice between Freedom and Slavery. She must make her choice...

Britain's paid propagandists have been calling me an enemy agent. I need no credentials when I speak to my own people. My whole life is one long persistent, uncompromising struggle against British Imperialism and is the best guarantee of my bona fides... All my life I have been the servant of India. Until the last hour of my life I shall remain one. My allegiance and loyalty have ever been and will ever be to India alone, no matter in which part of the world I may live... If you make a dispassionate and objective study of different theatres of War today, you will come to the same conclusion as me that nothing on earth can prevent the rapid collapse of the British Empire. Already the outposts in the Indian Ocean have passed out of the hands of British sea-power. Mandlay has fallen and fallen troops have been practically expelled from Burmese soil-Countrymen, when the British Empire is disappearing, the day of India's deliverance approaches. I want to remind you that in the year 1857 began India's first war of Independence. In May 1942 has begun her last war of Independence. Gird up your loins. The hour of India's salvation is at hand.

Quit India resolution and mass rally at Kuala Lumpur

On 11 August 1942, the news reached Malaya that the Indian National Congress had demanded at an A.I.C. meeting in Bombay that the British must quit India. Mahatma Gandhi had given a call 'Do or Die' to all patriots. 'Do not wait for a lead from leaders, do what you think is right, do what you think shall bring us freedom' was his message to the Indian people.

The Indians at Kuala Lumpur decided to hold a mass rally to express their appreciation and approval of the 'Quit India' resolution passed by the Indian National Congress and to express their indignation at the arrest of Mahatma Gandhi and other prominent national leaders. That day in the morning, Japanese Liaison Officer Lt. Nyui came to me and asked that the General Commanding Kuala Lumpur Area wished to know if I and my troops would be going to the rally. My reply was in the positive. He then went on to say that in that case we would have to march to the scene of the meeting carrying crossed Japanese and Indian national flags at the head of the column. He thought that this would be a sign of goodwill and show close cooperation between the two nations. I asked him to go and inform the General that if that was the condition, I would not take part in the rally. I told him that no Indian wished to carry the national flag of another nation. I further said if the Japanese intention was to show to the world that they could make the prisoners carry the Japanese flag by force then they ought to insist on this, otherwise not. Finally, I assured him that if we went to the rally we would march there only under our own national flag and would not carry any Japanese flags. He reported this to the General. The Japanese General not only allowed me to have my own way, but also issued orders that on that day no civilian was supposed to show or carry the Japanese flag.

We went to the rally held at a big maidan at Kuala Lumpur where approximately 45,000 people of all nationalities were present. Some high-ranking Japanese officers were also present there.

I was asked to deliver a speech on behalf of the Indian soldiers. I did so. In the course of the speech, I said, 'Nobody should ever have any misconception that the Japanese were going to make the I.N.A. a puppet force.' I added that if on arriving in India, we found that the Japanese had any designs of that sort, we would turn around and fight them most vigorously. I assured them all that rather than becoming a Japanese puppet, every single soldier of I.N.A. would perish fighting to uphold India's honour. This remark of mine thrilled the masses and there was wild cheering; perhaps it was too bold a statement to make at a time when Indians were terrified of the Japanese. A recording of my speech was also made. The next day, the Japanese General congratulated me on my speech, and said if the Japanese went to India with the intention of replacing the British we ought to fight them; otherwise we would be traitors in our own country.

Thus, during the period of June-September 1942, when I was commanding the Indian Prisoners of War in Malaya, I served them to the best of my ability. Several times I had to travel by goods trains, without food, and had to face insults and humiliation at the hands of junior Japanese Officers for the sake of the men I commanded. I refused to let the Japanese exploit the Indian Prisoners of War in any way, and at the same time secured for them the best treatment that was given to any Prisoner of War in East Asia.

I always upheld the honour and prestige of my country and refused to brook any racial superiority from the Japanese. I also induced the Japanese not to arrest any Indian soldier who had turned civilian during the war and was honourably earning his living.

Propaganda for the formation of the I.N.A.

After the return of the delegates from the Bangkok Conference, resolutions were discussed with only a few senior officers. They were kept secret from the others until the official ratification of these resolutions came from Tokyo.

Some selected officers were detailed to visit various camps and explain the proceedings of the Bangkok Conference to the men. Lectures on nationalism were intensified and all the ranks were informed of the seriousness of the step that they were required to take in joining the I.N.A.

During this period of intensified activities, Capt. Mohan Singh had to take some serious steps and adopt drastic measures against those who knowingly tried to undermine this propaganda amongst the ranks. Certain officers who proved to be stumbling blocks were made depart from their units. Detention camps were opened where such anti I.N.A. elements were segregated.

The Japanese Military Government in Malaya kindly permitted the I.I.L. to broadcast a programme of Indian propaganda over the Singapore Radio Station. K. P. K. Menon was appointed the propaganda-secretary of the I.I.L., while the Radio department was placed under Major Irshad Ali Sahibzada I.M.S. Messages from Indian soldiers and civilians to India and speeches by prominent members of the I.I.L. and the Army became regular features of this daily broadcast.

Prior to this, some army officers had been despatched to Saigon and Bangkok to take charge of radio programmes broadcast from these radio stations. Very interesting broadcasts from Saigon Radio Station were made by Colonel Ehsan Qadir, Colonel Nagar and Colonel I. Hassan, and were eagerly listened to by the people in India.

A paper called the *Azad Hind* was published daily from Singapore under the control of the I.I.L. This paper was published in English, Tamil, Malayalam, Roman Urdu and Gujarati.

Organization and formation of the I.N.A.

Shortly after the Bangkok conference, Major Fujiwara was transferred and he was replaced by a Colonel of the Iwakuro Kikan. This department used to issue instructions to Capt. Mohan Singh regarding the organization of the I.N.A. The Japanese informed Capt. Mohan Singh of the quantity of arms, equipment and transport they would issue to the I.N.A., and that the organization of the I.N.A. should conform to the means placed at the disposal of Capt. Mohan Singh by the Japanese.

Capt. Mohan Singh detailed Major M. Z. Kiani to work out the details of the organization. Eventually, it was decided that the I.N.A. should consist of 15,000 of all ranks, and the following units and formations were to be raised:

3 Guerrilla Regiments:
        Gandhi Guerrilla Regiment
        Azad Guerrilla Regiment
        Nehru Guerrilla Regiment
1 Special Service Group   Bahadur
1 Intelligence Group
1 Reinforcement Group
1 Regt. of Field Force   1st Hind Field Force
1 Artillery Unit
1 Armoured Fighting Vehicles Unit
1 Engineering Unit
1 M. T. Coy.
1 Medical Aid Party
1 Base Hospital
1 Officers Training school

Headquarters I.N.A. with General Staff and other administrative departments, including the propaganda department.

All details of arms and equipment, strength and organization, allotment of vehicles were worked out entirely by the General Staff branch of H.Q., I.N.A.

An Officers' Training school was established to train officer from amongst civilians and other ranks of the Army with a view to further expand the I.N.A. All instructors were Officers from the Indian Army.

As far as possible, old Indian Army units were not broken up but were absorbed in the various units of the I.N.A., as a whole. Certain amount of reshuffling of officers was inevitable; which was done.

The officers and men who did not join the I.N.A. were put under the control of a separate headquarter meant for the Prisoners of War camps. This headquarter was under the command of Major A. B. Mirza, Bahawalpore State Forces, who received all instructions from H.Q., I.N.A.

Organization I.I.L. centres and training of Indian civilians
After the Bangkok conference, under the auspices of the Council of Action, I.I.L. centres in East Asia were reorganized according to the resolution passed at the conference. Chairmen were appointed for each I.I.L. branch and a committee of local civilians was formed. The main job of these committees was to look after the welfare and relief of Indians residing in their respective areas. These committees also looked after the allotment and requisition of labour demanded by the Japanese.

No particular training on military lines was carried out by these committees in their respective areas, though lectures delivered and meetings were held to instruct the local Indians into being better citizens. It was decided by the Council of Action to open a training centre at Kuala Lumpur for the training of civilians for the I.N.A. A school was opened in Penang to train civilians in civic duties and other administrative jobs. On passing out, these cadets were sent to various districts in Malaya to promote and help the local committees in their functioning.

It was decided by the General Staff of the I.N.A., after consultation with the Senior Officers, that the training of the I.N.A. should be resumed on the same lines as that of the Indian Army since all the arms and the equipment given to the I.N.A. by the Japanese were from the Indian Army and on English Army pattern. It was also decided not to follow the Japanese method of training, but to adopt such methods which were more congenial to the Indian soldier, and were superior to that of the Indian Army. This, it was concluded, would be more useful in our new role as the member of the I.N.A. The policy for the training of the I.N.A. was laid down by the General Staff, but unit Commanders were given a free hand in the training of their units in accordance with their role in the battle. Initially, lack of training books and experience hampered the programme to some extent, but gradually officers worked out their own methods to train the soldiers. The General Staff of the I.N.A. subsequently published training manuals and pamphlets to help and guide the officers.

Stress was laid on developing a national spirit amongst all ranks. The sense of slavery which was embedded in the minds of the men of the Indian Army, and the mercenary spirit which proved to be a stumbling block were the first obstacles to be removed. Officers were especially instructed to impress upon the men under their command that they were Indians and the I.N.A. was an Army of the Indians, officered and manned by Indians, whose sole object was to help India in her fight for freedom which could only be achieved by developing a high sense of honour, responsibility, and national spirit.

The ranks were also trained and taught that they were Indians first, irrespective of class and creed. Gradually separate cookhouses and other religious barriers were done away within the I.N.A. Every sepoy and officer, no matter to what class and creed he belonged, lived, ate and worked together.

English words of command were abolished and words of command in Hindustani were adopted. The Congress flag was adopted as the symbol of the I.N.A. As far as possible no help in training was obtained from the Japanese.

My recall to Singapore in September 1942

In September 1942, I was recalled to Singapore and posted as Second in Command to Colonel Bhagat at the Officers' Training School. Later on, after the transfer of Colonel Bhagat, I was appointed as the Commandant of the O.T.S., which started functioning in November 1942, and was disbanded after a few days by the order of General Mohan Singh.

In my opening address to the cadets I said that independence was our birth-right, and to achieve it we had to fight the British. Later on we must be prepared to fight the Japanese too if they showed any intention of dominating India. I told them that the ex-Army men were quite justified in joining the *Fauj* as their oath of loyalty was to their country. Moreover, I said that they were certainly entitled to go their own way and implement their oath of service to their country as best as they could. If they thought that joining the *Fauj* was the best way of serving their country's interest they were thoroughly justified in doing so. I went on to say that India had outlived the smashing up of her repeated yearning for freedom; and that despite 150 years of foreign domination, she still yearned for her freedom. I told them she witnessed her best sons and daughters being ground down in poverty and misery for the crime of seeking freedom for their motherland. All of us who were fighting for the same cause were destined to the same ignoble fate at the hands of the same torturer. And yet, always a new generation had drawn unquenchable hope from the graves of the dead, and fought the same fight all over again. The cycle of fight and death had gone on and on, never ending, inexhaustible. Up to this time we had refused to be cowed down. With indomitable persistency we had kept alight the fire of liberty in our hearts. We had been reduced to a nation of 'Clerks and Coolies', but the fire within still burnt bright. Millions of our countrymen had been killed by famine and flood year after year, and yet we had managed to pass on the tiny spark of liberty to our children and grandchildren. And, again and again that tiny spark had burst out into flames. Once again we were summoned by history to play our part in a conflagration. And, we were once again ready to make ourselves living torches to set alight the walls of that vicious prison into which the British Imperialism had converted our country.

Personally, even at this stage, I was not fully convinced of the Japanese sincerity and my object was to create such a spirit among the officers at least that they would always be prepared to turn around and fight the Japanese, the moment they felt that the Japanese had any intentions of dominating their country, India.

Visit to the prisoners of war camp

One of the first things I did on arrival in Singapore was to visit all the Prisoners of War Camps. Although I was a member of the I.N.A., I had full sympathy with those Prisoners of War who had refused to join the I.N.A. In fact, originally it was with the intention of protecting them that I had joined the I.N.A. I found that during my absence they had been subjected to a certain amount of maltreatment and large numbers of them, specially the officers, were in Separation Camps.

At Seletar Camp, approximately 6,000 of them had signed up as volunteers in the I.N.A. in order to avoid hardship, and with the intention of obtaining arms and turning around against the I.N.A. I did not approve of this, as I had always felt that it was useless to enlist unwilling volunteers in the I.N.A. for there would always be the danger of their letting us down at a critical time. I, therefore, went and reported this to the G. O. C. General Mohan Singh, who refused to admit that any force or coercion was being used to enlist volunteers for the I.N.A. I took him to Seletar, where after talking to the officers he was convinced and he ordered lists of all such volunteers to be torn up.

The actual facts were that the local Indian Camp Commandants, in order to impress General Mohan Singh with their hard work, wished to produce long lists of volunteers and in their enthusiasm far exceeded their powers. It is quite likely that the full facts of such cases never even reached General Mohan Singh.

The dilemma

From the day that we first came in contact with the Japanese, most of us developed a great dislike for their way of dealing with people whose cause they professed to champion. This dislike intensified when we witnessed with our own eyes the organized looting and raping indiscriminately indulged in by Japanese soldiers. We often asked ourselves: 'Is the same thing going to happen in India when we take the Japanese with us?' In addition to this, the more we dealt with the Japanese the more suspicious we grew of their real intentions about India. For example, when we first organized the I.N.A. they issued us guns without any optical or mechanical instruments without which it was not possible to fire them with any degree of accuracy. No ammunition was entrusted to the I.N.A. and the tanks and armoured cars given were fit only for ceremonial parades and propaganda photographs. In fact anyone with any knowledge of modern weapons could see that the Japanese were deliberately not issuing proper arms and equipment to the I.N.A., and without essential equipment it was not possible for any army to succeed against a well-equipped modern fighting force. Perhaps, the Japanese never intended that the I.N.A. should be used for active fighting. In fact we felt that the Japanese were frightened of making the I.N.A. too powerful as they did not trust it. This attitude made us suspicious of the Japanese. We gradually began to lose confidence in them and doubted their professed intentions.

We also knew that the Indian National Congress was very strongly opposed to the expansionist policy of Japan. They were opposed to any scheme which would bring Japan on Indian soil. But, on the other hand, Netaji Subhas Chandra Bose in his broadcasts from Berlin was urging us to advance towards India and destroy the British Imperialism. We were also aware of the events that were taking place in Bengal and

Bihar and the ruthless measures that the British were adopting to suppress the 1942 agitations.

We were thus in a dilemma. We did not know what the right course to follow was. In fact, we were not sure whether when we arrived in India, accompanied by the Japanese, the people would welcome us or spit on our faces.

It was at this stage, early in August 1942, that General Mohan Singh sent Colonel Gill with a few selected and trustworthy officers to the Burma Front with the object of getting them to infiltrate into India. These officers, it was intended, should contact Indian leaders and inform us of the true state of feeling in the country.

On arrival at the front, however, a very prominent member of the party and a close and a trusted friend of General Mohan Singh betrayed the rest of the party by communicating with the British Forces and going over to them. On arrival in India, this officer is said to have concocted hair-raising stories of his heroic escape from Singapore. He also took away with him some very secret I.N.A. documents and records. He was amply rewarded for his treacherous conduct by being awarded the much-coveted honour of becoming a Member of the British Empire. Poor Colonel Gill was so heart-broken that he gave up the attempt and returned to Singapore in disgust. As a result of this incident, the Japanese grew even more suspicious of the I.N.A., and a feeling of mutual distrust grew up between the two armies. Another crisis came about some weeks later which culminated in the dissolution of the first I.N.A., and the arrest of General Mohan Singh.

Crisis in the I.N.A. and the I.I.L.

Early in January 1942, a party of officers and men from Kuala Lumpur under Major Ram Swarup was sent by General Mohan Singh to work with the Japanese Forces operating in Burma. Ever since then these parties were made to operate in various sectors on the Burma Front. The Japanese had divided these men into small groups of eight to ten men and placed them directly under the command of a Japanese officer. The Japanese used these men for propaganda and spying activities.

Arriving in Burma, Colonel Gill found all this very disturbing and greatly resented Indian soldiers being placed directly under the command of the Japanese Officers. He also gathered from his conversation with Japanese G.H.Q. Staff Officers that they intended to use the I.N.A. too in a similar role when the main body arrived in Burma.

Earlier in October 1942, an advance party of all I.N.A. units was sent to Rangoon to arrange for the reception of the I.N.A. due to arrive there in November or December 1942.

Another episode of some considerable interest took place in Rangoon in October 1942. The Indians, in accordance with the resolution passed at the Bangkok conference, asked the Japanese to hand over the property of absentee Indians to the Indian Independence League. The Japanese, who had taken control of all this property, refused to part with it. When the Indians insisted, Mr Yutani, a Japanese political advisor to the Iwakuro Kikan told the members of the League that the issue of Indian Independence was all nonsense as far as the Japanese were concerned; and Indians must not ask for too many concessions. This was a real eye-opener to those who believed in the sincerity of the Japanese promises.

On his return to Singapore from Burma, Colonel Gill apprised General Mohan Singh of the situation in Burma and strongly advised him not to send any more troops there unless the Bangkok Conference resolution was officially ratified by the Japanese Government. He warned General Singh that the Japanese were only out to exploit Indians. Finally, General Singh, who had done so much for the Japanese in the battles of Malaya and Burma, and who had trusted them implicitly in the initial stages, also began to doubt the real intentions of the Japanese. It was decided that no more troops would be sent to Burma until the resolutions passed at the Bangkok Conference were officially ratified by the Japanese Government. At the time, when this decision was being taken by General Singh, Japanese ships were already waiting in the harbour to transport the units of the I.N.A. from Singapore to Burma.

The refusal to despatch these units to the front at this juncture was too great a responsibility to be borne by one man, so General requested the president to call a meeting of the 'Council of Action', the supreme directing body for the I.N.A. and the Indian Independence League. At the meeting, in addition to all, General Iwakuro, the Head of the Japanese Liaison Organization was also present. Mr Raghvan asked General Mohan Singh why he had despatched I.N.A. troops (Advance Party) to Burma without referring the matter to the 'Council of Action' since the question of employing the I.N.A. in operational areas was of vital importance concerning India and the Indian Independence Movement. General Singh could give no satisfactory reply, and apologised for not informing the 'Council of Action', and promised to refer all such matters to the Council in future.

The 'Council of Action' then expressed the opinion that the *Ivoakuro-Kikan* (Japanese Liaison Department) was interfering too much in the affairs of the I.N.A. and the I.I.L., and that they were trying to use the Indian Movement for the purposes of Japan's aggressive intention regarding India. The Council firmly resolved to resist all such designs, and to run the Indian Independence Movement themselves without Japanese control or interference, hence in the best interests of India.

Sri K. P. K. Menon, a very fearless and patriotic civilian member of the 'Council of Action', then pointed out that the Bangkok Conference had been held five months ago and the Japanese Government had not yet officially ratified its resolutions. One of the essential preliminaries for the resolutions to be put into effect was that they had to be first officially ratified by the Japanese Government. Sri Menon pointed out that I.N.A. had been raised illegally and its activities should be suspended forthwith.

In the meantime, a serious crisis had also arisen in the I.I.L. as a result of the Swaraj Institute incident, which was briefly as follows: Mr Raghvan had started an institution at Penang with the object of training young Indians for national service. They were trained in sabotage work and were taught *Nippongo*. One night early in November 1942, some Japanese Army Officers, accompanied by *Iwakuro-Kiltan* officials, came to the Institute, gathered the boys, picked out the most promising ones, herded them into lorries and drove away. Despite the most strenuous efforts on the part of Mr Raghvan it could not be found out who was responsible for the removal of the boys, nor could their whereabouts be discovered. The 'Council of Action' formally protested to the Japanese General Headquarters but no satisfactory reply came forth. Eventually, Mr Raghvan threatened to close the institution unless the Japanese gave a public undertaking that such incidents would never be repeated, and the boys who had been taken away would be returned to the institute. This was a very bold step for a civilian to take. The Japanese as a nation do not believe in allowing any of their subjects to raise their voice against the State and it was, therefore, feared that the Japanese 'Gestapo' would probably quietly do away with Mr Raghvan. But, this brave man was not to be deterred. Eventually, the Japanese were forced to admit that the boys had been taken away by the Japanese. Mr Raghvan publicly condemned this high-handed action of the Japanese and told the Kikan that his institution was not a factory for producing spies for the Japanese. He told them that no Indian could be forced to work with the Japanese Army against his will, and in fact, he advised all Indians to refrain from doing so unless the 'Council of Action' gave the lead.

Eventually, on 29 November 1942, Mr Raghvan closed the Swaraj Institute as a protest against the high-handedness of the Japanese. The Japanese severely resented this, and declared that it was an insult to their Emperor. They then interned Mr Raghvan in his house in Penang and no one was allowed to see him. The arrest of Mr Raghvan, who was the head of the Malayan Branch of the Indian Independence League, had a very depressing effect on the Indians in Malaya.

Such was the atmosphere in which the 'Council of Action' met at Singapore and submitted a memorandum to the Japanese Government putting forward their demands and asking for an unequivocal reply by the Japanese Government to the Bangkok Conference resolutions. They warned the Japanese that if no satisfactory reply was received within a fortnight, they would dissolve the I.N.A. and the I.I.L.

General Iwakuro, however, advised the 'Council of Action' that it was not proper for them to submit such a strong memorandum to the Japanese Government, and that it was likely to be interpreted as an 'ultimatum'. On this, the Council decided to withdraw the memorandum, and General Iwakuro undertook to get an early reply from the Japanese Government for which purpose he sent special envoys to Saigon and Tokyo.

On this representation, Premier Tojo issued a statement that the Japanese had no territorial ambitions over India. But this did not satisfy the 'Council of Action' and the original memorandum was again submitted to General Iwakuro to be despatched to the Japanese Government. The main demands contained in the memorandum were: (1) The official ratification of Bangkok Conference Resolution; (2) Cessation of all unnecessary interference in the affairs of the I.N.A. and

I.I.L. by the Japanese; and (3) The Indian Prisoners of War to continue to be under the command of General Mohan Singh.

In October 1942, after the formation of the I.N.A., a new Japanese department took over control of all those Indian Prisoners of War who had either refused to volunteer for the I.N.A. or had not been absorbed in the I.N.A. General Mohan Singh wished to keep them under his command, as he felt that these Prisoners of War would serve as a reserve for the I.N.A. The Japanese however refused to agree to these demands and a fresh crisis arose. General Mohan Singh called a meeting of all senior I.N.A. officers and solicited their views on the subject. They were unanimously of the opinion that we should insist on our demands, and if the Japanese did not agree, we should disband the I.N.A.

On 8 December 1942, the Japanese, probably on the suspicion that they were at the back of the crisis, arrested Colonel Gill. They said that he was a British spy and that it was due to his instigation that Major Dhillon had deserted from Burma. They also arrested all the other members of the party who had accompanied Colonel Gill to Burma with the object of contacting Indian leaders.

Following the arrest of Colonel Gill, all the members of the 'Council of Action' resigned. In the Army, the feeling was growing that the Japanese had definitely gone back on their words, and that we should have nothing to do with them. The other members of my block, as well as I, who had no faith in the Japanese, considered this an ideal opportunity for ending all cooperation with them. We started an intensive propaganda campaign against the I.N.A. and advised General Mohan Singh to dissolve the I.N.A.

Mr Rash Behari Bose, the president of the 'Council of Action', was however of the opinion that all the difficulties and obstacles in the way of the Indian Independence Movement could be removed by direct negotiations with the

Japanese Government. He volunteered to proceed to Tokyo and settle all the differences with Premier Tojo who advised General Mohan Singh to exercise patience. But General Mohan Singh and other members of the 'Council of Action' refused to listen to him and the situation started deteriorating drastically.

During the middle of December 1942, Mr Rash Behari Bose made an effort to sort the matter out. He wrote a letter to General Mohan Singh and asked him to send some senior officers to meet him at his residence in Singapore for he wanted to explain the actual situation to them. General Mohan Singh, however, sent a very curt reply stating that no officer was entrusting in meeting him. Moreover, General Mohan Singh himself would not allow anyone to go and see him. The matter enraged Mr Rash Behari Bose who asked the Japanese to issue orders for the arrest of General Mohan Singh. Consequently, General Iwakuro was sent on 20 December 1942, to put General Mohan Singh under arrest. In the initial stages, the treatment meted out to General Mohan Singh by the Japanese was satisfactory. He was given a separate bungalow on St. John Island, near Singapore, and he was allowed personal staff of seven officers and men, including two A.D.Cs., cooks and orderlies. He was later transferred to Sumatra where, on the arrival of the British Forces, he reported to them and was brought to the Red Fort of Delhi. General Mohan Singh, who had anticipated all this, had issued secret instructions prior to his arrest ordering the commanders to dissolve the I.N.A. as soon as he was arrested. These instructions were carried out as per his orders. All arms were collected and dumped by the units, all party badges of rank were burnt, and all military training was suspended.

This led to a general antagonistic feelings against the Japanese and almost all officers and men decided to trust the Japanese never again.

A letter was addressed to the Japanese Liaison Department (Iwakuro-Kikan) by the I.N.A. informing them of the decision of all officers and men to be reverted to the status of the Prisoners of War. The Japanese, however, refused to recognize them as such, and said that as far as they were concerned, Indian Prisoners of War had been declared free persons once; therefore they could not be classified as the Prisoners of War again. On this, we expressed our intentions of exercising our rights as free persons to leave our camps; either to march to India, or settle down as civilians in Malaya, Thailand or Burma. The Japanese refused to allow us to leave our camps.

Mr Rash Behari Bose maintained that General Mohan Singh had a perfect right to resign from the command of the I.N.A.; but he had no right to dissolve the I.N.A., as it did not belong to him personally. It was India's army and *not* General Mohan Singh's. He also made a formal declaration that he had ordered General Mohan Singh to be arrested, and he had been deprived of his rank of General which Mr R. B. Bose had bestowed upon him, when he was appointed as the Commander of the Indian National Army.

This state of affairs lasted for approximately two months. In the meantime, an intensive propaganda campaign was started by Mr R. B. Bose and the Japanese together to motivate officers and men to continue in the I.N.A., which most of them did not wish to do at that stage. The Japanese, however, found a few junior officers who were prepared to work for them, and with their help they tried to raise a puppet I.N.A.

Lectures by General Iwakuro at B'JaJiri

In February 1943, after the Japanese had carried out a thorough propaganda campaign, the Japanese General Iwakuro, Head of the Liaison Department, called a meeting of all I.N.A. officers, approximately 300 of them, at Bidadari and delivered a speech. The salient points of his speech were:

1. That, the I.N.A. had been raised as a result of the decision taken by the Indian delegates who had assembled at Bangkok as representatives of Indian residents of East Asia.
2. That, the Japanese government sympathized with the desire of the Indians to fight for the liberation of their country, and had granted travel facilities to the delegates to meet at Bangkok and to decide on the ways and means of conducting their campaign for liberation.
3. That, a 'Council of Action' was elected by the delegates with Mr R. B. Bose as the President; and Bose had nominated Capt. Mohan Singh to command the I.N.A.
4. That, the Japanese Government had given a promise of all-out aid to the President.
5. That, General Mohan Singh could, if he so chose, resign Command of the I.N.A., but he had no authority to disband the I.N.A. without the sanction of the President, and that any attempt at disorganising it would be treated as mutiny.

It was a very critical time, and it was obvious that the Japanese were determined to keep the I.N.A. going, if necessary even by use of sheer force; and that they were looking for a few ring-leaders whom they wished to make scape-goats to frighten others so that they would continue as a part of the I.N.A. Everyone present, realizing Japanese intentions and their unreasonable attitude, decided to remain quiet. I could no longer stand it. I made Iwakuro admit that the I.N.A. had been raised by the Japanese by the use of force, deceit, and coercion, and that the people who had gone to Bangkok were not our representatives, and, as such, although legally we were bound by the Bangkok Conference Resolutions, normally the Japanese had no justification in forcing us to continue in such a moment, because in a seared movement meant for securing India's Independence there was no place for deceit and coercion. The Japanese General Consented and as a result everyone was allowed a free choice of either continuing in the I.N.A., or going out of it.

The next day, I was sent for by General Iwakuro at his bungalow for a 'heart to heart talk', as he called it. He told me that he had fully appreciated my arguments on the previous day's meeting and was anxious that a man like me should take up the leadership of the I.N.A. He asked me if I would accept it. I told him that I would *not* because I did not feel I had the necessary ability or the following, and that the people had lost all faith and confidence both in the Japanese as well as in our own leaders.

He then requested me to give my opinion on how a real and true I.N.A. could be raised – an I.N.A. which people would be willing to join. I made the following suggestions:

1. That the question of Indian Independence should be treated as something sacred, and everything pertaining to it should be based on truth and on unshakeable foundations; that the Japanese must not attempt to exploit us for their own selfish ends.

2. That there must be no coercion to induce anyone to join it; that anyone who came forward must do so of his own free will, and after fully realizing the consequences of doing so. I also suggested that people wishing to leave the I.N.A. should be treated kindly.

3. Finally, I told him that there was only one man outside India who could start a real I.N.A., and that was Netaji Subhas Chandra Bose. I insisted that by the real I.N.A., I meant a formidable fighting force, not merely a propaganda army.

He agreed with me and assured me that he would try his best to make arrangements for Netaji to come to Singapore from Germany. I informed him that a large number of officers and men would be willing to continue in the I.N.A. on the express condition that Netaji would come to Singapore, and until the time of his arrival no troops should be moved out of the island. It was on this condition that I decided to continue in the I.N.A. and was appointed the Chief of General staff to the Director of the Military Bureau.

In reorganizing the I.N.A., we set out to ensure that:

1. Anyone who wished to leave the I.N.A. was free to be so without any fear of reprisals against him.
2. Those who remained in the I.N.A. were to be prepared even to fight against the Japanese, if the Japanese proved dishonest.
3. That the Japanese shall not exploit us for their own benefit.

By this time the Japanese had taken over all the non-volunteers under their direct control and our main worry was the treatment that would be meted out to those officers. We feared that they would be sent to the Pacific Islands where the conditions were bound to be very unpleasant.

During the period of the crisis and after the arrest of General Mohan Singh, Mr R. B. Bose appointed a committee of officers to carry on the administration of all I.N.A. camps, and to maintain strict discipline among the troops. The committee consisted of. Lt Col. A. D. Loganadhan, Lt. Col. J. K. Bhonsle, Lt. Col. M. Z. Kiani and Lt. Col. Ehsan Qadir. This committee continued to function until the reorganization of the I.N.A.

Reorganization of the I.N.A.

It was realized by everyone that the greatest weakness in the first I.N.A. was that it was entirely a one-man show; therefore in order to organize a second I.N.A. on a more democratic basis, it was decided to institute a Directorate of Military Bureau to control all the activities of the I.N.A. The Director of the Military Bureau was a military officer who directly came under the President of the I.I.L. In addition to this, it was decided to set up an Army Headquarter under an Army Commander who would command the combatant units of the I.N.A. in the field. The President appointed Colonel J. K. Bhonsle as the Director of Military Bureau, and Colonel M. Z. Kiani as the Army Commander.

All those who were not willing to continue in the I.N.A. were given an opportunity of reverting to the status of a Prisoner of War, and about three thousand officers and men took advantage of this. In the reorganized I.N.A., these members were made up from amongst new volunteers from amongst the Prisoners of War and civilian recruits who were forthcoming in large numbers. The Japanese officially recognized the I.N.A. as an allied Army, equal in rank and status to the Japanese Array. They also promised to ratify the Bangkok Conference Resolutions.

A meeting of delegates from all over East Asia held to formulate plans for the reorganization of the I.I.L., and an Advisory Council was set up to assist the President. It was also announced at this meeting that on arrival in the Far East Netaji Subhas Chandra Bose would take over the Presidentship of the I.I.L.

A sketch showing the reorganization of the Indian Independence Movement and the Indian National Army are given in forthcoming pages.

Even after the reorganization of the I.N.A. the Japanese did not give up their original game of exploitation. In fact, they tried to intensify it and weakened the resistance to this exploitation by the I.N.A. and the I.I.L. They realized that General Mohan Singh had been successful in creating a crisis, because he had been given too much power. They, therefore, placed a scheme before Mr Rash Behari by which they succeeded in splitting the I.N.A. into two distinct divisions.

1. The Directorate of Military Bureau with General Bhonsle at its head. This Directorate controlled the general policy and finances of the I.N.A. It was under the President of the I.I.L., Mr Rash Behari Bose, who had no direct contact with the troops.

2. The Army, with General M. Z. Kiani as its Commander, who was responsible for its administration, training and discipline.

Thus the previous functions of General Mohan Singh were distributed between two I.N.A. commanders. This was not all. The Japanese, realizing that the Indian Officers were too shrewd for them and would never agree to Japanese exploitation started other training centres where civilian volunteers were trained for various duties, the most important of them was to supply recruits for the I.N.A. These camps came directly under the I.I.L. and had Japanese officers as supervisors. Colonel Ehsan Qadir was put in command of these camps. All the instructors were I.N.A. officers and men. In some camps, civilians were also employed to give political training to recruits. All these camps came directly under the President of the I.I.L. and not the I.N.A.

We, in the I.N.A., suspected that the Japanese were attempting to raise an I.N.A. from amongst the civilian population with the object of having a parallel organization to our I.N.A. and which, if the I.N.A. gave any more trouble, could replace it. Thus, in the I.N.A., the Japanese were trying to play with three different Commanding Officers at the same time. They did their best to play one Indian officer against the other; but, thanks to their integrity and to their loyalty to their country, the Indian officers staunchly refused to become stooges of the Japanese and were able to resist all their attempts at creating ill-well among the three heads of the I.N.A., and thereby facilitate its exploitation.

Against the Indian Independence League, which together with all its branches in Malaya had taken a prominent part in the crisis, the Japanese set up an organization called the Indian Youth League. This youth movement was launched with the *Kikan's* secret support and was little more than a pocket borough of the Japanese. They conducted a vilifying campaign against the civilian members of the 'Council of Action', who resigned in December, 1940, in order to stop the Japanese exploitation of Indians.

Thus, even after the reorganization of the I.N.A. and I.I.L., the Japanese still continued to interfere in their affairs with the difference that they did not do it explicitly as before. They only changed the method of approach. As a result the position continued to remain unsatisfactory. All these weaknesses were pointed out by General J. K. Bhonsle to Mr R. B. Bose, who fought valiantly against it in order to put an end to it. Mr Bose always advised us not to create any more trouble, as the time factor in our coming struggle would be vital. He assured us that Netaji Subhas Chandra Bose was going to come in the near future. This state of affairs lasted from March 1943 to July 1943, when Netaji arrived to take charge of the Indian Independence Movement from Sri Rash Behari Bose.

Sri Rash Behari Bose

After throwing a bomb on Lord Hardinge in 1911, this great revolutionary had escaped to Japan and found shelter under Mr Toyama, who was a spiritual leader of the Japanese. Sri Bose had been in Japan for approximately 30 years, when the greater East Asia war erupted. It gave him the real opportunity for which he had waited so long. Even before the outbreak of the war he had been constantly carrying on his revolutionary activities with the object of bringing about the emancipation of his motherland, whom he loved so dearly. He was responsible for organizing the '*Kama-Gata-Maru* Expedition' in 1921, where he succeeded in procuring a shipload of arms and ammunition and tried to smuggle it inside India in a Japanese ship, called the *Kama-Gata-Maru*. Unfortunately, the plan was discovered. *Kama-Gata-Maru* and all the Indian revolutionaries who were on board with all arms and ammunitions were captured by the British.

By his timely and far-sighted step in contacting the Japanese Vice-Foreign Minister and Field Marshal Sugiyama, Chief of Japanese Imperial General Staff, and getting them to agree *not* to treat Indians in Japanese occupied territories as enemy subjects, he saved the life, property and honour of thousands of his countrymen residing in the East, and earned their everlasting gratitude.

Netaji used to say that when they were children, Sri Rash Behari Bose was looked upon as a national hero, whose name used to inspire the younger generation. He remained the same great revolutionary throughout his life.

Sri Rash Behari Bose was absolutely incorruptible and held the honour and prestige of his country above everything else. The fact that he lived in Japan for over 30 years, with a price of one lakh rupees, which the British had placed on his head, dead or alive, and that he had married a Japanese woman from a very high and respectable family, did not make the slightest difference to his patriotism. He probably knew the Japanese better than any other Indian residing in East Asia, and he exerted considerable influence on higher Japanese military and political circles.

It is a peculiar custom in the Japanese Army that the local commanders, irrespective of how small they are, are given very wide range of powers, and each one of them feels that it is his personal duty to achieve something great in helping Japan to win the war.

It was inbred with this feeling that the Japanese Liaison Officers of the Hirakari-Kikan used such methods as suggested that the Japanese were out to exploit us: and it was not surprising that the Indian officers did not trust them and very frequently lost patience with them. But, Mr Rash Behari Bose, who knew the Japanese so well, was always confident that he would be able to bail out Indians of all troubles hag influencing the Japanese High Command in Tokyo. It was because of this that he advised us to have more patience.

On 4 July 1943, he very gladly handed over the charge of the Indian Independence Movement to Netaji Subhas Chandra Bose and retired to have a well-deserved rest. He died in Tokyo in January 1945 at the age of 62.

Initially about 17,000 officers and men volunteered to join the I.N.A. They signed the declaration to join the I.N.A. unconditionally, under the command of Capt. Mohan Singh, who was appointed G.O.C., I.N.A. The H.Q. of the I.N.A. was established in Bidadari camp in the month of September 1942.

It was agreed by Capt. Mohan Singh and other senior officers of the I.N.A. that the officers of the I.N.A. who were holding commission in the British Indian Army would relinquish their posts. They would then be given commission in the I.N.A., subject to the approval of the President of the 'Council of Action'. Accordingly, all officers ceased to wear badges of the ranks of the Indian Army. Subsequently, they all became Gazetted Second Lieutenants of the I.N.A. Gradually, they were promoted to senior ranks according to their old seniority.

The I.N.A. Headquarters was officially established on 1 September 1942. Capt. Mohan Singh assumed the command of the I.N.A. with Colonel N. S. Gill as the Supreme Advisor and Colonel M. Z. Kiani as the Chief of Staff.

CHAPTER FOUR

ARRIVAL OF
NETAJI SUBHAS BOSE IN EAST ASIA

After the crisis in the Indian National Army, General Iwakuro, Head of the Japanese Liaison Department known as 'Iwakuro Kikan', managed to convince his government that it was not possible to raise a real I.N.A. without the personal assistance and guidance of Netaji Subhas Chandra Bose. He therefore requested his government to make arrangements for Netaji Subhas Chandra Bose to come from Berlin to Singapore and take over the personal leadership of the I.N.A. General Iwakuro was informed by his government that it was not possible for Subhas Chandra Bose to come to Japan as the journey was most hazardous, and that there were only five per cent chances of his coming through it alive. The journey, they said, was to be performed by submarine and as all sea routes were constantly patrolled by the British and American warships there was practically no chance of the submarine getting through undetected. General Iwakuro again wrote to his Government insisting that it was imperative in the interests of the Indian Independence Movement that Netaji should undertake this journey however hazardous it may be. He further counselled them that it was not possible for the Japanese to do anything substantial for the Indian Independence without Netaji's personal guidance in the Far East. He wrote: 'I know there are impossible odds against his coming through safely, but all Indians here feel that without his guidance they cannot launch powerful struggle to secure India's liberation. If he cannot come through safely, then we would have to resign to the belief that Providence does not wish India to be free. If on the other hand, in spite of all the perils *en route* he comes through safely, then we would know that it is the will of God that India should achieve independence through his efforts.'

In any case, General Iwakuro asked the Japanese government to inform Netaji Subhas Chandra Bose of the wishes of Indians in East Asia, the risks involved in undertaking this journey and let him make a decision himself. The Japanese government agreed to this.

Consequently, the Japanese Ambassador in Berlin approached Netaji Subhas Chandra Bose and acquainted him with the wishes of Indians in East Asia, and the dangers that lay ahead of him in undertaking the journey. He frankly informed Netaji that there were only five per cent chances of his getting through safely and advised him not to take the risk as his life which was too valuable. Netaji replied that he would very willingly undertake the journey in spite of the dangers involved. He proudly said that if it got killed en route he would welcome such a death.

It is reliably learnt that Netaji boarded a German submarine which brought him as far as the seas round Madagascar. From there, a Japanese submarine, which had gone from Penang (Malaya) across the Indian Ocean to meet the German submarine, took him on board and brought him back to Penang, from where he flew by plane to Tokyo.

On 3 June 1943, Sri Rash Bihari Bose left Singapore for Tokyo to meet Netaji and brought him to Singapore. The night before his departure, Sri Rash Behari Bose gave a dinner party to several I.N.A. officers. The news of the arrival of Netaji Subhas Chandra Bose was kept a closely guarded secret. When asked about the purpose of his visit to Tokyo, Sri Rash Behari Bose told the officers that he was going to Tokyo to bring back a present for them.

On 20 June 1943, it was announced by Tokyo Radio that Netaji Subhas Chandra Bose had arrived in Japan. Throughout his journey from Berlin to Tokyo, Netaji was accompanied by a Muslim young man by the name of Mr Abid Ali Hasan, who was acting as his ADC It is learnt that Tokyo gave him a very rousing reception, worthy of a great revolutionary leader who had defied the might of the British Imperialism so many times.

On the day of his arrival in Tokyo, Netaji issued an important press statement in the course of which he said, 'During the last World War, leaders had been bluffed and deceived by the British politicians, and that was why we took the vow more than 20 years ago never again to be deceived by them. For many years my generation has striven for freedom and eagerly awaited the hour that has now struck the hour that is for the Indian people the dawn of freedom. We know very well such an opportunity will not come again for another hundred years and we are therefore determined to make the fullest use of it. The British Imperialism has meant for India moral degradation, cultural ruin, economic improvishment and political enslavement... It is our duty to pay for our liberty with our own blood. The freedom that we so win through our sacrifice and exertions, we shall be able to preserve with our strength. The enemy that has drawn the sword must be fought with the sword. Civil disobedience must develop into an armed struggle. And only when Indian people receive the baptism of fire on a large scale will they qualify for their freedom...'

On 21 June 1943, Netaji broadcasted his first speech over the Tokyo Radio. This speech was relayed in all I.N.A. camps. Netaji declared:

So far as India is concerned what is most important to all of us is the situation near India. During the whole history of the British in India, it had not struck one single British General that at any stage in the future, some enemy of the British may appear on the eastern frontier of India. The whole attention of the Britain's military strategists has, therefore, been concentrated on the North-west Frontier of India. With the naval fortress of Singapore in their possession, our rulers thought that India was safe in their hands. The dynamic advance of General Yamashita had opened the eyes of the world to the worthlessness of British strategy. Since then General Wavell has been making feverish attempts to put up fortifications on the eastern frontier of India. But what the Indian people are asking is this: "If it took them almost 20 years to build Singapore, and only one week to lose it, how long will it take the British C-in-C., or his successor to withdraw from his fortifications?" To us Indians, what is of primary importance is not what is happening in Tunis, Tumbuctoo, Lampedusa, or Alaska, but what is happening inside India and across our frontier. What is of primary importance to us is the much-advertised reconquest of Burma which has ended in shameful retreat. Even the fall of Singapore and the loss of Burma, the greatest disasters in British military history, could not bring about any appreciable change. British Imperialism remains inexorable. Men may come and men may go, empires may come and empires may go, but British Imperialism goes-on forever – that is what our rulers continue to think you may call it lack of statesmanship or political bankruptcy or midsummer madness, but this midsummer madness has its own explanation. The British Empire has grown out of India. The British people know, no matter to which political party they belong, that they need to reap all the resources of India. To them Empire means India. They are now fighting madly to preserve that Empire. Consequently, no matter what fate besets Britain during the course of this War, the Englishman will endeavour to the very last to keep his Empire ... i.e. to hold on to India. Therefore, if I may speak frankly, we see that it is not midsummer madness that British politicians refuse to recognize their plight; it is midsummer madness that we should expect Englishmen voluntarily to give up his Empire... No Indian should ever cherish the illusion that one day England will be induced to recognize India's independence. But that is not to say that British politicians will never again compromise with India. Personally, I expected another such attempt sometime this year. But what I want to point out to my countrymen is, that by compromise, British politicians will never recognize India's independence, but will only try to bluff the Indian people. Protracted negotiations are planned to side-track the campaign for independence and thereby undermine the national will, as they did between December 1941 and April 1942... Therefore, we should, once and for all, give up hope of any compromise with British Imperialism. Our independence admits of no compromise. Freedom will only be won when British and their Allies quit India for good. And those who really want liberty must fight for it and pay for it with their own blood... Countrymen and friends! Let us, therefore, carry on the fight for liberty, inside India and outside India, with all our strength and vigour. Let us continue the battle with unshakable faith till the day when British Imperialism will be broken up and out of its ashes India will once again emerge an Independent Nation. In this struggle there is no going back, and there can be no faltering. We must march onward and forward till victory is achieved and freedom won.

CHAPTER FIVE

MOVE OF THE AZAD HIND FAUJ TO BURMA

On 9 November 1943, having completed its training but to a certain extent with its deficiencies in arms and equipment, the first party of the No. 1 (Subhas Brigade) Regiment left Taiping by rail for Rangoon. The last party left Taiping on 24 November.

At the time of departure there were some very touching scenes at the railway station. All the sick and physically unfit soldiers whom the doctors ordered to be left behind at Taiping came to the station and lay down on rails in front of the railway engine and refused to allow the train to start unless they too were allowed to go to the front. They said, 'We have given a pledge to Netaji that we will sacrifice ourselves for the sake of our motherland. How then could anyone leave us behind and deny us this privilege?' It was only after a great deal of persuasion and on an assurance that they would be sent to join the Regiment as soon as they recovered, that they allowed the train to proceed.

The Regiment moved from Taiping via Penang to Chumpon in Siam (Thailand) by train; (2) Chumpon-Kawashi (Victoria point) a distance of 90 miles, some by route march and some by motor lorries; (3) Chumpon-Mergui, by steam boats and rivercraft; (4) Mergui-Tavoy-Ye, mainly on foot; and Ye-Moulmein-Rangoon by train.

The main body of the Regiment arrived in Rangoon early in January 1944.

The journey from Taiping to Rangoon took five weeks during which the men had to cover at least 400 miles on foot. Except for a few unarmed encounters with the Japanese, the journey was uneventful. The only extraordinary thing about the journey was that our soldiers, in their eagerness to reach the front as soon as possible, generally covered the distance in two days, a distance which the Japanese soldiers took five days to travel.

Our soldiers carrying an average load of 80 lbs. were covering 25 miles a day. In one or two instances, two of our companies 'Parwana' and 'Jangju', commanded by Capt. Amrik Singh, *Shaheed-e-Bharat*, and Capt. Santa Singh, respectively covered 30 miles a day.

At Waw, approximately 20 miles East of Pegu, at 11.00 hrs, our train was attacked by the British fighter planes. We suffered slight casualties-one soldier killed and two wounded – some Japanese who were travelling by the same train also suffered casualties. They had 8 soldiers killed and 6 wounded.

Thus Sepoy Jit Singh, a Garhwali, was the first battle *Shaheed* of the Regiment. He was cremated with full military honours at Waw.

Stay at Rangoon

On our arrival at Rangoon, the Regiment (Subhas Brigade) was accommodated in military Barracks at Mingladone, and final preparations for the next move to the front line were taken in hand.

Our difficulties at Rangoon were mainly administrative, which may be summarized as follows:

1. Transport: To transport the rations, ammunitions, battle casualties, etc., the Regiment had only five lorries. It had no proper workshop nor any supply of spare parts. The Japanese Motor transport companies helped whenever it was possible, but this assistance was very inadequate. Inspite of our most strenuous efforts to persuade the Japanese to give us more transport, we were unable to get any. There was even no sack-animal transport of any sort. The result was that the men had to carry everything, including reserve ammunition, heavy machine guns, and medicines.

2. Clothing: The I.N.A. was deficient of warm clothing. It was known that in the area of the Chin Hill and the Kaladan Valley where the unit was going into action the winter was very severe. The men had only one thin cotton blanket and one warm shirt to face this severe winter. All efforts to obtain great coats and other warm clothes failed.

3. Mosquito nets It was known that the area in which the Brigade was going to operate, i.e., the area of the Kabawa Valley-Ganga Tamu and the Kaladan Valley was infested with the most virulent type of malaria. Unfortunately, no proper mosquito nets could be obtained.

4. Emergency rations: We had no emergency-rations for the Azad Hind Fauj. But in Rangoon a special type of 'Shakarpara Biscuit' as emergency-ration was prepared for all the soldiers. In its preparation Netaji took very keen personal interest.

Netaji arrived in Rangoon on 4 January 1944, on a Japanese plane, and established his advance Headquarters there. He realized that the time for launching the offensive was very short. He took the keenest interest in every sphere of the final preparations for the Regiment to proceed to the front; he did for us everything that was humanly possible. He was up against a stone wall. The Japanese were not giving enough assistance to the I.N.A. that they would and should have given. They made all sorts of vague promises that the I.N.A. would be supplied with everything when it reached the front line, which of course, was never fulfilled. Anyhow, the main thing was to reach the front line as soon as possible and launch the offensive. The soldiers told Netaji and their officers not to allow any delay by worrying about providing them with warm clothing, transport, etc. They were anxious to get to the front, from where they said they would get everything from the 'Churchill Supply'.

Understanding with the Japanese army
Much more important than the administrative problems which confronted the I.N.A. was the question of promoting cooperation between the I.N.A. and the Japanese army.

On 7 January 1944, Netaji went to return the courtesy call on the Japanese Commander-in-Chief (C-in-C) in Burma, General Kawabe. I also accompanied Netaji on this visit. At that meeting, the question of the deployment of the I.N.A. and the basis of cooperation between the I.N.A. and the Japanese army was discussed. The Japanese C-in-C told Netaji that the Japanese army was ready to take the offensive as soon as Netaji ordered them to advance. General Kawabe's idea was that the I.N.A. forces should be split up into small groups and attached to all the larger Japanese formations.

Netaji told him that this was not acceptable to him as the splitting up of the 'Subhas Brigade' into small formations would result in the loss of its identity. Netaji insisted that no I.N.A. formation should be split into smaller formations than a Battalion and that the command of all I.N.A. units should remain entirely in the hands of Indian officers. This was ultimately agreed to by the Japanese C-in-C. It was also agreed that Japanese and I.N.A. units would follow a common strategy, as it had been previously discussed and agreed to by Netaji and the Japanese C-in-C. The I.N.A. was to be allotted an independent sector in the front. It was also agreed that every inch of Indian territory liberated would be handed over to the I.N.A. for administration and Major General Chatterji was appointed as the Governor designate of such liberated territories; besides this, all captured dumps of arms, ammunition and other stores, including machinery, were to be handed over to the Provisional Government of the Azad Hind.

The question of the status of the two armies was also discussed, and it was reaffirmed by General Kawabe that the I.N.A. would be treated as the army would be given an ally and equal status in every respect. It was, therefore, decided that saluting was to be on a reciprocal basis, that is, junior officers of the either army would salute the senior officer of the other army. Another difficult question arose related to the procedure to be followed in respect of officers of equal rank of the two armies. It had to be decided. Who would salute first – the Indian or the Japanese officer? The Japanese C-in-C was of the opinion that once the Japanese army was a senior army, the I.N.A. officers should salute first. Netaji took up strong objection to this procedure and told the Japanese C-in-C that he could not accept this proposition as it meant accepting an inferior status as a nation – a status he was not prepared to accept. Netaji, therefore, suggested that when Japanese and an Indian officer of the equal rank met they would both salute at the same time. This was also agreed to by the Japanese.

The question of whether the I.N.A. would be subject to the Japanese Army Act when operating under the direction of the Japanese General Headquarters was discussed next. The Japanese C-in-C informed Netaji that all Allied Armies in East Asia, such as the Mantchurian Army, the Nanking Army, the Burmese Army, and the Thai Army were all subject to the Japanese Military Law, and that it was only right that the I.N.A. too should be subject to it. In actual practice, the acceptance of this principle would have meant that the Japanese Military Police would have the authority to arrest any I.N.A. officer or soldier without referring the matter to Netaji. Netaji refused to agree to this too. He informed the Japanese C-in-C that the I.N.A. had its own Military Law and Army Act, and that he would not allow the Japanese to interfere in any way with its discipline and regulations. This made the Japanese C-in-C very upset and he said that he had no authority to take a decision on this issue. He, however, promised to refer the issue to the authorities in Tokyo, though he doubted very much if they would ever accept it. Netaji assured him that as far as he was concerned it was a matter of principle, and he would never accept the Japanese point of view. Later on, however, Netaji had his own way and the Tokyo Government had to submit to his demand.

Netaji finally summed up the situation by saying that he and other Indians in East Asia looked upon the impending offensive as primarily a battle for India's liberation; and as such, India's honour demanded that Indians themselves should exert their utmost and make supreme sacrifices. He told the Japanese C-in-C that it was his wish that the Indian National Army should form the spearhead of the advance into India, and that the first drop of blood to be shed on Indian soil should be that of a member of the I.N.A. Netaji also informed the Japanese C-in-C that he had told his soldiers and his countrymen inside India that the I.N.A. was coming to liberate them from British bondage, and that he had ordered his soldiers to shoot at sight anyone Indian or Japanese, who was seen looting or raping on Indian soil. The Japanese C-in-C appreciated these orders and agreed to issue similar orders to the Japanese Army as well. Netaji also told General Kawabe that the only flag that would be approved to fly over Indian territory would be the Indian Tricolour. At the end of the conference, the Japanese C-in-C assured Netaji that the Japanese Army would give all possible aid and assistance to the I.N.A. in Burma in all such matters as rations, medicines and evacuation of casualties.

Having settled these fundamentals of cooperation between the I.N.A. and the Japanese Army, Netaji returned to his headquarters and devoted himself to the task of providing the Azad Hind Fauj with all its essential requirements. He worked day and night, like one inspired, and created a tremendous wave of enthusiasm among the army as well as all the civilian population of East Asia, particularly in Burma, where a considerable number of Indians headed by Messrs Habib Betai and Khanna, gave their all to the Azad Hind Government. These two selfless patriots gave property worth several lakhs and became *fakirs* for the sake of their country. All that they expected and got was the title of 'Sevak-e-Hind'.

Netaji also took very keen interest in the welfare of his men, their food, accommodation, hospital arrangement, etc. and very frequently came to inspect them on outdoor training. In the meantime, he ordered the seat of Provisional Government of the Azad Hind and the supreme headquarter of the I.N.A. to be moved to Burma.

Azad Hind Fauj proceeds to the front
On 24 January 1944, General Katakura, Chief of the general staff to Japanese C-in-C in Burma, reported to Netaji and explained to him the whole strategy of the impending

offensive against the British forces on the Indo-Burma border, and the role that had been assigned to the I.N.A. in the proposed offensive. This meeting was held behind closed doors and in an atmosphere of absolute secrecy. There were only three persons present, Netaji, General Katakura and I. Netaji showed an amazing grasp of military science and was able to make a number of observations which were very much appreciated by the Japanese Chief of Staff, and subsequently agreed to by the Japanese G.H.Q. At that meeting General Katakura revealed that it was a part of the Japanese plan to launch a heavy air attack on Calcutta simultaneously with the advance of the land forces. Netaji disagreed to this proposition. He told the Japanese general that there should be no indiscriminate bombing on Indian civilians as it would lead to much panic and destruction. It would probably shake the confidence of the Indian people in him and the Japanese consented to this.

After the plan had been fully approved by Netaji, the No. 1 Subhas Brigade Regiment was placed under the direct command, for purposes of operations only, of the Japanese General Headquarters in Burma, which was known as on 'Mori Butai'.

On 27 January 1944, I called on the C-in-C and received final orders to move to the front. The Japanese C-in-C told me that my Brigade (the Subhas Brigade) was the first I.N.A. fighting force to go into action. Its activities would be watched very keenly by all to see whether the I.N.A. could bear hardships and fight as well as the Japanese Army. He said that he was going to put us through all the tests to determine the real fighting qualities of the I.N.A. I assured him that we were prepared to face any test and bear any hardship that came our way. Netaji then issued detailed orders regarding the role of No. 1 Guerrilla Regiment (the Subhas Brigade). He began to describe the relative positions and strengths of the British forces on the Indo- Burma Border, and the location and strength of the Japanese and the Indian National Army forces on the front. He told me that the main concentration of the British and American forces was at Sadiya-Imphal-Tamu and Tiddim, and that they were preparing to attack the Japanese forces with the object of recapturing Burma. He told me that there were powerful British forces at Aijal (probably one Brigade) and Lungleh (one Brigade,) which were threatening the left flanks of the Japanese forces, and were in a position to advance to Kalewa and cut off the main supply-line of the Japanese forces. Whereas the intentions of the Japanese Army was to attack and capture Tiddim-Tamu and Imphal.

The role allotted to the No. 1 Brigade was:

1. No. 1 Battalion (under the command of Major P. S. Raturi) was to proceed via Prome Taungup-Myo-Haung-Kyauktaw-Paletwa, to operate in the Kaladan valley, where the British had brought their much-praised West African Division.

2. No. 2 & 3 Battalions (under the command of their respected Battalion Commanders Major Ran Singh and Major Padam Singh) were to proceed via Mandalay and Kalewa to the Chin Hill area of Haka and Falam. The whole of this column was commanded by me.

    Further detailed orders regarding the deployment of the I.N.A. were to be issued by the Japanese North Burma Command at Maymyo. At the same time, some Japanese officers and NCOs were attached to each Battalion to act as liaison officers between the I.N.A. and the Japanese Headquarters. Their duties were to liaise with Japanese Headquarters and neighbouring units, to act as interpreters and to arrange the supply of rations, transport, medicines, etc., from the Japanese.

On 3 January 1944, Netaji delivered his farewell speech to the Regiment. It was one of the most inspiring and moving speeches that he had ever delivered in East Asia.

Three thousand soldiers in full military feet stood rigidly to attention for an hour and half and listened to every word he spoke with rapt attention. Netaji declared: 'You are the strength of my arms, the force with which I shall be able to protect rights, and everything depends on what you achieve on the battlefield.' He warned them seriously that as the first large formation of the I.N.A. to go into action, they would he put through various tests and hardships by the Japanese. He further warned them that anyone who did not feel fully prepared to face these hardships should decide to stay heck. The soldiers assured him that they would never bring shame on India's fair name by turning their backs to the front or retreating in the face of the enemy.

On 4 January 1944, advance parties of the No. 1 Battalion moved by train to Prome, and No. 2 and 3 Battalions to Mandalay.

In addition to the troops of No. 1 Guerrilla Regiment, there were already a large number of men belonging to the Bahadur and Intelligence groups on the front. They were organized in small groups of eight to ten I.N.A. men and were attached to various Japanese forces to help in the collection of information, interrogation of captured Prisoners of War and to do propaganda among the personnel of the British Indian Army through loud speakers, leaflets and pamphlets. These groups were distributed as follows in the various sectors under senior I.N.A. officers:

1. *Arakan Sector:* Under the command of Shaheed Colonel Misra Sardar-e-Jang and Major Mehar Das Sardar-e-Jang.
2. *Bishanpore sector:* Under Colonel S. A. Malik Sardar-e-Jang.

3. *Kohima Sector:* Under Shaheed Major Maghar Singh and
    Shaheed Major Ajmere Singh.

These parties distinguished themselves in fighting that
followed, and in collecting battle intelligence. In February
1944, the encirclement and almost complete annihilation of
the British 7th Division in the Maungdaw-Buthidang area
was due largely to the activities of the group commanded by
Col L. S. Misra and Major Mehar Dass. In this sector, Lt.
Hari Singh won the Sher-e-Hind medal, equivalent of British
Victoria Cross by slaying 7 British soldiers single-handedly. In
the Bishanpore Sector, the group commander Col S. A. Malik
especially distinguished himself, and reached within two miles
of Imphal. Colonel Malik also took over the administration
of the liberated areas of Manipore State. Parties under the
Command of Major Maghar Singh in the Kohima sector, also
did excellent work. Among those who especially distinguished
themselves were Shaheed Capt. Gurbachan Singh, Shaheed
Lt. Sohan Lai, Capt. Mohd Hussain and Lt. Asif.

Activities of No. 7 Battalion, the Subhas Brigade

Having received the final orders, the advance party of the
Battalion left Rangoon for Prome, on 4th February 1944, by
train. The main body of the unit left on the 5th and 6th under
the command of Major P. S. Raturi. The unit arrived at Prome
without any grave difficulty, although the railway line and
the bridge were very much damaged by the enemy's aerial
bombing. From Prome to Taungup, a distance of approximately
100 miles, the unit travelled on foot; and heavy baggage was
carried in Japanese lorries from Taungup to Myo Haung,
a distance of about 150 miles, the unit went on foot again,
leaving the heavy baggage to be transported by coastal boats.

At Taungup, our camp was heavily bombed by enemy
aircraft, and we lost 16 men. Some of the boats carrying

our equipment were machine-gunned and sunk by enemy fighter planes. The Battalion eventually concentrated at Kyauktaw where they formed the Battalion base in mid-March 1944.

A few days later, information was received that a whole Division of West African negroes was advancing south along the East Bank of the Kaladan River, and as they were advancing they were constructing a road along the way. Another road was being constructed from the West Coast to link up with the other road running parallel to the East Bank of the Kaladan River. The function of these roads was to meet at a place a few miles north of Kaladan village.

This place was known Tetma, and here the West Africans were trying to construct a bridge across the Kaladan River to link up the two roads. The task allotted to Major Raturi was to prevent the Africans on the West bank of the Kaladan from crossing over to the East bank and establishing a bridgehead.

Major P. S. Raturi started off with three companies consisting of approximately 300 men, but before he could reach Tetma the enemy had already crossed over the river in large numbers and had established itself in well-fortified hills on the East bank of the Kaladan. Major Raturi at once decided to attack the enemy. By a clever encircling movement through thick bamboo forests, he managed to encircle and annihilate the enemy in both these villages – Lower and Upper Tetma. Having captured these two villages, he decided to advance further up the Kaladan valley. His scouts reported that an enemy force, approximately one Battalion strong was entrenching itself on a prominent hill. Major Raturi decided to attack by the night, and followed by two companies of his troops, crawled right up to the enemy position. At a given signal, they all charged into the enemy trenches with fixed bayonets. There was very fierce hand to hand fight in which our men shouting 'Bharat Mata ki Jai', 'Netaji ki Jai', neither asked for nor gave any quarter. At last, bit by bit, the enemy started to give ground. The enemy collapse came suddenly. Realizing that they were faced with troops with a vastly superior morale, they left their trenches and made a mad rush to get to their boats in order to escape to the West bank of the river where their main forces, including the heavy artillery were concentrated. But, our men had no intention of letting them escape so easily. They followed them down to their boats and as the enemy was rowing across the river, they opened heavy machine-gun fire and capsized at least 16 of the escaping boats. The enemy artillery on the west bank opened up a heavy barrage on our men, who had no weapons heavier than rifle and grenades to reply to their artillery fire. As a result 14 men were killed and 22 wounded. When dawn broke out, all the soldiers who had crossed over to the East bank of the Kaladan had been forced back to the West bank. It was estimated that, in this battle, we inflicted at least 250 casualties on the enemy besides capturing large quantities of arms, ammunition and delicious food which our men had not tasted for a long time.

In the meantime, more Japanese troops arrived to reinforce our battalion, and together, we advanced on both sides of the Kaladan River. After a fierce fight, Paletwa, 50 miles further north, and later Daletme were taken over.

After a short rest to reorganize themselves, our troops were on the move again. From Daletme, approximately 40 miles to the west, they could see the Indian frontier, the sacred soil on which our soldiers longed to plant the national flag. Soldiers frequently approached their officers and said, 'Sahib our orders from Netaji are that we have to hoist the tricolour on Indian soil as soon as possible. Let us, therefore, not wait for any rest here.' By this time it was early May 1944. The nearest British port on the Indian side was Mowdok. Major Raturi decided to launch an attack on it as soon as possible.

Through constant retreat and harassment, the morale of the enemy forces was completely shattered, and that of our men was very high indeed. Our men had established a definite superiority over the enemy.

The attack on Mowdok was launched at night with a lightning speed. It came as a complete surprise to the enemy who fled, leaving behind large quantities of rations, like atta, ghee and sugar. There were considerable quantities of arms and ammunition including 3 mortars, which we needed very badly.

The entry of the I.N.A. on Indian territory was the most touching scene. Soldiers laid themselves flat on the ground and passionately kissed the sacred soil of their motherland which they had ventured out to liberate. A regular flag-hoisting ceremony was held amidst great rejoicing and the Azad Hind Fauj national anthem was sung with great gusto. The anthem was:

Subh Sukh chain ki barkha barse Bharat bhag hai jaga.
Punjab, Sind, Gujarat, Maratha, Dravid, Utkal, Banga,
Chanchal Sagar Vindh Himala, Nila Jamuna Ganga,
Tere nit gun gayen, Tujh se jiwan payen.

Sab tan paye asha.

Suraj ban kar jag par chamke Bharat nam subhaga.
Jai ho, Jai ho, Jai ho; Jaya, Jaya, Jaya, Jaya ho,

Bharat nam subhaga.

Subah sawere pankh pakheru, Teri hi gun gayen, Ras
bhari bharpur hawaen, Jiwan men rut layen.
Sab mil kar Hind pukare, Jai Azad Hind ke nare,

Piara desh hamara

Suraj ban kar jag par chamke Bharat nam subhaga.
Jai ho, Jai ho, Jai ho; Jaya, Jaya, Jaya, Jaya ho,

Bharat nam subhaga.

Sab ke dil men prit basae, Teri mithi, bani, Har sube ke
rahne wale, Har mazhab ke prani, Sab bhed aur fark mita
ke Sab god men teri a-ke,

Gundhen prem ki mala.

Suraj ban kar jag par chamke Bharat nam subhaga.
Jai ho, Jai ho, Jai ho; Jaya, Jaya, Jaya, Jaya ho,

Bharat nam subhaga.

After the occupation of Mowdok, various outposts around it
were established. About this time the situation regarding the
supply of rations had become very difficult. All our rations
were transported by river boats from the supply base at
Paletwa, where enemy aircraft were very active both by day
and night.

Keeping all this in view, as well as the impending counter
attack by the British forces from the direction of Maungdaw-
Buthidaung, the Japanese commander in Mowdok area
decided to withdraw his forces, and advised Major Raturi to
do the same. Major Raturi called a conference of his officers,
and explained the situation, and the decision of the Japanese
forces on their right and left flanks to withdraw. The officers
with one voice told Major Raturi, 'If the Japanese want to
withdraw let them do so. We have orders to get to Delhi –
Delhi lies ahead of us. Having once hoisted our national flag
on Indian soil, how can we strike it and retreat before the
enemy when we have defeated him wherever he has met us.

No Sir, the Japanese can retreat because Tokyo lies that way; our goal – the Red Fort of Delhi – lies ahead of us. There is no going back for us.'

Having taken stock of the quantity of rations and the military situation, Major Raturi decided to leave one company under the command of Capt. Suraj Mal at Mowdok to guard the flag and decided to withdraw the remainder of his forces nearer the supply base. The role of this company was more or less a 'suicidal role.' Facing them were the British, strengthening their forces and preparing to attack our men sooner or later. Our army had occupied a portion of Indian territory and it was determined to hold on to it. The Japanese, admiring the spirit of our men, decided to leave one platoon of their own troops in the same area to share the fate of the I.N.A. These Japanese troops were put under direct command of Capt. Suraj Mal. It was probably the first time in the history of the Japanese Army that their troops had been placed under the command of a foreign officer.

Major Raturi, Capt. Suraj Mal, and the other officers and men of the I.N.A., through their gallantry and self-sacrifice, convinced the Japanese that when it came to fighting for the honour and liberation of their country, Indians were as brave, if not braver, than any other soldier in the world. The Japanese, who once doubted if the I.N.A. could ever face another fight and bear any hardship, were so impressed that they voluntarily placed their own troops under the command of an Indian officer. The Japanese C-in-C in Burma went to Netaji and bowing before him said, 'Your Excellency, we were wrong. We misjudged the soldiers of the I.N.A. We know now that they are no mercenaries, but real patriots.'

Capt. Suraj Mal and his small band of gallant men stayed at Mowdok from May to September 1944. During this period, they were attacked by the British forces almost every day, but not even on one occasion did they retreat one step.

One instance of the type of fight our men had to go through is given below:

The Azad Hind Fauj had a small outpost of 20 men at Labawa, which was commanded by 2nd Lt. Amar Singh. One morning at about 0800 hrs. the enemy, approximately 150 strong, attacked this post. They had heavy artillery and mortars to give themselves covering fire and to put down a smoke screen.

Our men, who were armed only with machine guns and rifles and had a very limited quantity of ammunition, held their fire and allowed the enemy to come nearer. All of a sudden they opened rapid fire on the enemy inflicting heavy casualties and forcing them to retreat. At about midday the enemy attacked again. The attack was preceded by intense artillery and mortar shelling; and the attack was launched after a smoke screen had been laid all around the post.

This attack was also met by our men in a very cool, calm and determined manner; and once again the enemy had to withdraw, leaving a number of dead around our post. That day the enemy appeared determined to capture our post, but our men were equally determined not to allow them to do so. Our men – each one of them – were fully prepared to lay down their lives rather than let the enemy oust them from their post. At about 1700 hrs, the enemy made a third attack on the post. This attack was more determined than the two previous ones, and this time it was preceded by aerial bombardment. Six enemy fighter planes circled over our post for over an hour dropping heavy calibre bombs, and later on machine-punned our trenches. They used 20mm bullets which are generally used against heavy-armoured vehicles, like tanks and armoured cars. This was followed by intensive artillery and mortar shelling, and the enemy thinking that their aeroplanes and artillery had probably annihilated our post, advanced rather boldly, but God was on our side. We had suffered only one casualty during all this. Our men withheld their fire and almost from point blank range opened deadly and accurate firing on the enemy. The enemy who had expected practically no opposition was taken aback and once again they beat a hasty retreat to lick their wounds. By this time, Capt. Suraj Mal, who was in command of the main camp a few miles away, rallied about fifty men and came to the assistance of the Labawa post. On arrival there, he found our men in great spirits and not a bit shaken by the repeated attack of the enemy. Suraj Mal decided to return the enemy's call, and to go and attack their base a few miles away. It was nearly dusk when he, together with his fifty men, crawled up to the enemy base and charged into their camp. The enemy were not expecting this at all, and their soldiers ran helter-skelter in all directions, causing considerable confusion in their camp. After successfully raiding the enemy camp and capturing considerable quantities of arms and ammunition, Capt. Suraj Mal returned to his camp. The enemy was so shaken by this bold move of Capt. Mai that we had no trouble from them for some lconsiderable time.

While this was going on, Major Raturi had to arrange the supply of rations to Capt. Mal's party. He had to train his own men to row boats and deliver rations to the Kaladan. In addition to this, the battalion was also allotted an anti-parachute and anti-guerrilla job. For this it had to disperse its force – one company at Sarai, one company at Apukawa and one company at Kyauktak.

In September 1944, after the failure of Imphal Campaign, Netaji issued orders to all his forces to fall back. The No. 1 Battalion was ordered to return to Rangoon. The men at first refused to obey these orders. They thought those could not have come from Netaji; but after they were convinced, they agreed to return to Rangoon – victorious in every battle but heartbroken to have had to retreat. The Battalion concentrated at Rangoon in the middle of November.

In action, the Battalion lost its adjutant-Capt. Kabul Singh, a gallant soldier and thirty other *shaheeds*. During the operations, the Battalion suffered terribly from malaria, and dysentery and at the time of their arrival in Rangoon, almost every single person was suffering from malaria.

The advance parties of the Regimental Headquarters and the two Battalions moved from Rangoon by train to Mandalay on 4 and 5 February 1944. On the way, owing to the railway bridges being blown up by enemy aircraft, the men had to cover considerable distances on foot.

Major Mahboob Ahmad, Major Ram Sarup and I started off from Rangoon by car on 5 February and arrived at Mandalay on 8 February.

On 10 February, I went to Maymyo to meet General Muta Guchi who was commanding all the Japanese forces in North Burma. He explained the role of my regiment in the operations that were going to start shortly. His plan very briefly was that the No. 1 Regiment should proceed to the Haka-Falam front and take over the defence of that sector. There were two British brigades operating on that front – the Lushai Brigade and the Aijal Brigade.

The task of the No. 1 Regt was: (a) to prevent these brigades from advancing on Kalewa and thereby threatening the main supply-line of the Japanese forces operating against Tiddim-Tamu, and (b) to carry out offensive operations on the Haka-Falam front in the direction of Lungleh with the object of deceiving the British of the real point of attack. I was told that as soon as the main offensive was started by the Japanese my regiment would be given an opportunity of leading the advance into India.

Having received instructions, I returned to Mandalay on 12 February. By that time most of the personnel of the No. 2

& 3 Battalions had arrived at Mandalay. From there, we had to despatch two companies to Pakokou to bring rations on bullock carts via Pawk-Tilin-Gan Gaw-Kan to Nauchawng which was to be the Regimental base.

On 14 February, with the Senior Staff Officers of the Brigade, I left Mandalay by car for Mutaik, the Headquarters of the Japanese Division operating in the Chin Hill area. This Division was known as the 'Yumi' or 'White Tiger Division.'

I.N.A. troops from Mandalay left for Kalewa in parties of approximately 300 men and performed the journey from Mandalay to Yeu by train or on foot and from Yeu to Kalewa in lorries or on foot.

On 16 February, I arrived at Mutaik and went to meet the Japanese Commander of the Yumi Division in cooperation with whom the No. 1 Regt (the Subhas Brigade) had to operate in the Chin Hill area. He explained the local situation to me. According to him, in the Chin Hill area the enemy strength was one Division (17th Indian Div) at Tiddim, one Indian Brigade at Aijal, one Indian Brigade at Lungleh, and one Brigade consisting of Chins and Gurkhas known as the Lushai brigade which was split up into guerrilla bands and was harassing the Japanese garrison around Haka Falam. Their main Headquarters were located at Tibual. Salen, approximately 40 miles west of Haka, and Shurkhwa, approximately 50 miles south of Haka. In addition to these, they had a regular network of smaller posts all round Haka and Falam. These Chin guerrillas, approximately 3,000 strong, under the command of British officers were making the stay of Japanese garrisons very difficult at Haka and Falam.

The Japanese had one battalion and one company, approximately 600 men, at Falam; and one company at Haka, approximately 200 strong. Other Japanese troops were located in the area of Fort White and Kangyi.

The No. 1 Guerrilla Regiment of the I.N.A. was to take over the Haka-Falam sector from the Japanese, and prevent the enemy from capturing Haka and Falam by cutting off the main Japanese supply lines Kalewa-Fort White and Kalewa-Tamu.

The Japanese General was of the opinion that the British were preparing to launch a huge offensive with the intention of recapturing Burma. For this, the enemy had amassed large reserves of men and material at Imphal and Tiddim and had built an excellent road from Imphal to Tamu, called the Road to Tokyo.

The British plan, according to him, was to advance from (a) Imphal-Vimpalel-Tamu to Kalewa; (b) from Tiddim via Fort White to Kalewa; and (c) the Lushai Brigade and other troops in Lungleh area would orderly advance via Haka-Kan-Gangaw-Tilin Pauk to Pakokou on the Irrawaddy. The main task of the No. 1 Guerrilla Brigade was to prevent this. He went on to say that the Japanese plan was to attack the British just before they launched their main offensive and upset all their plans by capturing Imphal.

I told the Japanese General that I did not appreciate the idea of their allotting an out of the way sector to the I.N.A. and that I wanted to, as I had been promised, form the spearhead of the advance into India. He told me that he had received instructions from his General Headquarters that the I.N.A. was to be tested first and that a separate and independent sector was being allotted to us. He also warned me that that sector was probably the hardest one to hold, not so much from the point of view of enemy strength, but because of the tremendous difficulties of terrain and ration supply.

I had also been warned about this test by Netaji and our soldiers were anxious to prove their worth whatever the obstacles in our way might be. I, however, made the Japanese General promise that as soon as the main offensive was launched, my troops would be given an opportunity and the honour of leading the advance into India.

I returned to my Headquarters and issued orders to Major Ran Singh, who was commanding the No. 2 Battalion, to despatch a detachment to take over Falam from the Japanese.

The regimental base was to be established at Nauchawng (Myitha Haka). I arrived at Myitha Haka on 24 February with Senior Staff Officers of the Regimental Headquarters. By that time approximately 500 men of the No. 2 Battalion under Major Ran Singh, had arrived there. The rest of the Brigade was still coming up in small parties from Yeu and Kalewa.

On 25 February, Major Ran Singh sent the Awal Company under Lt. Sikander Khan with approximately 100 men to take over the defence of Falam from the Japanese.

On arrival at Myitha Haka, I found out that there were no rations at Falam and that we would have to make our own arrangement to supply rations to our troops at Haka and Falam. The supply point was at Myitha Haka where Japanese lorries would come to deliver rations at the Regimental Headquarters. From here to Falam, a distance of approximately 50 miles, and to Haka, approximately 85 miles away, we had to arrange our own means of transportation. There was only a hill track connecting Haka Falam with the regimental base. We had no transport of any kind to help us to carry our rations. The Japanese garrison was supplied with rations by their animal transport companies, and they also used coolies for the purpose, but we were told that no transport was available for carrying the I.N.A. rations. The result was that our men had to carry their rations on their heads to supply their comrades who were fighting in the front line.

Haka-Falam is a very mountainous area. Falam is situated at a height of 6000 feet and Haka at 7000 feet. Our valiant soldiers had to labour hard to clamber up those lofty heights, carrying heavy weights on their heads to prevent their comrades in the front line from being starved to death. Rations were of very poor quality indeed. All that we could get with the greatest difficulty to supply to our troops in the front line was salt and rice, and even these they failed to receive on several occasions. Sugar, milk, tea and meat were luxuries which our men hardly ever tasted.

In order to build up a chain of supply centres, we had to establish six posts each approximately eight miles apart. Rations were carried from post to post. Every man had to do approximately 16 miles a day and it was a most painful business to see them being treated in this way. We all realized that these meagre rations meant slow but sure death. The Japanese could have, if they wanted to, help us in this respect, but they did not do so and I am of the opinion that they did it deliberately. They had seen the spirit and determination of our men and had realized that they would stand no nonsense from the Japanese. In actual fact, as Field Marshal Terauchi had told Netaji long before in Singapore, the Japanese did not want large formations of the I.N.A. to come to the front; and now that they were there, the Japanese wished to break their spirit and weaken their bodies by putting impossible obstacles in their way. All that they wanted to do was to break the morale of the I.N.A. and tell Netaji that his army could not face the rigours of a hard campaign. But our soldiers had been forewarned by Netaji and they had promised to face all hardships. For them, there was only one course, to do or to die. They carried on their work without complaint or even a murmur. The Japanese were putting us through a terrible test indeed.

When the men of the Awal Company arrived at Falam, they carried on their backs all the heavy machine guns, light automatics reserve ammunition, all their clothing, leading and 20 day rations. In actual fact, every soldier including the officers, carried on their backs an average weight of 85-90 lbs (38.5-40.5 kgs).

Immediately after their arrival, they took over the defence of the Falam area from the Japanese. At that time, there were approximately 600 British and Chin guerrillas in the immediate vicinity of Falam. We had heard a lot about these Chin guerrillas, and in fairness to them, I would say that they had created a very favourable impression on the Japanese by their skill in jungle warfare. On several occasions they had successfully ambushed the Japanese supply columns and bodily carried away some Japanese soldiers. The name of one Major Manning was particularly well known, and, I might say, feared by the Japanese. This British officer was an expert in guerrilla warfare and had been in the Chin Hill several years before the outbreak of the war. He knew the people of the Chin Hill and their language very well. He even had a Chin wife. The inhabitants of the Chin Hill, therefore, cooperated whole-heartedly with him and gave him all the information regarding the disposition and movements of our troops.

The task of the Awal Company was not an easy one. I would have liked to have kept many more troops at Falam but this was not possible on account of the scarcity of ration; 100 men were the maximum we could maintain at Falam.

It was bitterly cold there and our men had only one warm shirt and one thin cotton blanket. They would spend their nights sitting around the fire as it was impossible to sleep because of the severe cold. Many of our sentries guarding strategic heights were unable to stand the bitter cold and freezing blizzard and collapsed at their post – never to recover again. There was also an acute shortage of medicines and medical staff. This company had only one Naik and two nursing Sepoys as the medical staff. Through daily wear and tear, the men's boots were in a very poor state, and some men had no boots at all. Their clothes after a few months of rough life, were in tatters and there was no hope of any replacements. But, in spite of all this, the men kept up their spirits wonderfully well although their health was fast deteriorating, particularly of those in the plains, around Myitha Haka, where due to malaria 60 per cent of the men were hospitalized. Myitha Haka is situated in the heart of the Kaba valley which was known to the British as the 'Death Valley'. In this valley, our men had no mosquito nets. Anyhow, our men accepted it all. They had undertaken to perform a task and they meant to complete it.

On 11 March, I went to the Divisional Headquarters at Hvigon, where I met Major Fujiwara, the Japanese officer who had handed us over to Colonel Mohan Singh at the Farrer Park. He was acting as the Intelligence Officer of the North Burma Command. He told me that the Japanese in cooperation with certain units of the I.N.A. had attacked and surrounded Tiddim. I told him that I had been promised by the Japanese C-in-C that we would be given the opportunity of leading the attack. I insisted that some troops of my brigade should get an opportunity of taking part in the attack. He agreed, and asked me to call up the No. 3 Battalion, which was concentrated at Kalewa, 20 miles away. I telephoned Colonel Thakur Singh, Regimental Second-in-Command to bring the troops to Kyigon. They marched all night and by day break, had covered 20 miles. They were ordered to proceed to Fort White and attack Tiddim, but before they could get there, Tiddim had already fallen.

On 17 March, I received the information that a strong column of enemy troops was operating in the area of Klankhua, approximately 40 miles west of Falam. I at once ordered Lt. Sikander Khan to take his company and contact the enemy. I further instructed him that if the enemy troops were Indians they were not to open fire on them first. He was to ask them to come over and join us in the fight for India's freedom, and only if they fired first, the fire was to be returned. Accordingly Lt. Sikander Khan, with approximately 80 men of the Awal Company, set out on the mission on the night of the 19-20 March. Over high and precipitous mountains, they walked all night and at dawn were in the vicinity of a village named Zomual. Here, they halted for a short rest while sentries were posted all round. A short while later one of the sentries reported that a strong fighting patrol of the enemy was approaching. Lt. Sikander Khan at once decided to capture or annihilate this enemy force. Brisk orders were issued and in a flash all the men were in position ready to ambush the enemy. The enemy, who never expected our men to be there, walked straight into our ambush. Lt. Sikander Khan pounced forward and pointing his revolver at the patrol commander's chest asked him to surrender, which he did together with all his force. We captured one officer and 24 men of the Lushai Brigade, complete with all their arms and equipment.

On interrogation, Lt. Sikander Khan found out that our prisoners were the men of the Lushai Brigade and that Major Manning, the expert guerrilla fighter, was also in the same vicinity and that two powerful columns – one of Lushai Brigade and the other of Punjabi troops were advancing on the either side of the track to Falam. Lt. Sikander Khan decided to capture Major Manning alive and to forestall this move of the enemy on Falam.

Major Manning was, at that time, down below in Nullah. Lt. Sikander Khan laid an ambush for him and then asked one of the captured prisoners to ask him to come up to where they were. Manning came to us unsuspectingly as the first ambush was carried out so quietly that the people in Nullah knew nothing about it. He was preceded by his orderly as he came up the hill. The orderly was quickly captured as he was turning round a corner; but when Manning came near, Lt. Sikander Khan could not restrain himself. He at once pounced upon him and pointing his revolver at him ordered him to surrender. Manning, who was carrying a Sten gun at once opened fire at him. Lt. Sikander returned fire with his revolver which unfortunately misfired. A Bren gun which was fixed there also misfired and jammed. Manning then threw down his Sten gun and ran down the hill. Lt. Sikander was close at his heels but he managed to escape.

Lt. Sikander Khan then attacked the enemy force and drove it back several miles. The enemy was so shaken that they beat a hurried retreat and gave up all ideas of advancing on Falam for a long time. Lt. Sikander Khan returned to Falam on 2 March with all the prisoners, arms, and ammunition. His own force did not suffer a single casualty. Intensive patrolling then continued.

In the meantime, a small reserve of ration was built up at Falam, and it was now possible to send a garrison to take over the defence of Haka.

On 28 March 1944, the Parwana Company of the No. 2 Battalion under the command of Lt. Amrik Singh arrived at Falam from Myitha Haka. They carried with them on their backs, all heavy machine guns, reserve ammunition, and one month's rations. A few buffaloes caught in paddy fields were also used as beasts of burden, and helped us to carry some of our rations.

The road between Falam and Haka, a distance of approximately 35 miles, was under constant watch by enemy guerrillas. They had established a strong hold in a village called Chunsong, approximately 10 miles away from the road, from there, they operated against Japanese supply columns. They were a constant source of trouble and anxiety to the Japanese but the Japanese, probably considering their strength at Haka to be insufficient, never attacked this post.

The Parwana Company left Falam on 30 March. They were approximately 150 strong. I accompanied them from Falam. Next day, on 31 March, I received information that the enemy at Chunsong was preparing to attack us. I decided to attack them first. The attack was led by Lt. Lehna Singh, who surrounded the village at night and after a fierce struggle drove the enemy out of their stronghold capturing a considerable quantity of good rations.

On 3 April 1944, we took over the defence of Haka from the Japanese garrison which returned to Falam and later to Tiddim.

Conditions at Haka were even harder than those at Falam. Ration supply was becoming an acute problem. The strength and the activities of the enemy demanded that there should be a strong force at Haka, but the ration scarcity made it necessary to maintain the minimum number of men to be fed at Haka which was approximately 85 miles from the supply point. The choice before us therefore was, (a) to have a large force at Haka and risk it being starved to death, and (b) to have a small force and risk its being annihilated by the enemy. A conference of officers was held and it was decided to adopt the second course. It was bitterly cold at Haka which was situated at a height of 7,000 feet. Some of the piquets held by our men were living at a height of nearly 8,000 feet.

On 5 April 1944, I went to inspect camp piquets and asked the commanders there about the status of rations. They all said that they were getting satisfactory rations. I was surprised to hear that reply. On return to the camp, I found that these men had not had proper food for the last two days and they had been living on a type of mountain grass known as Lingra. Such touching incidents happened hundreds of times.

Opposite our lines only a few miles away, we could see British Dakotas dropping rations to their troops by parachutes. Our men knew where to look for really good rations. They never complained about not receiving enough rations. All that they always complained about was not being given enough opportunities to attack the British posts to capture rations.

On the Haka front, the enemy was very active and more numerous than at Falam. Their main centres were at Surkhua, Zokhua, Klang, and Sopum. There were approximately 7,200 enemy guerrillas around Haka as compared to our 150 men of the Parwana Company.

Capt. Amrik Singh, the Commander of the Company, was told that the best way to defend Haka was to snatch the initiative from the enemy and to keep on attacking the British continuously, and thereby forcing them to go on the defensive.

This plan worked well. Thanks to the excellent leadership of Major Mahboob Ahmed, Major Ran Singh and Capt. Amrik Singh, all of whom carried out a most intensive patrol activity even behind the enemy lines forcing them to be defensive. It was by no means an easy task. In the early stages the enemy resisted hard.

On 14 April, our post at Klang Klang was heavily fired upon by the enemy. As soon as the noise of firing was heard in the main Haka camp, Capt. Amrik Singh at once took out a strong patrol and went in search of the enemy, who retreated so far that our men could not even establish contact with them.

On 16 April, the enemy, in much large numbers, attacked our post on Klang Klang Road. They were approximately 100 strong, whereas our post consisted of only 20 men. The enemy used three mortars and machine guns. They completely encircled our post and some of them came up to within fifty yards of our defences. This post was commanded by Lt. Lehna Singh, who, realizing that the situation was becoming very grave, decided to charge at the enemy. Leaving 10 men to defend the post, he collected a party of 10 men and charged straight at the machine gun post which the enemy had established near the piquet. He captured this position and opened deadly flanking fire on the remainder. Realizing the danger, the enemy decided to beat a hurried retreat. Lt. Lehna Singh, with this little force, followed the British troop for over 10 miles shouting and challenging them to stop and fight; but the enemy was in no state to accept the challenge and gave our men no chance to catch up with them.

On 30 March, Major Mahboob Ahmed, the Brigade Adjutant, went to inspect our troops operating on the Tiddim front. He found that, after the fall of Tiddim, the Japanese had put them on to widen the road. The officer in charge, who happened to be a junior officer had agreed to do this, but Major Mahboob at once stopped this and ordered his troops to return to the regimental base. He sent a full report of the incident to me. This distressed me a lot as I was not at all convinced that the Japanese were sincere to us. An entry in my diary on that date reads, '"Boobies" report is distressing… I wonder what is going to be the outcome of this one-sided co-prosperity.'

About this time in mid-April, both sides were very active. The enemy were massing troops to capture Haka Falam. I was also able to increase my strength. It was a struggle in which both sides were trying to snatch the initiative.

On 23 April, I took out a patrol with the object of reconnoitring area for an attack on the enemy posts in the area. We advanced very cautiously and crept up very near to the enemy positions. All of a sudden our sentries reported a strong patrol of the enemy advancing towards us. I decided to annihilate this party and ordered Lt. Lehna Singh to lay an ambush for them. Lt. Lehna Singh took his men and posted them on either side of the track. The enemy patrol walked up unsuspectingly and ran right into the ambush. The entire patrol was either killed or captured alive. Owing to our most intensive patrol activities, we forced the enemy to withdraw to their posts and beat a general retreat along the whole front.

On 28 April, in response to my letter requesting Netaji to allow us to attack Imphal, I received information that the No. 1 Division of the I.N.A. consisting of the Azad and Gandhi Brigades were attacking Imphal, and that the No. 1 (the Subhas Brigade) should be ready to push through and get across the Brahmaputra as soon as possible. I was told that the fall of Imphal was a matter of hours and our soldiers were waiting most anxiously for the order to cross over from Kohima to the other side of the Brahmaputra into the heart of India.

On 10 May 1944, I issued orders to various commanders to attack a British stronghold at Klang. This stronghold of the British was located approximately 20 miles west of Haka, on the top of a mountain ridge. It had a very commanding position and the only track leading up to it was a very narrow one and completely commanded by the post. All other approaches were extremely difficult, being almost like sheer cliffs. Here on this apparently impregnable stronghold the main British garrison was stationed and from there they were carrying out guerrilla activities. We also learnt that there were plenty of rations there. The Japanese, who had been at Haka before us, had not found it a practical proposition to attack this post. Some of the Japanese liaison officers with me at Haka came to request me not to attempt to attack that post as it was almost impossible to capture it without the support of artillery and aeroplanes of which, unfortunately, we had none.

On 12 April, I took out the commanders who were to take part in the raid on Klang post for a reconnaissance of the area. That day we covered over 28 miles and returned to Haka at night. In the evening I was informed that I was required to report immediately at the Japanese Divisional Headquarters at Indaingyi for fresh orders as to the change in the role of the regiment.

From Haka, I issued orders to the 3rd Battalion over the telephone at Nauchawng, 90 miles away, to move immediately to Ukhrul.

I left Haka on 14 May with Major Ram Sarup and some men, and marched to the Brigade Headquarters for Nauchawng. It was a distance of 85 miles which we covered on foot in just over two days.

In the meantime, I had issued instructions that the raid on the Klang Klang post was to be carried out under the direction of Major Mahboob Ahmad. The main party left Haka on the evening of 14 May. At about dusk they attacked the first British outpost which was a covering post to Klang. This post was captured; without much opposition. The advance then continued at night and at about 0400 hrs. in the morning of 15 May they reached the vicinity of the British stronghold. Major Mahboob Ahmad tried to encircle the post but this was found impossible due to steep cliffs. The track leading up to the post was very well covered by the guns in the post. The situation looked very difficult. Major Mahboob then decided to launch a frontal attack. Taking a small group of 8-10 men with him, and Capt. Amrik Singh, Shaheed-e-Bharat, he began to creep up, inch by inch a very steep mountain side. Fortunately for the party, the moon had also come up and they were able to see well than during the earlier part of the night. It was a very hazardous task, and even a little slip would have sent them tumbling to death hundreds of feet into the nullah.

Luckily for them the enemy was not expecting them on this side of the fortress as they had considered it impossible for anyone to attack from that direction. After a long and nerve-wrecking climb, they came right up to the enemy trenches, closely followed by their men. The worst part of the climb was now over. But, as soon as they had come up, the enemy spotted them and opened the most intensive barrage of fire. Our men took cover and returned the enemy fire. Our machine guns, which had been very cleverly cited gave covering fire to our men. The fire of our machine guns was so accurate that the enemy guns were soon silenced and the attacking party of Capt. Amrik Singh was able to advance further. But this was not for long. The enemy in other trenches nearby opened heavy rifle and machine-gun fire. Capt. Amrik Singh carrying hand grenades in both hands rallied his men and with one cry of 'Jai Hind,' a cry that rent the skies and shattered the nerves of the enemy, charged straight into the enemy defences. He threw both hand grenades on the enemy post and silenced it for ever. They had now pierced the enemy's perimeter and fighting was going on inside the camp. After a very hard struggle, the enemy left the post and fled downhill, followed by volleys of accurate fire from our soldiers. As daylight broke out, the peak which had been the scene of the bloody fighting at night was enveloped in a shroud of thick fog but gradually as the sun came up the mist cleared, and through the clouds, the people at Haka saw the Tricolour fluttering proudly over the stronghold which only the night before had been in the hands of our enemies.

A signal was then flashed back to Haka by Major Mahboob stating, 'Have captured the enemy's fortification after great opposition. The enemy having suffered severe casualties evacuated the post, leaving behind large quantities of most delicious tinned fruits, butter and jam. They also left behind large quantities of arms and ammunition.' This message was then flashed to the Regimental Base at Falam, from where instructions were sent back to Major Mahboob to destroy the enemy camp and return to Haka, as soon as possible, as the role of the Brigade had been changed.

The new orders for the Brigade were:

'That the main body of the Brigade would proceed to Kohima and would be preferred, on the fall of Imphal, to advance rapidly and cross the Brahmaputra into the heart of Bengal.'

The responsibility of holding and defending the Haka-Falam front and preventing the British guerrilla forces from cutting off the main supply route of the armies fighting around Kohima and Imphal was still to be that of the No. 1 (the Subhas Brigade) Regiment. Accordingly, I left approximately 150 men at Haka and 300 men at Falam to perform this duty. I fully realized by this time that it was too late then. The monsoon had almost broken out and the British forces, though surrounded by the Japanese in Imphal, had been considerably strengthened by the arrival of a fresh Indian Division that had been transported by planes. By this time, most of the Japanese Air Force had been transferred for fighting in the Pacific area. In addition, a powerful force of the British was counter attacking from the direction of Dimapore and Kohima. The Japanese garrisons in that area were being very hard pressed and it was to assist them that the Japanese asked the No. 1 Regiment to proceed to Kohima. Our soldiers were overjoyed to hear of the new role assigned to them because they had been living in the hope of such a day.

At this time, the troops which had been in the plains of Kalemyo were suffering, almost without exception from malaria, and about 70 per cent of them were hospitalized; but when the time came to ambush, all the sick men from the hospital came and occupied the lorries. They were determined not to be left behind. Most of the journey from Myitha Haka to Tamu was done in motor lorries belonging to the Japanese army.

From Tamu our men walked to Humine Oukhrul, and then to Kharasom and Kohima. On arrival, our men hoisted the Tricolour on the lofty mountain tops around Kohima. The British whose strength had increased considerably were counter attacking more and more vigorously every day. Our men were holding out most gallantly and beating back attack after attack.

By this time heavy monsoons had set in. Our only supply line – an unmetalled hill rose – was completely washed away and all supplies ceased to reach us. Our rations were exhausted and the men were living on paddy which they managed to collect in very small quantities from abandoned Naga villages. They mixed this paddy with jungle grass and ate it after boiling. They had not even little salt to add to this peculiar diet. They, however, lived on this for several weeks, and a time came when they became extremely weak, but no one ever thought of retreating in the face of the British.

All the medicines were finished. The doctor had nothing with which he could treat his patients, and to make matters worse, in those jungles there were millions of huge flies which attacked men and beasts alike as soon as they had the slightest wound and within half an hour there were hundreds of maggots in their wounds, and in most cases there was no other alternative for the men than to say 'Jai Hind' and shoot themselves.

It was under these circumstances that on 4 June, I met the Commander of the Japanese Forces operating in that area. He informed me that the role of his Division, to which my Brigade was also attached, had been changed and that they were going back to Ukhrul. He asked me to do the same. These orders came as a complete bombshell to me. I told him that it was impossible for me to obey those orders. We had hoisted our tricolour on Indian soil. How could we uproot it and retreat before the British whom our men had defeated in every battle? Also our men were unwilling to budge even an inch. Realizing this Japanese Commander decided to mislead me and make me retreat on a false pretext.

He told me that the I.N.A. and the Japanese forces around Imphal had failed to capture it, and that he had been ordered to attack and capture Imphal in cooperation with the No. 1 Regiment. He asked me to select my role. As I wrote in my diary, my choice was, of course, to attack Imphal. What I was given to understand was that as soon as we captured Imphal, we would advance again. On this assurance I was able to persuade my men to withdraw to Ukhrul from where we were to attack Imphal along the road from Ukhrul to Imphal. I returned with my unit to Ukhrul from where I sent out reconnaissance parties to find out possible routes for attacking Imphal. The Japanese General arrived a couple of days later. I went and met him at the Divisional Headquarters. He informed me that the situation had changed for the worse and that owing to the heavy monsoon, it was impossible for the supply services to supply rations to troops in that areas. He was, therefore, falling back on Tamu and Sittaung where it was possible to get rations by the only means of transport left to the Japanese, the Chindwin river. I informed him that I thought he had betrayed me by issuing false orders and requested him to transfer my brigade immediately to join the No. 1 Division of the I.N.A. which had been fighting around Palet since early April. He promised to do so.

On 22 June, he issued orders to me to withdraw to Tamu and re-join the No. 1 Division of the I.N.A. Hence we started on the trek back again. This retreat from Kohima was perhaps one of the most difficult retreats that any army in the world had had to face. Torrential rains had washed away all tracks. The men made fresh tracks which soon became almost a knee-deep mass of mud, in which many of the men got stuck and died there itself. At that time there was no transport of any kind with us. Almost every man was suffering from dysentery and malaria. No one had any strength left in him to help anyone else. It was a question of every man for himself and the devil take the hindmost. In that retreat, I saw men eating horses which had been dead for four days. There were hundreds of dead human bodies of the Japanese and Indian soldiers lying on either sides of the road. These were the men who had died either through exhaustion, starvation or diseases while those who being unable to face this ordeal any longer had taken their own lives by shooting themselves, which they preferred instead of falling prisoners in the hands of the British.

It was at this stage that the wily British thought that they would be able to subvert the I.N.A. soldiers whose morale they estimated would be completely crushed due to unimaginable hardships and suffering. They dropped leaflets from aeroplane signed by their commander. The substance of these pamphlets was, 'Soldiers of the I.N.A. have no ammunition, no medicines or ration; you are living on jungle grass like wild animals. Come over to us, we will give you excellent food, clothing and medical attention as well as substantial pay and reward. Why have you become so stone-hearted? Your children are waiting for you. Come to us and we will send you on three months leave. This is our real promise to you. Do not be frightened to come to us. We will welcome you.' This was indeed a very tempting offer at a time when our soldiers' condition was so terrible. But our soldiers, without a single exception, had only one reply to this. They said, 'We would much rather live on jungle grass like wild animals and remain free man rather than have luxurious food and be among our children, as British slaves and dishonourable men.' They preferred death to dishonour.

Through knee-deep mud and slush, under constant shell and machinegun fire, the valiant soldiers of the Azad Hind Fauj trudged back.

There was nothing that the officers could do for their men at such a time, except to set a personal example, and, by words of encouragement, inspire their soldiers to hold on. After travelling several hundred miles from Kohima, the soldiers of the Subhas Brigade arrived at Tamu. Many of them died on the way. But those who were still alive had only one hope that was of being sent to the Palel front to assist their comrades of the Gandhi and Azad Brigades. But destiny had another disappointment in store for them. On arrival at Tamu, they were informed that they were not being sent up to join the No. 1 Division, as they were to form the general reserve in the hands of the Japanese Commander-in-Chief. We were disillusioned and deceived by the Japanese once again.

A few days later, I was informed that all the Japanese forces and the Indian National Army would withdraw to the East bank of Chindwin. This order broke men's hearts; and they finally, realized that our assault had failed.

A strong deputation of officers and men came to me and suggested that the only honourable course left open to them was that all those who were still fit enough to walk a few miles should attack the enemy and perish fighting. The sick – they all realized – would die anyhow. I agreed to their plan, but the Japanese Liaison Officer came to know of it, and sent a frantic message to Netaji who issued strict and final orders to me to come back. As a soldier, there was no other alternative for me but to obey these orders and return to Kalewa. In this connection, Netaji issued a Special Order of the day which read as follows:

Comrades of Azad Hind Fauj,

In the middle of March this year, advanced units of the Azad Hind Fauj, fighting shoulder to shoulder with their valiant allies, the Imperial Nippon Forces, crossed the Indo-Burma border and the fight for India's liberation thereupon commenced on Indian soil.

The British Authorities, by ruthlessly exploiting India for over a century and bringing foreign soldiers to fight their battles for them, had managed to put up a mighty force against us. After crossing the Indo-Burma border, inspired by the righteousness of our cause, we encountered these numerically superior and better equipped, but heterogeneous and disunited forces of the enemy and defeated them in every battle. Our units, with their better training and discipline and unshakable determination to do or die on the path of India's freedom, soon established their superiority over the enemy, whose morale deteriorated with each defeat. Fighting under the most trying conditions, our officers and men displayed such courage and heroism that they have earned the praise of everybody. With their blood and sacrifice, these heroes have established traditions which the future soldiers of free India shall have to uphold. All preparations had been completed and the stage had been set for the final assault on Imphal when torrential rains overtook us, and to carry Imphal by an assault was rendered a tactical impossibility. Handicapped by the elements, we were forced to postpone our offensive. After the postponement of offensive, it was found disadvantageous for our troops to continue to hold the line that we then had. For securing a more favourable defensive position, it was considered advisable to withdraw our troops. In accordance with this decision, our troops have withdrawn to a more favourable defensive position. We shall now utilize the period of lull in completing our preparations, so that with the advent of better weather, we may be in a position to resume our offensive. Having beaten the enemy once in several sectors of the front, our faith in our final victory and in the destruction of the Anglo-American forces of aggression has increased tenfolds. As soon as all our preparations are complete, we shall launch a mighty offensive against our enemies once again. With the superior fighting qualities dauntless courage and unshakable devotion to duty of our officers and men, victory shall surely be ours.

Many of souls of those heroes, who have fallen in this campaign inspire us to still nobler deeds of heroism and bravery in the next phase of India's War of Liberation. Jai Hind.

To withdraw from Tamu to Kalewa, the Japanese General Headquarters issued the following orders to me: 'The No. 1 Regt. will withdraw to Kalewa a distance of 150 miles.

'From Tamu the Regiment will withdraw to Ahlow a distance of 25 miles. All the sick men were to be carried there under the Regimental arrangement.'

From Ahlow, the Japanese promised to provide river transport for 400 seriously sick soldiers. The remainder were to walk from Ahlow to Teraun, from where river transport for the whole regiment was to be provided as far as Kalewa.

About this time, the soldiers of the Gandhi and Azad Brigades had also been ordered to fall back on Kalewa. They were given the road Tamu-Yezagyo-Kalewa as the route of withdrawal.

At Tamu we were able to collect a few bullock-carts with the help of which we transported our sick men to Ahlow on Yu River.

Here we found the river flooded and there was not even a single boat to transport our sick. On this river bank, we were held up for seven days. Eventually, with the help of some Burmese boats, our men got across. At this stage our rations were completely exhausted and there appeared to be no prospects of receiving any fresh supplies. Whatever little was available in the local village the Japanese had already commandeered for their own troops, and the I.N.A. was left to fend for itself. It was at this stage that I made an entry in my diary on 7 July 'Men did not receive any ration... 4 Garhwalis have died of starvation. We have approached the Japanese to do something for our rations. They seem not to take the least notice of it. I do not know what is the idea behind this deliberate starvation of our men.'

Under these circumstances, our men had to trek back in torrential monsoons with no shelter except a small ground through knee deep mud, and through thick tropical forests infested with deadly malaria mosquitoes and poisonous leeches.

By this time, all administration services had completely broken down. Doctors had no medicines left to treat anyone and most of the doctors and the medical staff were themselves suffering from malaria and dysentery. At that time, in the surrounding forest and on the track were millions of huge flies feasting on the human dead. There were some terrible scenes and no description can depict a real enough picture of it, and no one who has actually witnessed those scenes can ever forget them.

On one occasion during the retreat, I met a soldier who had been wounded in action. He had walked back several miles and now he could walk no more. He fell out on the side of the road and waited for death to come to him and relieve him of his miseries. There were hundreds of maggots in his wound and it would not be long before he died. I stopped by his side. He opened his eyes and looked at me and tried to get up, but he had no strength left for that. He signed to me to sit down by his side. He had a message which he wanted me to convey to Netaji. With tears rolling down his young cheeks, he began, 'Sahib, you are going back. You will see Netaji, but I will not. Please convey my "Jai Hind" to him and tell him that I lived up to the promise I made to him. Please also explain to him the **way** in which death came to me. Tell him how I was eaten alive **by** maggots but please assure him that in this great suffering I found a strange peace and happiness. Peace and happiness because I realize, that all this suffering is for India's sake. For the liberation of my motherland.' It was only one of the hundreds of similar instances that took place every day. It is very difficult to explain what had brought about this change in our soldiers. Up to the very time of their death, the thought of their Netaji and the promise they had made to him was upper most in their minds.

I know of hundreds of other instances where soldiers, suffering from dysentery and Beriberi with their legs and faces all swollen up, had fallen out, completely exhausted and it looked as if they would never be able to walk an inch further. Their officer would come up to them and say, 'Have you forgotten the promise you made to your Netaji – the promise that you would bear all hardships like a brave man. Our Netaji is waiting for us 50 miles down the road at Kalewa. Do you not wish to go and see him?' Saying this, the officer would command the soldier to get up and walk. These words used to have an almost magical effect on our exhausted soldiers. I have seen some of them crawling forward on their hands and knees determined to cover the last 50 miles just to have one glimpse of their Netaji. Many of them were just able to complete the journey and as soon as they arrived there they collapsed and died happily because they had that last glimpse of their beloved leader.

At Ahlow, the Japanese came to us and told us that the regiment should march to Teraun where river transport for everyone would be made available. Carrying all our sick, now numbering approximately 600, we marched off to Teraun, a distance of 25 miles. A large number of men died on this route as a result of exhaustion and starvation. Finally, the remaining ones arrived at Teraun, the place where we had been promised that river transport would be available for the whole regiment.

On arrival at Teraun we found to our great disappointment that not a single boat was available to transport us across the Yu River.

Teraun was a small camp, situated on the bank of the Yu river, on a hill-track running from Tamu-Yuwa on the Chindwin River. It also had a small Japanese supply base. This route had previously been used by the Japanese patriots and infiltration parties.

Due to torrential rains, the Yu River was flooded. Since its bed was of a rocky and precipitous nature there were several rapids in it and only the most experienced and daring boatmen could have dared to row on it, and that too only in special boats on certain occasions when the water level of the Chindwin river was higher than that of the Yu river, and Chindwin water flowed into the Yu.

Here again, we were held up with no hope of getting across. Things looked very grim for us indeed. Rations were running very short. The men were receiving only salt and ¾ lb. of rice a day. We were told that the reserve in Japanese supply would run out any day, and there was no hope of securing a fresh supply.

The men were sent in all different directions in search of boats and eventually some boats arrived from Ahlow and transported fit men across the river. They were then ordered to March to Yuwa and from there to Kalewa, where motor transport was made available to carry them to Mandalay and other stations.

The greatest problem was that of 400 seriously sick men who were quite incapable of walking even a mile. Eventually, I decided to leave these 400 men there and proceed to Yuwa and arrange for river transport to fetch these men down from Teraun. This proved to be a very difficult task and it took one month for us to evacuate our sick from Teraun during which period approximately 50 per cent of them perished through enemy bombing, disease and starvation.

Once the sick men were able to reach Yuwa, the rest was easy as there were some country boats available to take the men down to Kalewa where an I.N.A. camp had been started and medical aid, rations, and motor transport were also available.

On arrival at Kalewa, the units of No.1. Division were distributed in Burma as follows:
Divisional H.Q. Mandalay.
1. Subhas Brigade at Budalin.
2. Gandhi Brigade at Mandalay.
3. Azad Brigade at Choungoo.
Most of the officers and men were taken straight into hospitals at Monywa and Maymyo.

Haka-Falam Garrison after May 1944
In mid-May 1944 after the attack and capture of Klang Klang post by Major Mahboob Ahmed, the main force of the brigade was ordered to proceed to Kohima, but the responsibility of defending the Haka-Falam front was still to be that of No. 1 Regt. (the Subhas Brigade). Consequently, a small detachment of approximately 100 fit and 150 sick was left at Haka under the command of Lt. Ranjodh Singh, while a similar detachment was left behind at Falam.

A skeleton supply, medical and control staff under the command of Major Thakur Singh was left at the Regimental base at Nauchawng.

As soon as the main body of the regiment left Haka Falam the enemy became very active on that front. Our posts were being attacked almost daily.

The I.N.A. Klang Klang post was the scene of much bitter fighting. The morale of the enemy had risen considerably of late and they made determined efforts to capture our post and the Haka Base. But thanks to the daring and fortitude of our men, these attacks were always beaten back and offensive operations against the enemy continued by our forces.

Early in August 1944, after the failure of our assault on Imphal and the subsequent retreat, the British forces on the Haka front made a most determined attack to capture our Klang Klang post and the garrison at Haka. They amassed approximately 600 men and started attacking Haka from all directions. One strong detachment of the enemy encircled the Klang Klang post and occupied the mountain ridge between Haka and the Klang Klang post with the object of preventing any help from reaching our post.

The enemy launched attack after attack well supported by artillery and aircraft but our men held on. In the meantime realizing the critical situation that faced our men at Haka, Lt. Ranjodh Singh decided to leave a small detachment in Haka to hold the enemy attacks from the East. And with the remaining fit men, approximately 60 in number, he decided to counter attack the enemy who was besieging our Klang Klang post. He realized that the time was of the utmost importance and unless help reached the Klang Klang post quickly, it might be overrun by the enemy. Rallying his men around him, Lt. Ranjodh Singh, explained the critical military situation to them. He said, 'Our post is completely encircled by the enemy and unless we relieve the pressure on them, they may all be annihilated. We must go to their aid and save them or we must all perish together.' These words were enough for our men who fixing their bright steel bayonets on their rifles and led by their gallant commander charged into the enemy who were holding the ridge between Haka. There were approximately 300 enemy soldiers on the ridge. Our men were fighting against one to five odds, and against much superior arms and equipment – but their spirit was irresistible. With shouts of 'Netaji ki Jai' and 'Jai Hind', they dashed up the steep mountain ridge held by the enemy. There was a fierce hand to hand fight in which we suffered severe losses, but eventually the enemy had to withdraw to the next ridge. Lt. Ranjodh Singh's blood was boiling. He had seen several of his comrades fall by his side and he had no intention of breaking off the engagement yet. After reorganizing his small force, he again attacked the enemy and drove him off from that ridge as well. The contact with our besieged post was also established. Lt. Ranjodh Singh then proceeded to attack the enemy who had encircled the post and after a severe fight was able to drive them back. In this engagement the enemy left twenty-two dead on the battlefield. A large quantity of arms and ammunition was also captured by our men.

About the middle of August orders were issued to Lt. Ranjodh Singh to evacuate Haka Falam and re-join the rear Regimental Headquarters at Nau Chang. Amid torrential rains his men retreated to Falam, carrying all their sick and wounded on their shoulders. On arrival at Falam, they found that the suspension bridge over the Manipore River had been blown up by enemy guerrillas, and that owing to heavy floods, it was quite impossible to cross the Manipore River. There was no alternative for them but to return to Haka and attempt to reach Nau Chang via Kan. But this route, too, they found completely blockaded by the enemy, who had now closed round them from all directions. They had, therefore, to return to Falam again but this time, luckily for them, the Manipore River was not that heavily flooded and they were able to construct a temporary bridge and cross over to reach

Nau Chang early in September. From there, they retreated to Kalewa and re-joined the remaining soldiers of the Brigade returning from Kohima.

By this time our relations with the Japanese, which never at any time had been cordial, became very strained. All of us were of the opinion that the Japanese, by not extending proper cooperation to us and by hampering our operations, had betrayed us and were mainly responsible for our failure in capturing Imphal and for the extremely heavy casualties suffered by us. The feeling that existed at the time may be judged from the last word of dying I.N.A. officer who said to me, 'Sahib, please see that my grave is not next to that of a Japanese.'

During the retreat there were several instances where serious clashes took place between the Japanese and our men, and at Kindat and Yuwa we had regular machine-gun battles.

When the Haka Garrison was returning to Kalewa, the Japanese captured one of our small detachments of approximately ten men in the early hours of the morning. After tying them up to the trees, they bayonetted them as enemy spies. Most of them died but a few lived with as many as ten bayonet wounds to tell the ghastly story. When the facts of this incident were reported to Netaji, he was much enraged and took up the matter to settle it directly with Tokyo Headquarters.

It is difficult to explain why the Japanese behaved with the I.N.A. in such a manner. The only explanation that I can think of is that in the earlier stages of the battle the Japanese were too sure of themselves and of capturing Imphal. It is quite likely, in fact probable, that they had certain designs on India. Hence, they were afraid of allowing the I.N.A. to become too powerful and one day turning around and fight the Japanese in case of their betrayal. This, they may have had judged by their intimate contact with the I.N.A. officers and men.

I can quite confidently assert that even Netaji did not trust the Japanese. His idea was that the I.N.A. must be made as powerful as possible and that our surest guarantee against possible Japanese betrayal was our own strength. Netaji considered, and quite rightly too, that our strength would go on increasing immensely as we advance further inland into India and that we must be prepared at all times to fight all aggressors be they British or Japanese. His appreciation was that in their own interests the Japanese could not afford to antagonize India and create a similar situation as they had created in China where huge Japanese forces had been lodged.

I arrived at Kalewa from Kindat early in September 1944 and then proceeded to Yeu and Budalin to reconnoitre for the regiment. Around 23 September 1944, I proceeded to Mandalay and reported to Netaji. This was our first meeting after I had left Rangoon for the front in February 1944.

Activities of No. 1 Division during the Imphal operations

After the brilliant activities of the I.N.A. in the Arakans and in the Chin Hill, under the distinguished leadership of Shaheed Major L. S. Misra, Sardar-e-Jang and Major P. S. Raturi, Sardar-e-Jang, the preliminary doubts of the Japanese regarding the fighting capacity of the I.N.A. were dispelled, and Netaji's hands were considerably strengthened. He was then in a position to force the Japanese to send more I.N.A. units to the front. The mobilization and preparation for the final move to the front of the other units of the No. 1 Division were immediately taken into hand.

Subsequently, the No. 2 Guerrilla Regiment (the Gandhi Brigade) and the Divisional Headquarters moved to Burma early in March, and after a short rest at Rangoon they started moving to the front early in April. The route and condition under which they travelled were the same as those faced by the Subhas Brigade.

The Division was commanded by Major General (then Colonel) M. Z. Kiani, who was undoubtedly one of the most brilliant and daring commanders of the I.N.A. The Gandhi Brigade was commanded by Colonel I. J. Kiani, who was a cousin of General Kiani. It was a formidable combination and great things were expected from them. Colonel I. J. Kiani was well known for his perseverance and doggedness.

While moving to the front, they were told by the Japanese that they were too late, and that in all probability Imphal would fall before they arrived there. So by extremely hard and forced marches, they arrived at Kalewa early in April 1944. Here Colonel Kiani and the Divisional Commander were too late to take part in the attack on Imphal as it had either already fallen or would have done so in a few hours' time. They were advised to leave all their heavy baggage, including machine guns and hand grenades at Kalewa and reach Imphal as soon as possible. All that they required, their Japanese Liaison Officers told them, was one blanket, a rifle and fifty rounds of ammunition. The rest they were assured would be available in huge quantities at Imphal. In this state, the Gandhi Brigade rushed to the front eager not to be left behind at the time of the final assault on Imphal. It was the desire of every officer and man to be the first in that assault.

On arrival at Tamu, the Divisional Commander found out that Imphal had not fallen yet and that fierce fight was going on in the vicinity of Palel. He contacted the Japanese commander on the Palel front and in cooperation with him and with Major Fujiwara (of Singapore fame) who was now a Staff officer in the Japanese General Headquarters, it was decided that the No. 1 Division would have an independent sector to the west of the main Tamu-Palel road, and from there carry out guerrilla activities against the enemy forces on the Tamu front and against the enemy aerodrome at Palel.

The divisional headquarters were established at Chamol and the regimental headquarters at Mithan Khunou.

The Tamu-Palel road being the most important line of advance, the British had amassed very powerful forces on this front. They had one division holding this front with one brigade to the east of the road with a strong point in the neighbourhood of the Laimatol Hill. One brigade was to the west of the road with strongest points on Yapu ridges and one brigade in support in the neighbourhood of Palel aerodrome. These units were strongly supported by artillery and aeroplanes. Thus the Gandhi Brigade was faced by most powerful British forces and had to bear the brunt of some of the heaviest fighting in that area without any artillery or air support and with the additional disadvantage of having left behind at Kalewa all their heavy equipment including machine guns, hand grenades and entrenching tools.

In addition to the I.N.A., there was one Japanese Brigade, supported by artillery, operating on the main road and to the east of it.

Attack on Palel aerodrome

Early in May 1944, Major Fujiwara came to General Kiani and informed him that the Japanese were going to launch a general attack on the Palel aerodrome and wanted to know if the I.N.A. would also like to take part in the attack. He assured General Kiani that the capture of Palel by the Japanese forces was almost a foregone conclusion, but he was keen that the I.N.A. should also participate in it. Consequently, a plan of attack on the Palel aerodrome in cooperation with the Japanese forces was worked out by General Kiani and orders were issued to Colonel Kiani to put it into execution.

A striking force of approximately 300 strong under the command of Major Pritam Singh, was detailed to carry out this operation. The force started off, armed only with light automatics and rifles carrying only one day's rations with them. They covered approximately 40 miles over very steep and rocky mountains and successfully managed to infiltrate through the enemy's forward defences and reached the suburbs of the Palel aerodrome. The attack was planned to take place at about midnight, so for the day they lay very low, hiding themselves among thick shrubs in deep ravines. As soon as darkness fell, they started to advance in the direction of the aerodrome. On arriving near it, Major Pritam Singh found that there were strong piquets posted on the hills around the aerodrome. He realized that it was not possible to attack the aerodrome without first attacking those piquets. He, therefore, detailed one party under Capt. Sadhu Singh to encircle and capture one of those piquets and the remainder under another officer to infiltrate through and attack the aerodrome.

The British piquet was a very strong one and had machine guns fixed in it. Our soldiers advanced very silently under the cover of darkness and with fixed bayonets made a surprise night raid on the enemy post. The enemy was caught completely at a loss. They put up their hands and said in Hindustani to our soldiers, '*Sathi Ham ko mat maro.*' The I.N.A. soldiers had orders not to shoot or kill any Indian soldiers, unless they were attacked first. The officer halted our men, and accompanied by Lt. Lai Singh and Lt. Mohan Singh entered the post to accept its surrender. In the meantime, the post commander asked our officer, 'What is that you want?' Lt. Lai Singh, who was in front and was armed only with a Naga spear replied, 'I want the blood of those two English officers who are hiding in that corner.' Saying this, he charged at them. The men inside the piquet opened fire on them and Lt. Lai Singh was mortally wounded. But before he fell, he had killed with his spear both those officers. Realizing that they had been treacherously misled, our men under the command of Major Pritam Singh made repeated attacks on the British post but it was so heavily surrounded by barbed wire that they were unable to capture it. By this time it was nearly daybreak and Major Pritam Singh decided to call a halt and to retreat to his Regimental Headquarters.

In the meantime, the other party had successfully infiltrated through and captured the aerodrome, but they found no trace of the Japanese there and since they were not strong enough to hold the aerodrome by themselves, they withdrew after destroying all the aeroplanes concentrated there.

While all this was going on, Colonel Kiani with the remainder of his brigade, had advanced and occupied Upaw ridge so as to be in a position to support Major Pritam's Singh force. As soon as the daylight broke the enemy artillery and aeroplanes became very active and carried out a ceaseless bombing and shelling on our forces for the whole day. Our men, under Major Pritam Singh, had had nothing to eat for the last three days. On that day the Gandhi Brigade suffered very heavy casualties and we lost approximately 250 men.

One very notable feature of this operation was that Major Ali Akbar Khan, who was the Regimental Medical officer of this brigade, went right up to the front line. During the heaviest bombing and shelling, he went from man to man dressing their wounds and carrying out minor operations. He had no immaculate instruments of surgery. All he had was a pair of ordinary scissors and a cut-throat razor, and with these he carried on his duty in that pandemonium and hell, quite oblivious of his personal safety in a manner that any country would feel proud of. His death in September 1944, in the I.N.A. hospital at Monywa, deprived the Azad Hind Fauj of one of its best and most loved officers. This attack on the aerodrome came as a rude shock to the British who now decided to counter-attack and drive back the Gandhi Brigade from Mithan Khunou.

Seaforth highlanders attack Mithan Khunou

After the Palel Aerodrome attack, the enemy patrol activity increased very considerably. One daring British officer managed to creep up to our sentries on several occasions to shoot them at their posts. Colonel Kiani then laid an ambush for him and finally disposed him off.

A few days later, the British battalion, strongly supported by heavy artillery, attacked our foremost company in the vicinity of Mithan Khunou. The leading platoon of our company was commanded by a young Second Lieutenant, Ajaib Singh, who had been trained at the I.N.A. Officers' Training School in Singapore.

The Scottish soldiers of the Seaforth Highlanders, knowing that they were up against the I.N.A., attacked fiercely. The soldiers of the I.N.A. had also been waiting for this day. It was the first battle of the Gandhi Brigade against white troops, and at the very sight of them they became wild. Challenges were thrown out by both sides, and a grim battle at close quarters ensued. The British soldiers came almost up to the trenches occupied by our men, but time and again, they were beaten back with heavy losses.

After their first setback, the British fell back and after reorganizing their troops they attacked again, this time supported by artillery and aeroplanes; but the gallant platoon of the I.N.A. led by their brave commander, held firm and continued to beat back attack after attack. Eventually being unable to make any headway against the I.N.A. soldiers, the enemy called a halt and withdrew to their defences. Ajaib Singh had no intention of ending the engagement yet. Rallying his men, and collecting ammunition from the dead and wounded British left behind by the attackers, Lt. Ajaib Singh advanced from his position and approached the nearest British defence post and shouted to them challenging them to come out and fight and not hide behind their defences and barbed wire fences. The British accepted the challenge and another grim battle ensued, this time with British on the defensive. Lt. Ajaib Singh had captured a large number of rifles and grenades in the first engagement and he wished to use them against the British, but he did not have the proper ballistite grenade cartridges. So, against all rules and regulation of military training he used 303 ball ammunitions to fire rifle grenades. This worked well, and in that engagement he fired as many as fifty grenades. When darkness fell, Lt. Ajaib Singh, having returned the enemy's courtesy call, came back to his lines. His small force had suffered severe losses, but he had inflicted far greater losses on the enemy. In addition, he had taught them to be more respectful and cautious when attacking the Azad Hind Fauj. In the day's engagement, the enemy suffered at least fifty casualties in killed and wounded; while our losses were ten killed and a few slightly wounded. The remarkable feature of this engagement was that majority of the I.N.A. troops participating in it were raw Tamil recruits from Malaya. It was their first engagement, but they acquitted themselves most creditably and smashed the British theory of martial and non-martial classes. They proved in this engagement that Indians, whether classed as martial or non-martial by the British, could, when aroused, fight most heroically and make supreme sacrifices for the liberation of their motherland.

By this time heavy rains had set in and made the ration and ammunition supply the most difficult problem. Due to the lack of proper food and medicines, the health of the troops deteriorated rapidly and by the middle of June 1944, they had become so weak that they could hardly walk a few miles; but despite this, they stuck to their posts and in the face of repeated British attacks never retreated even an inch before them. At about this time the tide of the battle had turned. The British had managed to substantially reinforce their beleaguered garrison in Imphal, and were now in a position to launch the main offensive.

Their first move was to capture the heights occupied by the men of Gandhi Brigade around Mithan Khunou. This time it was an attack launched by a whole British Brigade, 3,000 strong, supported by heavy artillery and aeroplanes. Our old rivals, the Seaforth, again led the attack.

By a clever encircling movement, they surrounded one of our companies commanded by Capt. Rao, and it looked as if they would annihilate our force. The situation looked extremely grave. All the commanding heights and strategic points were in enemy hands. Besides this, the strength of the Gandhi Brigade was very much depleted owing to widespread illness and battle casualties. In this particular action there were 600 I.N.A. men opposing approximately 3,000 well-fed British soldiers having infinitely superior arms and equipment. Our men fought most heroically. Colonel Kiani, the brigade commander, himself was in the area of the company that was encircled by the British. He realized that unless the strategic heights were recaptured by them his garrison would be annihilated. He, therefore, issued orders to his officers to take possession of those heights at any cost. Lt. Mansukh Lall was ordered to recapture one of the heights. He was commanding a platoon consisting of approximately thirty men. With this small force he counter attacked without any artillery covering fire, and recaptured one of the strongest posts occupied by the enemy. While leading his small, and semi-starved force up the steep ridge, he was wounded 13 times; through exhaustion and loss of blood, he staggered and fell to the ground. His men seeing their gallant commander fall hesitated and slowed down their pace. Lt. Mansukh Lall, like a tiger that is mortally wounded but is determined to make the last charge, roared to his men and exhorted them to continue their advance and not to worry about him. They were very near the summit, and making a last supreme effort, with thirteen bullet wounds in his body, he rose to his feet and personally led the final assault on the height which was to decide the fate of the Gandhi Brigade that day.

The enemy, having no stomach for a bloody hand to hand fight, did not relish the idea of facing the cold bright steel bayonets of the men of the Azad Hind Fauj, and retreated, leaving the height in possession of the I.N.A. men. The most important point was thus recaptured and the unit saved.

While this company under the command of Lt. Rao was fighting to break the steel around it, another company under the command of Lt. Ajaib Singh was sent forward by the Battalion Commander to counter attack the British and to extricate Lt. Rao's company. This company advanced and by a very clever manoeuvre encircled the British troops who were besieging the Brigade Headquarters and Lt. Rao's company. The enemy were taken completely by surprise, and realizing that their line of retreat had been cut off, broke off the engagement with Lt. Rao's company and tried to break through Lt. Ajaib Singh's company; but all possible routes of withdrawal had been blocked. They were caught between two rings of fire and suffered extremely heavy casualties. It was a terrible massacre. The whole battalion was strewn with the dead bodies of 'tommies' and it was estimated that in this engagement, the enemy lost at least 250 men, killed or severely wounded. This battle of annihilation lasted throughout the day and when evening came, the enemy broke off the engagement and retreated to lick their wounds. In this battle, our men had dealt such a crushing blow to the enemy's morale that for some considerable time afterwards, they did not dare to attack any of our posts.

By this time it was nearing the end of June 1944. Extremely heavy monsoons had started and the Tamu-Palel road, the only line of supply was washed away by torrential streams. Our men did not have adequate protection from rain and all supplies of rations and ammunition was cut off. The situation was extremely grave, and it looked as if our men would have to fall back due to lack of supplies. Colonel Kiani had, however, no such intention. He said, 'If we cannot be supplied with rations from Tamu, we must make arrangements for collecting rations in our own area.' He was at that time occupying approximately 200 square miles of Indian territory. All this territory was being administered by him, through the Azad Hind Dal unit sent up by Netaji, which had been especially trained in the administration of 'liberated areas'.

He called a conference of all the prominent Naga chiefs and explained the gravity of the ration situation, and told them that unless sufficient rations could be collected locally, his troops would have to withdraw to Tamu. The Nagas implored Colonel Kiani not to retreat and said, 'You are the army of India's liberation. You must not go back. We are extremely short of food ourselves, but we will collect whatever we can for you. We will live or starve to death together.'

They returned to their areas and brought back whatever rations they could collect. But, it was not an easy matter for a mountainous and unproductive area to maintain a large force of approximately 2,000 men for a long period. These rations were soon exhausted, and again in few days the rations' situation became as grave as before.

The Nagas, who were a hill tribe residing in mountains all around Imphal, were most helpful to our troops. They were a brave and patriotic tribe and cooperated with us in every possible way. They helped and guided our patrols, brought back valuable information regarding the movements and disposition of the enemy, and supplied rations. Some of them were extremely bitter against the British. Their Queen, they said, had been arrested and taken away to India by the

British. One remarkable feature of the Naga character was that they refused to cooperate in any way with the Japanese, and for doing so in the Japanese occupied areas some of them had to pay heavy penalties. They said, 'We do not want the British, neither do we want the Japanese in our area. All that we would like to have is our own Raja, Netaji Subhas Chandra Bose.'

At about this time, a very unfortunate incident took place. Major B. J. S. Garewal, the Second-in-Command of the Gandhi Brigade, being unable to face the hardships of the battle any longer, deserted to the British side. His desertion was a very sad blow to the morale of our troops. He had done extremely good work in training the Gandhi Brigade in Malaya and during the actual fighting in the early stages of the Imphal campaign.

Early in July 1944, having reorganized and being fully informed of the conditions under which our men were fighting, the enemy attacked again. They managed, with the aid of some local spies, to infiltrate through our much depleted lines and encircled the entire Gandhi Brigade. By this time, due to heavy battle casualties, disease and starvation, our front line strength had diminished from 2,000 to 1,000 men, and these too were in poor health. The enemy launched a particularly fierce attack against the Brigade Headquarters. The situation looked very grave, but Major Abid Hussain, who had now replaced Major Garewal as the Brigade Second-in-Command, managed to break through the encirclement with one company. Not withstanding his small force, Major Hussain counter-attacked and after a fierce battle was able to extricate the Gandhi Brigade from a very dangerous and critical situation.

In the evening, the Gandhi Brigade counter-attacked the enemy who had captured the Mithun heights. In this battle Major Hassan, Lt. Rama Rao and Capt. Taj Mohammad displayed outstanding gallantry, and were awarded the much prized medal of Sardar-e-Jang.

By early July the entire face of the campaign had changed. The Azad Hind Fauj and the Japanese forces that had been holding Kohima had fallen back on Tamu. To the west of Imphal, the Japanese and the I.N.A. forces which had been attacking Imphal from the direction of Bishanpore had to fall back on Tiddim, and there was a danger that the line of retreat of the Gandhi Brigade might be cut off. In addition to this, after the retreat of our forces from Kohima, the British rushed huge reinforcements of men and material to Imphal, with the object of starting a large-scale offensive against the Japanese in Burma. The full impact of this fell on the Gandhi Brigade, which was eventually ordered to retreat to Kalewa along the main Kalewa-Tamu Road. The condition under which the retreat was carried out were the same as those experienced by the Subhas Brigade.

Activities of the Azad Brigade

Soon after the departure of the Gandhi Brigade from Malaya, the Azad Brigade also moved. It arrived in Rangoon during the later part of April 1944, and after a short rest, it proceeded to Tamu via Kalewa. On arrival at Tamu in mid-May, its commander, Colonel Gulzara Singh, went and reported to the Divisional Commander, General M. Z. Kiani, at Chamol and received instructions regarding the employment of his brigade from him. The task allotted to the Azad Brigade was that of carrying out intensive guerrilla activities against the British forces around Palel. The area of operations allotted to them was to the East of the Tamu-Palel road, with the Brigade Headquarters in the vicinity of Mintha.

The Azad Brigade went into action and prepared the bases of operation, but before they could launch a large-scale offensive against the enemy, the rains set in, and Colonel

Gulzara Singh had to order his unit to withdraw under orders from the Divisional Commander. Thus the Azad Brigade withdrew to Kalewa via the main Kalewa-Tamu road at the same time as the Gandhi Brigade.

Activities of the I.N.A. units during Imphal campaign
No. 1 – Engineering Company

This company moved into Burma in early 1944, and was sent to the Homalin–Thawiugdut sector. It was originally commanded by Lt. Shinde, but later Capt. Pritam Singh took over its command. During the operations, they were allotted the task of building bridges and repairing the Tamu-Humine-Ukhrul road. They did excellent work throughout the operations and kept the road in good state of repair throughout the monsoons. They withdrew with the rest of the I.N.A. forces to Kalewa.

No. 2 – Motor Transport Company

This company was raised in Singapore in August 1943 soon after Netaji's arrival. Most of its personnel was made up of the civilian volunteers, who in response to Netaji's call, joined the company in large numbers. Some of the drivers who owned private cars and lorries, donated these to the I.N.A. and joined as ordinary drivers. They were placed under the command of Capt. Harnam Singh, a very able and hardworking officer, who by his tact and ability created an excellent morale throughout his unit. They were moved to Burma in September 1943.

During the operations, they oscillated between Mandalay and Kalewa, and did excellent work in transporting men and materials to the front. In July 1944, when the No. 1 Division had to retreat to Kalewa, the No. 1 M.T. Company was operating between Kalewa and Yeu. It was during this time (July-October 1944) that they did their best work. Facing torrential rains, they undertook the evacuation of the No. 1 Division to Yeu. The men returning from the front were in a terrible state of health, but for the excellent work done by this company most of them would have perished on the way. They had only about twenty old lorries with which they had to evacuate approximately 7,000 men to a distance of 100 miles, on very difficult roads, through knee-deep mud and across streams which were generally flooded. The majority of these lorries were in workshops most of the time, and it was indeed a very creditable task to keep them on the road after all. In addition to this they had great difficulty in obtaining petrol and engine oil, and it was mainly through the efforts of Zora Singh, a civilian from Rangoon, and Colonel R. M. Arshad that these items could be procured mainly from the black market. Our allies refused to issue any spare parts or engine oil to our lorries. Later, during the evacuation of the No. 1 Division from Mandalay to Pyinmana, they did most creditable service in evacuating two large hospitals, supply and ordinance depots and approximately 2,000 sick men.

The company and its commander deserve to be congratulated for their excellent work throughout.

By the end of September 1944, the units of the No. 1 Division had concentrated in the rest areas, as under:

Divisional Headquarters	Mandalay
No. 1 (the Subhas Brigade)	Budalin
No. 2 (the Gandhi Brigade)	Mandalay
No. 3 (the Azad Brigade)	Choungoo

I.N.A. Base hospitals were located at Maymayo and Manywa.

Thus ended the main I.N.A. and Japanese offensive which had been started in March 1944. During this period, the I.N.A. with much inferior equipment and an extremely poor supply system, was able to advance as much as 150 miles into

Indian territory. While the I.N.A. was on the offensive, there was not a single occasion on which our forces were defeated on the battlefield, and there was never an occasion when the enemy, despite their overwhelming superiority in men and materials, was able to capture any post held by the I.N.A. On the other hand, there were very few cases where the I.N.A. attacked a British post and failed to capture it.

In these operations the I.N.A. lost nearly 4,000 of its men.

It is very well known by everyone that it was only on account of sheer bad luck that the I.N.A. and the Japanese failed to take Imphal. They came very near to capturing it; and at one time they were only two miles away from it. The British themselves tried several times to evacuate their forces from Imphal and retreat to Dimapore, but they failed as the road at Kohima was blocked by the I. N.A. and the Japanese. Had this road been left open to the British, they would certainly have retreated from Imphal. But our objective was to capture all the British forces and war material intact at Imphal.

Imphal is situated in plains surrounded on all sides by huge mountain ranges running through which are narrow roads. These were the only lines of retreat for the British forces to follow, and once these roads were blocked, the escape of the British forces from Imphal became impossible.

Netaji's own idea was that the I.N.A., as it was then, was not powerful enough to undertake a full-scale invasion of India, and at the same time fight successfully against a possible Japanese betrayal. He was, therefore, of the opinion that the 5 British divisions composed of nearly 1½ lakhs of Indians must be captured intact so that they could be persuaded to join the I.N.A. to fight for India's liberations. Moreover, with the captured war material the deficiencies of the I.N.A. artillery and other essentials could be made up.

With all the lines of retreat cut off, the British forces were obliged to fight with their backs to the wall. They had only two alternatives either to surrender unconditionally or to fight on. They decided to fight on, although the situation was very critical for them. They formed a 'box defence', a special type of defence in which armoured cars and tanks are put all round the camp to form a steel ring, inside which the infantry takes shelter. Unfortunately for us, the Japanese Air Force which had been holding complete air superiority in the earlier stages of the battle, was obliged to move to the Pacific Islands, where the Americans had attacked and intensive naval and air fighting was in progress. It was indeed very unfortunate that the Japanese Air Force had to be transferred, because had it stayed on, it would have been possible for it to smash the British 'box defences.' At the same time taking advantage of the absence of the Japanese Air Force, the British brought one full division by air from the Arakans. Had the Japanese Air Force been there, it would probably have made it impossible for the British to bring this division from the Arakan front. For nearly three months, the British forces in Imphal were supplied materials by air. A superior Japanese Air Force would have made this impossible and would probably have led the British to surrender. Another reason for our failure to capture Imphal was that we started the offensive too late. The Japanese General's staff thought that they would be able to capture Imphal by the middle of May at the latest, and that soon afterwards the monsoons would start, giving us time to consolidate our gains so as to make a British counter-offensive impossible. On the other hand, if the situation was favourable, the Azad Hind Fauj and Japanese forces at Kohima could advance and cross the Brahmaputra into Bengal and Bihar. Unfortunately, this calculation went wrong and when the monsoons started, the I.N.A. and the Japanese were still struggling to occupy Imphal. Eventually, towards the end of June 1944 it had become almost impossible to supply rations and ammunitions to our forces fighting on the front. Rain and mud were the two great enemies that forced us to abandon our siege of Imphal.

Lastly, and with a clear conscience, I can say that the Japanese did not give full aid and assistance to the Azad Hind Fauj during their assault on Imphal. In fact, I am right in saying that they let us down badly, and had it not been for their betrayal of the I.N.A. the history of the Imphal campaign might have been a different one. My own impression is that the Japanese did not trust the I.N.A. They had found out through their liaison officers that the I.N.A. would not accept Japanese domination in any way; and that they would fight the Japanese in case they attempted to replace the British. The Japanese were frightened of making the I.N.A. too powerful. They were too confident of themselves and thought that they would be able to capture Imphal without any assistance and or much difficulty. I quote the words of the Japanese Commander-in-Chief at Maymyo during the course of a conversation with me to support this. In February 1944, when asked what he thought of the British forces in Imphal, he said, 'Of the British forces I think nothing.' Of course he was speaking from the past experiences. He was one of the chief commanders who had forced the British to surrender in Singapore.

Thus ended our first offensive, I am afraid, in a tragic fashion.

At the end of September 1944, Netaji was at Yeu, where he met the troops returning from the front line. A few days later, he returned to Mandalay, where he held a conference of Divisional and all Brigade commanders of the No. 1 Division. At this conference all commanders were unanimous in their conviction that the Japanese had let us down, particularly the Hikari-Kikan, the Japanese Liaison Department attached to the I.N.A. It was, therefore, resolved that this department should be done away with and we should have direct dealings with the Japanese Government in Tokyo and with the Japanese General Headquarters in Burma.

Early in October 1944, Netaji went to Maymyo where we inspected the base hospital. There were nearly 2,000 patients in that hospital, most of whom were in a terrible condition due to septic gunshot wounds, dysentery and malaria. There was a detachment of the Rani of Jhansi Regiment girls working as nurses in this hospital. Their number was of course most inadequate compared to the amount of work they had to do. One of them Bela Dutt, a young Bengali girl of sixteen years, was at a time looking after eighty-five cases of acute dysentery. She used to wash their clothes, give the men a sponge-bath, and help them to dress. I will never forget the day when Netaji was going round the hospital from bed to bed. How each one of those sick soldiers adored their nurses! They told Netaji, 'Even our mothers and sisters could not have looked after us better.' There were tears in Netaji's eyes. He complimented Bela on her work and went on.

She was looking after 85 patients and she knew by heart the full history of each case! That day in recognition of her excellent work she was promoted from Naik to Havaldar.

I admire the Rani of Jhansi Regiment girls for their courage, fortitude and devotion to duty. Their hospital was bombed and machine-gunned almost daily by the British aircraft; at least on two occasions some of them were buried under the debris of their house. But nothing seemed to affect the morale of these brave daughters of Mother India.

Another incident that befell during that visit to the hospital was when Netaji went up to a soldier who was in an extremely bad state due to Beriberi. His face was all swollen. Netaji jokingly said to him, 'When are you going to get well.'

His reply was prompt, 'Netaji, I will be absolutely fit the very day you give us orders to advance again.'

While inspecting the hospital Netaji found that there was an extreme shortage of medicines, especially for dysentery. Feeling sorry for the diseased men, Netaji decided to give them a treat. He ordered *jallaibi* to be prepared in his house and sent to the hospital. The next day, he went to the hospital again and asked a dysentery patient if he had received his share of *jallaibi* and how he liked it. The soldier replied: 'Netaji I thoroughly enjoyed it; in fact it has done me more good than the doctor's medicine. Please send me some more.' After this Netaji was known as a *Jallaibi Doctor.*

Netaji returns to Rangoon
On 11 October 1944, Netaji left Mandalay for Rangoon, after inspecting all the front line troops. He was accompanied by his personal staff and the Divisional and Brigade Commanders of the No. 1 Division. While at Mandalay, Netaji had received on an official invitation from the Japanese Government to visit Tokyo on 9 October for discussions on certain vital points concerning our future course of action. Such discussions between the Japanese Government and Netaji were quite common. The Japanese had developed a great respect for Netaji's ability as a statesman and they used to consult him not only in matters relating to India, but also on other important matters related to the Japanese Foreign Policy. We, on our side, also welcomed the invitation as it had given us an opportunity to decide upon our future course of action in the light of the experience gained on the battlefield during the operations around Imphal.

On arrival in Rangoon, a meeting of the cabinet was held. Netaji, explaining the war situation to the civilian members of the cabinet, said:

We started operations too late. The monsoon was disadvantageous to us. Our roads were submerged. River traffic had to be against current. Against this the enemy had first-class roads. Our only chance was to take Imphal before the rain started: and we would have succeeded if we had more air support and if their forces in Imphal had not special orders to make a stand to the last man. If we had started in January we would have succeeded. In all sectors, till the rains began, we either held the enemy or advanced. In the Arakan Sector the enemy was held. In the Kaladan Sector, we routed the enemy and advanced. In Tiddim we advanced. In Palel and Kohima also we advanced. In the Haka Sector we held them. And these all, in spite of the numerical superiority that the enemy had, plus equipment and rations.

When the rains came, we had to postpone the general assault on Imphal. The enemy was able to send mechanized divisions and thus was able to retake the Kohima-Imphal Road. The question then arose where we should hold the line. There were two courses open: either hold on to the Bishenpur-Palel Line and not allow the enemy to advance: or fall back and hold a more advantageous position...

What are the lessons we have learnt from this campaign? We have received our baptism of fire. A body of ex-civilians who were ordered to withdraw when the ammunition was exhausted, preferred not to withdraw, and with fixed bayonets they charged the enemy. They came back victorious...

Our troops have gained much confidence must now make arrangements to take them over. We have learnt the tactics of the enemy. We have captured enemy documents. The experience gained by our commanders has been invaluable. Before the campaign started, the Japanese had no confidence in our troops and wanted to break them up into batches attached to the Japanese Army. I wanted a front to be given to our men and this was ultimately given. Our Divisional Commander and other Officers have gained much experience from this campaign.

We have also learnt our defects. Transport and supply were defective owing to the difficult terrain. We had no front line propaganda. Though we had prepared personnel for this, we could not use then owing to the lack of transport. Henceforth, each Unit of the I.N.A. will have a propaganda unit attached to it. We wanted loud speakers but the Japanese failed to supply them to us. We are now making our own.

After this it was unanimously resolved that we would continue the fight to the better end, until the emancipation of our country was achieved. It was decided that we would fight the British wherever we met them. For this purpose, and in view of the increasing strength of the enemy it was considered necessary to intensify our own efforts and to bring about a total mobilization of all resources of the Indians in East Asia.

One great weakness that we discovered during our operations around Imphal was that we were too dependent on the Japanese for rations, medicines, etc. It was, therefore, decided to eliminate all these shortcomings in future operations. A supply department was started and Sri Parmanand was appointed as the Supply Minister. The next resolution asked for the abolition of the Japanese Liaison Department – the Hikari-Kikan – through which we dealt with the Japanese Government and for the establishment of direct contact with the Tokyo Government. It was, therefore, decided to start a new department of the Provisional Government of the Azad Hind – the Foreign Department, and General Chatterji was appointed as the Foreign Minister. An exchange of Ambassadors with Japan was also agreed upon.

Lastly, for direction of all future operations of the I.N.A. a War Council was elected. It was considered that the Cabinet was too large for this task, and the necessity of a small and more efficient council was felt. The following were the elected members of the War Council:

1. Netaji
2. General Bhonsle
3. General Chatterji
4. General M. Z. Kiani
5. Colonel Aziz Ahmad
6. Colonel Ehsan Qadir
7. Colonel Habibur Rehman
8. Colonel Gulzara Singh
9. Sri Parmanand
10. Sri Raghavan
11. Colonel I. J. Kiani
12. Colonel Shahnawaz Khan

In accordance with the decision to intensify our war efforts, a recruiting campaign to increase the strength of the I.N.A. was started. Training centres for civilian recruits at Ipoh, Kuala Lumpur, Penang, Singapore, and Rangoon were expanded. As a result of this, the strength of the I.N.A. increased considerably and ultimately it reached a figure of 50,000 strong. At the same time the No. 2 Division was ordered to move, and a third division under the command of Colonel G. R. Nagar was raised. Advanced units of the No. 2 Division began to reach Rangoon early in October 1944.

Netaji left Rangoon for Tokyo early in November accompanied by General Chatterji, General Kiani and Colonel Habibur Rehman. Before his departure, Colonel Aziz Ahmad was appointed to officiate as the Supreme Commander in his absence, and I was appointed Commander of the No. 1 Division in place of General M. Z. Kiani who was appointed

স্বাধীনতা আমাদের জম্ম গত অধিকার

Charged with slogans of 'Jai Hind' and 'Swaraj is my birthright', young Indians
rejoiced the success of Azad Hind Fauj and Netaji Subhas Chandra Bose, who
was able to unite the people of India as never before.

The Cabinet of the Provisional Government of Azad Hind (Free India). Netaji Subhas Chandra Bose, standing third from left with Lakshmi Swaminathan (later Sahgal) of Rani of Jhansi Regiment, to his right.

'Men, money, and materials cannot by themselves bring victory or freedom. We must have the motive power that will inspire us to do brave deeds and heroic exploits.'

– Netaji Subhas Chandra Bose.

Postal stamp released on the 67th birth anniversary of Netaji Subhas Chandra Bose.

Surrendered Indian National Army (INA) troops at Mount Popa, Myanmar.

Netaji Subhas Chandra Bose arrives to a warm reception at Haneda Airport, Japan, on 31 October 1943.

Participants of the Greater East Asia Conference.
Left to right, front row: Zhang Jinghui, Wang Jingwei, Hideki Tojo,
Wan Waithayakon, José P. Laurel, Netaji Subhas Chandra Bose.
The conference was held in Tokyo on 5–6 November 1943.

UNITY   FAITH   SACRIFICE

AZAD HIND

161 & 163, Cecil St., Syonan.

ENGLISH EDITION
Organ of the Indian Independence League Headquarters.

Tel. Nos. 3491 & 3492 Ext. 7

NETAJI WEEK SPECIAL

Vol. 2—No. 156.   WEDNESDAY, JULY 4, 2603, SYOWA 20   Price 25 Cents.

Prodigious Sacrifices Of E.A. Indians For Freedom Struggle Can't Go In Vain

Independence Movement Set With Noble Mission Of Political Salvation & World Peace

(By H.E. N. RAGHAVAN)

IF to-day, there is a spirit of despondency abroad, it is entirely un-Indian. India's sons and daughters are made of sterner stuff. Freedom has never been won by the chicken-hearted; it is the prize of the brave. If we are, we have been defeated, we can as well write off our usefulness to India. Neither Imphal nor Rangoon can seal the fate of Hindustan. On the other hand, the events of the last two years and more shall brace us to greater efforts than hitherto. The History of the Indian Freedom Movement is not devoid of setbacks and setbacks, which India converted into stepping stones. In East Asia, the political achievements of the last two years cannot but instil into us the fullest faith and confidence in our Mission. The conversion of our Movement from an ordinary political undertaking into a fighting organisation capable of handling the great task we have set out to perform, the unification into one whole, one solid brotherhood and under one banner, the far-flung Indian communities of East Asia, the awakening of the masses, men, women and children alike, the infusion of an unquenchable thirst for freedom into their hearts, the faith and enthusiasm which they have spontaneously displayed in the Cause of our motherland, the prodigious sacrifices they have made at her call—all these cannot but indicate that we are on the eve of a great revolution with Indian liberation as its imminent goal. All these cannot go in vain. Every action has a re-action, and nothing good disappears without its results. The spirit with which Indians all over East Asia, from Manchukuo to Otawa and from Burma to Philippines, came forward to place their all at the Altar of their country's Freedom, cannot die merely because British Imperialism is once again making some headway here or there. During the last two years Indians have made themselves not only heard, but felt. They have risen to unprecedented heights in the service of their country and in the estimation of the world. Indian Independence can no longer be in doubt. The events in Burma which necessitated the withdrawal for the time being, of the Provisional Government of Free India from Rangoon, cannot make any difference to the attainment of our objective. When the Indian Independence Movement was originally launched in East Asia, there was no question of besieging Imphal or holding up the British on the banks of the Irrawaddy. They were but later developments in our battle for Freedom. A capable commander thinks out various plans to bring

(Continued on page 3)

"To This Vision I Offer New Life and Light
To This Nation A Sword For The Fight"—Josh.

NETAJI'S MESSAGE TO INDIANS

Two years have elapsed since a new life was infused into our countrymen in East Asia. It is necessary for us to take stock of our past achievements and failures and tighten our belts in order to face the responsibilities of the future. A long and bitter struggle lies ahead of us. At home and abroad, some of our countrymen, being overwhelmed by difficulties, have begun to lose heart and are thinking of how to compromise with our enemies. For those who are stout-hearted, brave and unflinching, the task has, therefore, become more arduous. We now need another gigantic moral effort to overcome despondency and weakness in every form and rise to greater heights of courage and self-sacrifice.

During the last twenty-four months we have made much progress towards our goal, but we have also suffered some reverses, as in recent months. But no setbacks can undo our positive achievements. The Indian people have now a Government and an Army of their own and under the aegis of that Government, the armed struggle for India's independence was launched by the Azad Hind Fauj on the 4th February, 1944. So long as India remains enslaved, that struggle will go on. The Azad Hind Fauj will fight to the last man and to the last round.

Standing on the threshold of another year of intense activity and sacrifice, I want to remind my countrymen in East Asia that if we are true revolutionaries, we can never be disheartened or depressed. If we continue to work in the spirit of true revolutionaries, we shall never fail, and victory will be ours in the end.

The roads to Delhi are many and Delhi remains our goal. "Chalo Delhi" will be our slogan, so long as India is not free. And "total mobilisation" remains our programme for the future. I want from my countrymen in East Asia more men, more money and more materials

Azad Hind Fauj Blaze Trail Across Indo-Burma Border With Their Blood

East Asia Indians Made History By Sheer Heroism & Sacrifice For Country's Freedom

(By H.E. Major-General M. Z. Kiani)

INDIANS in East Asia are today celebrating the Second Anniversary of the most eventful day in their history. Two years ago, today, our beloved Netaji Subhas Chandra Bose set foot on this island and assumed the active leadership of these millions of our countrymen in East Asia. Since then epoch-making events have followed each other in rapid succession.

For the first time in modern history a Government of Free India was established and recognised by nine friendly Powers. A national army, several thousands strong, armed with modern weapons, trained and officered entirely by Indians was formed and recognised as an army of Free India. War was declared on India's oppressors, the British and their allies, the Americans. Netaji's philosophy of militant nationalism, backed by the nation's total mobilisation programme was put into action.

The Rani of Jhansi Regiment, the only fighting unit composed entirely of women, was raised and part of it sent to the Burma front. The Indian National Army, morally and materially supported by the three million East Asia Indians, went into action against India's enemies and with their blood blazed the trail for all Indians to follow. The blood that has flowed from the wounds of our heroes of the Azad Hind Fauj, on the hills and in the valleys of the Arakans, Manipur and Assam has finally cemented the bond of unity and brotherhood between all classes and creeds of Indians.

We may well be proud of these achievements although we have not yet reached our goal, but we have already made history. How has this been possible? Firstly, because our cause is just. It can be said without any exaggeration that in the world today there is no other cause as just as ours. We are a nation of 388 million

(Continued on page 3)

during the next twelve months. Our losses in men and money have to be replenished. By our deeds and by our valour and tenacity, we have to put heart into those who are now disheartened and depressed. And above all, we have to continue the armed struggle for India's liberation, under all circumstances, until the Indian masses are roused and the long-expected revolution breaks out inside India. Only when the awakened masses of India take up the fight and march with us to Delhi—and only when our tricolour national flag flies over the Viceroy's House in New Delhi—will our task be over. Till then, we must labour and we must fight.

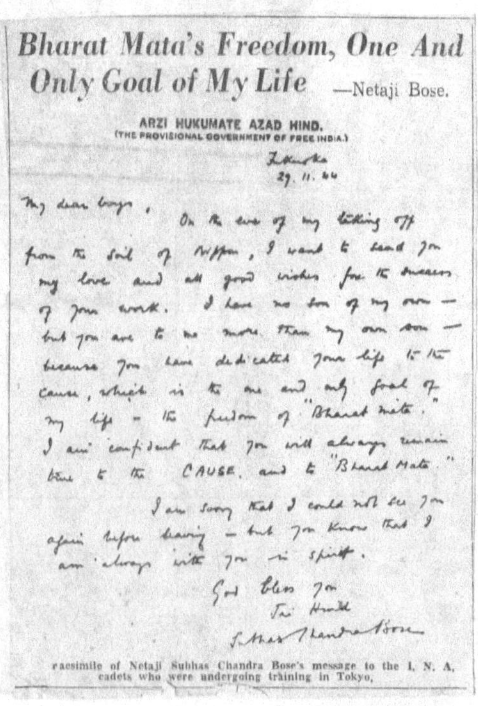

Bharat Mata's Freedom, One And Only Goal of My Life —Netaji Bose.

ARZI HUKUMATE AZAD HIND.
(THE PROVISIONAL GOVERNMENT OF FREE INDIA.)

Tokio
29. 11. 44

My dear boys,

On the eve of my taking off from the soil of Nippon, I want to send you my love and all good wishes for the success of your work. I have no son of my own — but you are to me more than my own son — because you have dedicated your life to the cause, which is the one and only goal of my life — the freedom of "Bharat Mata."

I am confident that you will always remain true to the CAUSE and to "Bharat Mata."

I am sorry that I could not see you again before leaving — but you know that I am always with you in spirit.

God bless you

Jai Hind

Subhas Chandra Bose

Facsimile of Netaji Subhas Chandra Bose's message to the I. N. A. cadets who were undergoing training in Tokyo.

Netaji Subhas Chandra Bose's letter to his fellow comrades, written on 29 November 1944.

General Shahnawaz Khan being felicitated in Calcutta after the Red Fort trails.

Some of the most prominent reasons for Indian soldiers and
civilians joining the INA included nationalism, feelings of betrayal
by the British, and racial discrimination. It was under the leadership of
Netaji that men and women came together to fight for their birthright.

The Red Fort trials of General Shahnawaz Khan (left), Gurbaksh Singh Dhillon
(centre) and Prem Sahgal (right) introduced Indians to the INA's role in the
fight for independence, generating sympathy for INA nationwide. With war
cries of 'Chalo Dilli' and 'Lal Qile Se Aayi Awaaz, Dhillo, Sahgal, Shahnawaz',
the court martial of these three war heroes was a watershed moment
in the freedom struggle of India.

General Secretary to the War Council. Netaji also issued orders that all the I.N.A. troops around Mandalay were to withdraw to Pyinmana a distance of 200 miles. I returned to Mandalay in December 1944, and took the evacuation of No. 1 Division in hand. We had to surmount great difficulties. Transport was most inadequate. Railway lines were almost always non-operational due to heavy bomb-raids. Eventually, by the end of January 1945, the evacuation of the No. 1 Division and the hospitals in Maymyo and Monywa was completed and a new Divisional Camp was established at Pyinmana.

By this time Netaji and his party had returned from Tokyo. The Japanese Government agreed to all the points put up by Netaji. It was therefore decided to send the No. 2 Division of the I.N.A. to take part in the operations in the vicinity of Popa hill.

NETAJI'S WEEK

(Extracts from the diary of a Rebel daughter)
4 July 1944

Subhas Babu arrived from the front on the 2nd. He has been touring the whole front for the last two months and has personally inspired the soldiers of the Fauj.

Today begins 'Netaji Week'. Last year, today, Subhas Babu took over the leadership of the East Asia movement at the Syonan Conference. Fourth of July! Three million Indians stood united behind Subhas Babu on the 4th of July last year and swore that 'Freedom or Death' shall be their slogan.

The Jubilee Hall was packed to capacity once again today. Loudspeakers were also installed outside on the road. The whole scene looked paved with human heads instead of cobble-stones. The road outside, the steps, the hall and its lobbies, every nook and corner was packed with struggling humanity.

Our achievements during the last twelve months can now be summed up:

1. We have been able to mobilize men, money and materials in accordance with the programme of 'Total Mobilization.'
2. We have trained our Army for a modern war and have expanded it considerably.
3. We have organized a women's section in our Army called the Rani of Jhansi Regiment.
4. We have set up our own Government, the Arzi Huku-mat-e-Azad Hind, and have obtained recognition from nine friendly powers.
5. We have acquired our first Free Territory in the Andamans and Nicobar Islands.
6. We pushed forward our Headquarters to Burma, and in February 1944, we launched our War of Independence. On 21 March, we were able to proclaim to the world that our troops were already in India.
7. We have considerably expanded the work of our Press Propaganda-Publicity Department.
8. We have set up a new organization called the Azad Hind Dal, to take over the task of administration and reconstruction in Free India.
9. We have set up a Bank of our own in Burma – the National Bank of Azad Hind Ltd. We have placed orders for our own currency to circulate in Free India.
10. We have been able to give a good account of ourselves in every sector of the fighting front and our troops have been pushing on inside India, slowly but steadily, in spite of all difficulties and hardships...

There was a time when people had some doubt as to whether the Indian National Army would go into action, and whether, if it went into action, it would really defeat the enemy troops. That test we have passed, and naturally it has given us unbounded confidence in ourselves…

Since the fighting began on the soil of India, this war has become our own war, and the feeling that the war has become our own war has brought a new inspiration not only to our troops who are actually fighting, but also to those who are behind the lines.

Until now, I have not received any complaint from our troops regarding the hardships that they are suffering. There has been only one complaint from the men and that is when there has been delay in sending them forward. For example, I recently visited a hospital where there were men who have either been wounded, or stricken with malaria or some other disease. All these troops expressed their desire to be sent back to the front as soon as they were well. These are men who fought at the front and they know the conditions there, and yet they were absolutely cheerful and optimistic. Without indulging in any exaggeration, I can say that this feeling of unbounded optimism prevails among all Indians in East Asia…

There is still another reason which strengthens our optimism, and that is the situation inside India. As you are well aware, so far there has been no compromise between the Congress Party on the one side and the British Government on the other. When Mahatma Gandhi was suddenly released some time ago, many people were speculating as to whether the release was purely on grounds of ill-health or it was a prelude to a compromise. Now it is quite clear that the sudden release of Mahatma Gandhi was ordered purely on medical grounds and that there is no political motive involved. As long as there is no compromise between Mahatma Gandhi and the British Government, we have no reason to feel anxious… Our task will be made much easier if there is no compromise inside India between the Congress and the British Government. So far there is absolutely no sign of compromise, and what is exceedingly encouraging to us is that the statements Mahatma Gandhi has made until now all point in one direction, and that is that he sees no reason to alter the attitude he took up about two years ago when he sponsored the 'Quit India' resolution...

Therefore, I come to the conclusion that the situation inside India remains exceedingly favourable to us. One can easily understand that so long as the Congress does not compromise and does not surrender to the British Government, the general attitude of the people will remain anti-British. As our operations advance, people will soon realize that there is no other way of achieving freedom than fighting for it, and they will decide to participate in the war and to give us all assistance to conduct our war.

People had listened to the speech of Netaji spellbound. It took nearly an hour and a half for the crowd to disperse after the meeting was over. Such was the enthusiasm!

5 July 1944

Today was the second day of the Netaji Week. The Fauj soldiers in Rangoon held a parade with Subhas Babu taking the salute. It was an imposing spectacle. The turn-out of our Regiment was perfect, and Subhas Babu paid us a high compliment.

Netaji spoke to the Fauj soldiers:

The formation of the Azad Hind Fauj has been a source of extreme worry and anxiety to our enemies. They tried to ignore its existence for a time, but when the news could no longer be suppressed, their organ – the anti-India Radio at Delhi – started propaganda to the effect that Indian prisoners-of-war, under Japanese control, had been coerced into joining the army. This propaganda could not, however, endure long, because the news began to infiltrate into India that large number of Indian civilians from all parts of East Asia were joining the Azad Hind Fauj. The experts of the anti-India Radio had therefore to alter their tactics. They then started fresh propaganda to the effect that Indian prisoners-of-war had refused to join the Azad Hind Fauj and that, thereupon, Indian civilians were being forced into joining that army. It did not probably strike the wise-acres at Delhi that if it was impossible to coerce prisoners-of-war into joining the army, it was even more impossible to coerce free civilians into becoming soldiers...

Anybody who has a grain of common sense will realize that though a mercenary army can be organized by coercion, a Volunteer Army can never be so organized. You can perhaps force a man to shoulder rifle, but you can never fight him to give his life for a cause which is not his own.

At an early stage our enemies used to say that the Azad Hind Fauj was no army – that it was a mere propaganda stunt – and that it would never fight. Later on, the anti-India Radio at Delhi began to shout that the Azad Hind Fauj had not crossed the frontier of India. Now that frontier has been crossed and the battle for India's freedom is being waged on Indian soul, enemy propagandists have taken recourse to a last desperate trick. They are now inventing fictitious dates supposed to have been given out by us for our entry into Delhi and are abusing us for not reaching our destination according to schedule...

I have already told you that the Azad Hind Fauj is composed both of ex-Army men as well as of ex-civilians. I may inform you further that it is composed not only of men but also of women...

Friends, the Azad Hind Fauj is an army which is not only composed of Indians, but it has also been trained by Indians. That army is today fighting under Indian officers.

The Azad Hind Fauj is the military organ of the Provisional Government of Azad Hind. The Provisional Government and its Army are the servants of the Indian nation. Their task is to fight and liberate India. When that liberation is achieved, it will be for the Indian people to determine the form of government that they desire. The Provincial Government will then make for a permanent Government in Free India, which will be set up in accordance with the will of the Indian people. For that glorious day we are now toiling sweating and fighting.

Shouts of 'Jai Hind' rose from thousands of throats; the soldiers lifted their rifles and placed them high on their shoulders and gave resounding slogans of 'Chalo Dilli' and 'Jai Hind'.

Then Netaji referred to the brave exploits of our heroes in the Arakan fight, and decorated M – with the medal 'Sardar-e-Jang' for efficient leadership of the Fauj on the Arakan front. He also decorated Lt. P – with 'Vir-e-Hind' for high standard of patriotism, courage and devotion to duty on 5 February.

6 July 1944

Netaji addressed Gandhiji on the radio today.

He spoke as if he would speak to his father, straight from the heart, without hiding a word of his joys and sorrows, without hushing a single discordant note.

Mahatmaji,

After the sad demise of Srimati Kasturba in British custody it was but natural for your countrymen to be alarmed over the state of your health... For Indians outside India, differences in method are like domestic differences. Ever since you sponsored the Independence Resolution at the Lahore Congress in December 1929, all members of the Indian National Congress have had one common goal before them. For Indians outside India, you are the creator of the present awakening in your country... The high esteem in which you are held by patriotic Indians outside India and by foreign friends of India's freedom, was increased a hundred-fold when you bravely sponsored the 'Quit India' Resolution in August 1942...

It would be a fatal mistake on our part to make a distinction between the British Government and the British people. No doubt there is a small group of idealists in Britain – as in the U.S.A. – who would like to see India free. These idealists, who are treated by their own people as cranks, form a microscopic minority. So far as India is concerned, for all practical purposes, the British Government and the British people mean one and the same thing. Regarding the war aims of the U.S.A., I may say that the ruling clique at Washington is now dreaming of world domination. This ruling clique and its intellectual exponents, talk openly of the 'American Century'. In this ruling clique, there are extremists who go so far as to call Britain the 49th state of the U.S.A...

I can assure you, Mahatmaji, that before I finally decided to set out on this hazardous mission, I spent days, weeks and months in carefully considering the pros and cons of the case. After having served my people so long, to the best of my ability, I could have no desire to be a traitor, or to give anyone a justification for calling me a traitor... Thanks to the generosity and to the affection of my countrymen, I had obtained the highest honour which it was possible for any public worker in India to achieve.

I had also built up a party consisting of staunch and loyal colleagues who had implicit confidence in me. By going abroad on a perilous quest, I was risking not only my life and my whole future career, but what was more, the future of my party. If I had the slightest hope that without action from abroad we could win freedom, I would never have left India during a crisis. If I had any hope that within our lifetime we could get another chance – another golden opportunity – for winning freedom, as during the present war, I doubt if I would have set out from home...

There remains but one question for me to answer with regard to the Axis powers. Can it be possible that I have been deceived by them? I believe it will be universally admitted that the cleverest and the most cunning politicians are to be found amongst Britishers. One who has worked with and fought British politicians all his life, cannot be deceived by any other politician in the world. If British politicians have failed to coax or coerce me, no other politician can succeed in doing so. And if the British Government, at whose hands I have suffered long imprisonment, persecution and physical assault, has been unable to demoralize me, no other power can hope to do so... I have never done anything which could compromise in the least, either the honour or the self-respect or the interests of my country...

There was a time when Japan was an ally of our enemy. I did not come to Japan, so long as there was an Anglo-Japanese Alliance. I did not come to Japan, so long as normal diplomatic relations obtained between the two countries. It was only after Japan took what I considered to be the most momentous step in her history, declaration of war on Britain and America, that I decided to visit Japan of my own free will. Like so many of my countrymen, my sympathies in 1937 and 1938 were with Chungking. You may remember that as President of the Congress, I was responsible for sending out a medical mission to Chungking in December 1938...

Mahatmaji, you know better than anybody else how deeply suspicious the Indian people are of mere promises. I would be the last man to be influenced by Japan if her declarations of policies had been mere promises...

Mahatmaji, I should now like to say something about the Provisional Government that we have set up here. The Provisional Government has, as its one objective, the liberation of India from British yoke, through an armed struggle. Once our enemies are expelled from India, and peace and order is established, the mission of the Provisional Government will be over... The only reward that we desire for our efforts, for our suffering and for our sacrifice is the freedom of our Motherland. There are many among us who would like to retire from the political field, once India is free...

Nobody would be more happy than ourselves, if by any chance our countrymen at home should succeed in liberating themselves through their own efforts, or if by any chance, the British Government accepts your 'Quit India' resolution and gives effect to it. We are, however, proceeding on the assumption that neither of the above is possible and that an armed struggle is inevitable... India's last war of independence has begun. Troops of the Azad Hind Fauj are now fighting bravely on the soil of India and in spite of all difficulty and hardship, they are pushing forward slowly but steadily. This armed struggle will go on, until the last Britisher is thrown out of India and until our Tricolour National Flag proudly floats over the Viceroy's house in New Delhi.

Father of our nation! In this holy war for India's liberation, we ask for your blessings and good wishes.

9 July 1944

Today, in front of thousands of spectators, Netaji announced the great sacrifice of Sri H – a Muslim multi-millionaire. He has presented his jewellery, estates and properties worth about a crore of rupees to the I.I.L. for the freedom struggle. Netaji awarded him the medal of Sevak-i-Hind. He is the first to receive it.

Reports from India are very promising. But our Staff Officers are expecting a long and hard struggle before the British quit India. The British are bound to fight desperately in their last effort to save the empire. Minus India, Britain would become a third-rate power. They know it.

Subhas Babu talks in inspired language when he talks about victory. His faith is really very deep. I tremble at the thought; if something were to go wrong with our plans, would he be broken – too sorely affected? He has put all his eggs in this one basket: Azadi. All of us in East Asia are doing it. God will protect us.

10 July 1944

Subhas Babu delivered a thundering speech at the public rally.

The audience was nearly 30,000. He outlined the strategy of our movement in the following terms:

We know that so long as the British Army in India is not attacked from outside, it will be able to suppress the revolutionary movement in the country. The Azad Hind Fauj has, therefore, set up the 'Second Front' in India's war of emancipation. When we advance further into India and the people see with their own eyes, the British forces falling back, they will get the confidence that Britain's downfall is at hand. Then only will they risk their necks and come and join hands with our advancing forces to liberate the country. Together we shall then pursue the British and expel them from the soil of India…

Friends! Only a fool would minimize the strength of the enemy. We have seen heterogeneous armies of our enemies in the Arakans, in the Kaladan and Haka sectors, in the Tiddim area and in Manipur and Assam. As we anticipated long ago, their rations and equipment are superior to ours, because they have been looting India in order to fight us. We have, nevertheless, beaten them everywhere. Revolutionary armies everywhere in the world have to fight under conditions similar to ours but they, nevertheless, triumph at the end. Their strength does not come from beer and rum, tinned-pork and bully-beef – but from faith and sacrifice, heroism and fortitude. The Azad Hind Fauj – unlike the British Army in India – has been trained to fight under conditions of extreme difficulty and hardship, and it will never let down the 388 millions of Indians for whose liberation it is now fighting…

CHAPTER SEVEN

NETAJI'S VISIT TO FRONT-LINE TROOPS

On 18 February 1945, Netaji arrived at Pyinmana to inspect the troops of the No. 1 Division at Pyinmana, and the No. 2 Division at Kyauk Padang and Popa. At this time most of the officers and men of the No. 1 Division were physically unfit and only about 20 per cent had any arms at all. It was quite clear that for some considerable period this division would not be fit to take part in any operation.

Netaji told me that the No. 2 Division had started moving to the front early in February and that unfortunately the Divisional Commander Colonel Ariz Ahmad, at the last minute, had been injured in a bombing raid. He, therefore, ordered me to proceed to Popa and take over the command of the No. 2 Division.

Having bid farewell to my troops, with whom I had been throughout Imphal operations and of whom I was very proud, I left Pyinmana, with Netaji and his personal staff to proceed to Meiktila and later to Popa. On the morning of 20 February, our party arrived in an Indian village named Indo approximately 20 miles south of Meiktila and halted there for the day. During the day, enemy aircraft were so active that it was almost impossible for any car to move on the road, and even at night, lorries and cars had to move without lights for fear of being spotted and shot by planes.

While resting in this village, we received information that the enemy had broken through the front held by the No. 4 (Nehru Brigade) Regiment at Nyaungu and Pagan in the vicinity of Pakokou. We were informed that our units had suffered very heavy casualties and the enemy was advancing on Meiktila.

Netaji decided to proceed to Meiktila at once and to try and close up the gap created by the advancing British forces. The party arrived in Meiktila on the evening of 20 February 1945. This party consisted of Netaji's personal staff, including one Japanese Major acting as the interpreter, and 20 armed soldiers acting as his personal body guards.

At the time, the situation on the front was very confused indeed. Heavy fighting was going on at Kyaukse. Mandalay had been occupied. The British forces, with the full weight of their armour were pushing down south along the main Mandalay-Meiktila Rangoon road. The Japanese forces fighting around Mandalay had been caught in the plains by the British tanks and aeroplanes and they had been moved down mercilessly. Those that had survived retreated towards Maymayo and into the Shan States to take shelter in the mountains. On the west of Meiktila, the British forces had crossed the Irrawaddy at several places and heavy fighting was going on at Myingyan, Pakokou, Nyaungu and Pagan. The enemy was attempting a thrust towards Meiktila, which was the nerve centre of the Japanese rail and road communications, and once Meiktila was captured the entire

Japanese force in Burma would have been paralysed. It was therefore, considered most inadvisable for Netaji to stay in Meiktila, especially because it had no proper defences and practically no troops to defend it.

All of us requested Netaji to leave Meiktila and to give up his idea of proceeding to Popa where fighting was in progress. He refused to listen to us, but eventually I managed to get him to agree to allow me to proceed to Popa first, study the military situation and then come back and report to him, and then, take him with me to Popa. In the meantime, Netaji was to proceed to Kalaw and inspect an I.N.A. hospital there.

Major Mahboob Ahmad, the Military Secretary to Netaji, and I left Meiktila on the night of 21-22 February. We started at about midnight. Netaji came to see us off and gave us full instructions on the plan and course we were to follow in the fighting. At that critical hour, when it was absolutely clear even to a lay man that the fight for Burma was over and that the defeat of the Axis powers was only a matter of days. Netaji was supremely confident of our victory. He said, 'Even if the Axis powers lay down their arms, we must continue our struggle. There is no end to our struggle until the last British quits the shores of our country.' He was of the opinion that the British should not be allowed to advance or break through our front, even if all the I.N.A. soldiers were killed. What he wanted most was that the I.N.A. *shaheeds* should leave behind such a legend and tradition of heroism that future generations of Indians would be proud of them. After assuring him that his wishes would be carried out and that as long as one soldier of the I.N.A. was alive, the British would not advance on our front, we left for Popa. We arrived at Kyaukpadang at 0500 hrs. on 22 February 1945, and met Colonel Dhillon, the commander of the No. 4 Regiment, and after issuing full instructions to him, proceeded to Popa to inspect the Divisional Headquarters and the No. 2 Infantry

Regiment, under the command of Colonel P. K. Sahgal. I took over the command of the division and issued orders to the Brigade commanders, allotting them different tasks, full details of which were to follow later.

On 25 February, Mahboob Ahmad and I returned to Meiktila and reported the situation on the Popa front to Netaji. I explained to him that owing to the confused state of fighting it was not proper for Netaji to proceed any further, as it was too dangerous. This discussion took place in an open field on a bright moonlit night, well after midnight. We could see the flashes of heavy gunfire and of machine guns. The situation was extremely critical. British tanks might have broken through any minute and would have captured Meiktila, with Netaji there. Major Rawat, Colonel Mahboob and I pleaded with Netaji to make him give up his idea of proceeding to Popa. Just at that moment, a Japanese officer arrived and informed us that British tanks and armoured columns had broken through and had occupied Pyinbin. They were then advancing on Taungtha, approximately 40 miles to the north west of Meiktila. He also appealed to Netaji to leave Meiktila that very night and go further south to Pyinmana, where there were troops of the No. 1 Division to put up a fight in case the enemy advanced. He further informed Netaji that there were no troops at all between Taungtha and Meiktila. I told Netaji that a distance of 40 miles was nothing for an armoured column, and that it could be covered in two hours at the most and we had no troops to push them back. Twenty men who formed Netaji's personal guard were armed only with rifles and could not put up any resistance to an armoured brigade. I strongly appealed to Netaji to leave Meiktila; but he would not listen to anything. I lost patience and said to him, 'Netaji, you are being very selfish. Just to show your personal bravery you are risking your life; but you have no right to risk your life in this way. Your own life does not belong to you; it is a precious trust of India, which is in our keeping, and I am going to make sure that the precious trust of India is not endangered in this way.' I pleaded, 'Netaji, just think what would happen to the I.N.A. and the Indian Independence Movement, should anything happen to you.'

He listened to me very calmly, because he knew that all that I said came from the very depths of my heart, and was prompted by my extreme anxiety for his safety. He just smiled and said, 'Shahnawaz, it is no use pleading with me. I have made up my mind to go to Popa and I am going there. You do not have to worry about my safety, as I know England has not yet produced the bomb that can kill Subhas Chandra Bose.' This last statement appeared particularly true as Netaji seemed to lead a charmed life. That afternoon, the place he was living in was heavily bombed by sixty B-25S. They caused terrible devastation all round, and it was difficult to imagine how Netaji escaped without even a scratch.

All of us had failed to persuade Netaji not to proceed any further, but once he had made up his mind, no one could make him change it. Yet, all of us were convinced that it was the most dangerous thing for him to go to Popa. We were in a terrible fix. At last Major Rawat, Netaji's adjutant, thought of a plan. It was nearly two in the morning. If we could delay Netaji's departure from Meiktila by about two hours, it would be daylight and his departure, at any rate, for that day would be delayed. Consequently, Rawat started his delaying tactics. Netaji was in a hurry to start, but Rawat, who was ordered to type out a very important letter took a long time over it. He then hinted to Netaji's driver to invent some engine trouble in his car. That night we received urgent telegrams from General Kiani and the Commander-in-Chief of the Japanese forces requesting Netaji to return to Rangoon immediately. Netaji was becoming very impatient and was losing his temper with everyone, but Rawat and the driver pretended that they were doing their best to start as early as possible. Eventually it was five in the morning, and I know that we had delayed his visit for another day, and had given us more time to study the military situation. At 05:30 hours, we managed to persuade Netaji to lie down and have a little sleep in a small grass hut in the nearby village, and the Japanese Liaison Officer Major Takashi went off to obtain the latest information about the movements of enemy forces. He returned at 08:00 hours and reported that a mechanized brigade of the enemy had arrived at Mahlaing – 10 miles north of Meiktila – and that it had cut off the road from Meiktila to Mandalay and from Meiktila to Kyaukpadang. He told us that the enemy was preparing to advance and that there being no covering troops between Meiktila and Mahlaing the enemy was expected to occupy Meiktila any minute. He said that we were too late already and that our line of retreat the Meiktila-Rangoon road had probably been cut off. We were in a dilemma. There were two courses open to us: (i) to stay on where we were and die fighting because our force was so small that there was no earthly chance for us to hold up the enemy's advance; or (ii) to make an attempt to escape from Meiktila despite the fact that the main road had been cut off by the enemy. Netaji's idea was 'that we should make an attempt to break through, and even if the enemy had established a road block across our line of retreat, it was better for us to get killed there. It was indeed a brave decision, because besides the possibility of an enemy road block, it was almost suicidal to travel on that road during the hours of daylight. There was practically no cover from air attack on that road and there were numerous enemy planes always patrolling overhead. Anyhow, Netaji had taken the decision and we had to abide by it.

Within ten minutes we were ready to start. There was only one car available for immediate use then, and only four people could go in it. I left the choice of those four men entirely to Netaji. For me, it was difficult to decide what I should do. On one side were my troops fighting valiantly at Popa and Kyaukpadang against heavy odds who were expecting me there, and in spite of the fact that the road was blockaded by the enemy I had a strong desire to go round the road block and reach my troops at Popa. On the other hand was my personal loyalty and duty to my leader. His life was in great danger. How could I leave him at that moment? I could not choose between these two conflicting duties and I left the decision to Netaji. Netaji decided that his Japanese Liaison Officer and his personal Medical Officer, Colonel Raju, should accompany him leaving a place for only one more person. Netaji said that we might have to fight our way through. It was, therefore, essential that the person who accompanied him should be such as to be able to fight his way through. Eventually Netaji turned round to me and said, 'You must come with me.' I bowed before his decision and filled up the car with grenades and ammunition fully realizing that the chances of escape were very slender indeed. But we were all prepared for it. None of us spoke, but we knew exactly what the others were thinking. Everyone looked cheerful. One thing was certain, the enemy would never capture us alive. When we got in the car and started off, Netaji was sitting with a loaded Tommy gun in his lap. Raju had two hand grenades ready. The Japanese officer was holding on to another Tommy gun and I had a loaded Bren gun in my hand. We were all ready to open fire instantaneously. The Japanese officer stood on the foot board of the car to be on the lookout for enemy aircraft. Raju sat next to the driver to locate any road blocks put up by the enemy, while Netaji and I sat at the back watching both sides of the road.

Our first objective was a small Indian village called Indo, approximately 20 miles south of Meiktila. We were on the road for about 40 minutes, but by some miracle not a single enemy plane turned up, neither did we encounter any road block. We arrived safely at Indo and decided to spend the rest of the day there. No sooner had we entered the village than British fighter planes arrived and started machine gunning the village. We had escaped almost certain death by about five minutes. It is not possible for those persons who have not actually been subjected to aerial bombardment or machine-gunning to imagine what a terrible thing it is to be caught in the open by enemy fighter planes. Some of them had as many as twelve machine guns in them. Neither did they have any scruples regarding the use of 22 and 40 m.m. armour piercing cartridges on our soldiers. These cartridges arc approximately 10 inches long and are used to destroy railway engine and heavy tanks, and when used against human beings make a terrible mess of the human body.

At this time, Indo village, as also the rest of the area in the neighbourhood of Meiktila, was infested with enemy spies and agents. I therefore requested Netaji to leave the village and come out into the jungle. We first took shelter in a cactus hedge near the village, but we were soon spotted and one very suspicious looking person came to our resting place, and after thoroughly studying the place, went away. I told Netaji that I suspected that the man was a British spy and that it was necessary to change our position. Netaji agreed and I took him away into a thick jungle approximately a mile away from the village. No sooner had we arrived at our new position than two British planes arrived and started circling very low over the very cactus hedge where Netaji had taken shelter. I pointed out those planes to Netaji and jokingly said to him, 'Netaji, they are looking for you.' The Burmese who had seen us in the hedge was after all a British spy. We spent that day in the jungle. We were feeling quite hungry and so I went and brought some grams from a field nearby, and Netaji lived on it for the day.

That day, we were visited by numerous enemy aircraft, but luckily none spotted us. As a precaution against enemy artillery-shelling and air attack, I had a small trench dug for Netaji. On one occasion some enemy planes arrived and started circling very low at tree-top height above the bushes where we had taken shelter and it appeared as if they had either spotted us or had been warned of our presence by the British spies. Both of us took shelter in that trench when all of a sudden I saw a huge black scorpion crawling about on the side of the trench hardly an inch from Netaji's neck. Netaji also saw it, but we dare not move for the fear of giving away ourselves to the enemy aircraft. After a minute or so the planes went away to search another patch of bushes. Fortunately, we had not been spotted. We then killed the scorpion.

In the evening, as soon as the sun went down, Netaji sent for me and told me that he intended to go back to Meiktila again. As there were still some I.N.A. soldiers left there he did not like to go back without making proper arrangements for their evacuation. Eventually, he agreed to proceed to Pyinmana, while I returned to Meiktila. I reached Meiktila at about 22:00 hours on 26 February and found heavy fighting going on in the town. There was a large Japanese hospital in Meiktila with approximately 1,000 bed-ridden patients. The enemy advance was so rapid that the Japanese had no time to evacuate them. They, therefore, detailed an officer with a guard to shoot all those who could not walk. This order was carried out.

After evacuating all the I.N.A. stores and personnel in Meiktila, I returned to Pyinmana where I found Netaji waiting for me. I met him on 1 March 1945 and found that he had prepared a plan of operation in case the enemy reached Pyinmana. At that time it looked very probable that the enemy would push down rapidly from Meiktila towards Pyinmana and Toungoo. Netaji's plan was to form one brigade known as the 'X' Regiment out of the remnants of the No. 1 Division, and with this force he intended to occupy a defensive position a few miles north of Pyinmana. He told me that he had decided to stop at Pyinmana and fight his last battle against the British there. For the remaining sick soldiers, he issued orders that they should be evacuated to another camp 10 miles to the rear and if the British broke through the defence of the 'X' Regiment they were to surrender themselves. For the 'X' Regiment his orders were that they must fight to the last man.

Colonel Thakur Singh, a daring commander who had been my second-in-command during Manipore operations, was selected to command the 'X' Regiment. Colonel R. M. Arshad was put in command of the remaining personnel of the No. 1 Division. Netaji called a conference of all senior officers and started issuing his orders. When he had finished I assured him that his wishes would be carried out, but it was not necessary for him to stay behind at Pyinmana and make it his last battle. All of us requested him to return to Rangoon, and from there exercise control and command over all the I.N.A. troops, including the No. 1, No. 2 and No. 3 Divisions. We also assured Netaji that the enemy would probably first consolidate his gains in Meiktila and then advance, which would probably take him a fortnight. Netaji having studied the situation agreed and ordered me to proceed to Rangoon and then to Popa via Prome-Yennangyaun-Kyaukpadang. This route was still open and it was possible for me, having safely brought back Netaji to Rangoon, to re-join my division.

When we arrived in Rangoon, we received information that four senior staff officers of the No. 2 Divisional Headquarters had deserted to the British from Popa. This upset Netaji very much. He called me at midnight and told me how much ashamed he was of the action of those staff officers. He explained that he realized that owing to the turn of the tide of battle and due to British victories some officers had become demoralized. He gave me a free hand in the selection of all my staff officers, and in turn I gave him an assurance that in future there would be no more desertions among the troops. I looked around and selected the best available set of staff officers. They were Major Ram Sarup, Major Mehar Das, Major Ajaib Singh and Major B. S. Rawat. We left Rangoon on the evening of the 7th March, 1945. Before we left I took all the staff officers to pay our respects to Netaji. We had dinner with him, and after dinner Netaji talked to us. He said, 'I know we have lost the battle of Burma, but that should not dishearten us in any way. We have to continue fighting to uphold the honour of India. All of you have been given the proud privilege of being called upon to take charge of fighting at a most critical hour in the history of the I.N.A. ... The honour of the I.N.A. is now in your hands and I am sure you will prove worthy of the trust that has been placed in you.'

When we bid farewell to him on the steps of his porch, there were tears in his eyes. Perhaps he realized that we were going on a very hazardous mission and that we would probably not meet again.

On behalf of all my staff officers, I asked Netaji to have full confidence in us and assured him that we would uphold the honour of India under all circumstances. We reached at Popa on 12 March 1945.

Formation and activities of the No. 2 Division

The No. 2 Division was raised at Singapore in December, 1943 and Colonel N. S. Bhagat was appointed its commander. Originally, it consisted of the old field force, i.e.

No. 1 Infantry Regiment

Heavy gun Battalion

Armoured Fighting Vehicles Battalion

Div. Signals

Div. Engineers

The units of the No. 2 Division were armed with much heavier weapons than the No. 1 Division, which was intended mainly for guerrilla operations. The No. 2 Division was meant for taking part in field operations. Their Infantry units had 3" mortars, anti-tank guns and rifles and heavy machine guns.

The original idea was that for the fighting in the mountainous areas around Imphal guerrilla operations were necessary, and as soon as Imphal was captured and the fighting entered the plains of India, the No. 2 Division, with its heavier weapons would be brought up.

In April 1944, the division was moved to Ipoh, and a new regiment, No. 5 Guerrilla Brigade was raised and allotted to the No. 2 division. This regiment was under the command of Colonel Roderigues. After a short but intensive training, units of this Division started moving to the front. The Divisional Headquarters moved from Ipoh in July 1944, and arrived in Rangoon in early November 1944. Before the move of the Divisional Headquarters from Ipoh, it was found necessary by Netaji, for certain internal difficulties, to change the commander of the No. 2 Division; and Colonel Aziz Ahmad who was commanding the Nehru Brigade in Burma was recalled to Malaya and appointed its commander.

Concentration of the division at Rangoon

In May 1944, the No. 1 Infantry Regiment, under the command of Lt. Colonel S. M. Hussain, left Jitra for Burma. It used the same route as the units of the No. 1 Division. By this time, enemy air force and submarines had become very active. They were continuously bombing railways, bridges and troop concentrations on the route in order to stop reinforcements reaching the front line. The sea journey from Kwashi (the Victoria point) to Mergui had become particularly dangerous. It was constantly being watched by enemy bombers and submarines and a ship carrying all the heavy armament, including mortars, anti-tank guns and machine guns of the No. 1 Infantry Regiment was torpedoed and sunk, with the result that when the infantry arrived in Rangoon it had only rifles and a few light machine guns with it. It was consequently rendered absolutely unfit to proceed any further without being reequipped.

Our troops had to cover this journey from Thailand to Rangoon, mostly on foot, with the result that it took the No. 1 Regiment almost four months to reach Rangoon.

The Divisional Headquarters and the No. 5 Guerrilla Regiment left Ipoh in July 1944. By the end of December 1944, the troops of the No. 2 Division had concentrated in Rangoon. At about the same time the No. 4 Guerrilla Regiment (Nehru Brigade), which had previously been a part of the No. 1 Division, was transferred to the No. 2 Division. This brigade, under the command of Colonel Ahmad had arrived in Mandalay in May 1944, and on the transfer of Colonel Ahmad to Malaya, Colonel Arshad took over its command. Later, Major A. K. Rana, was appointed its commander, who in turn was replaced by Major Mahboob Ahmad. This brigade did excellent service during the evacuation of the No. 1 Division from Kalewa to Mandalay.

Operational activities of the No. 2 Division No. 4 Guerrilla Regiment (The Nehru Brigade)

In early October 1944, the Nehru Brigade was transferred to Myingyan in the Irrawaddy under the command of Major Mahboob Ahmad. There, it was ordered to prepare defence works to prevent the British forces, crossing the Irrawaddy on that front. A few days later, Major G. S. Dhillon took over the command of the unit from Major Mahboob Ahmad, who was appointed Military Secretary to Netaji in Rangoon.

This unit was much weak in strength and was poorly equipped. It was armed only with rifles, light automatics, mainly Lewis guns and a few Bren guns. This unit had a large number of Tamil soldiers who had been recruited and trained in Malaya. Work had started and good progress was being made at Myingyan, despite constant attacks by British aircraft. In December 1944, our units suffered heavy casualties due to enemy bombing.

Late in January 1945, Major Dhillon received the following information regarding the movements of the enemy: (a) That one British Division had crossed the Irrawaddy in the vicinity of Malaya; (b) that the 2nd British Division had arrived at Saigon and bridgeheads had been established at Minbu and other places in the vicinity; and (c) that one division having advanced from Kalemyo, down the Gangaw valley, was advancing along the Kan-Gangaw-Tilin-Pauk road, and was in the vicinity of Pakokou, looking for likely places to establish bridgeheads across the Irrawaddy in the vicinity of Nyaungu and Pagan.

On 29 January, Major Dhillon received the following order:

'No. 4 Guerrilla Regiment will move immediately to Myatigu and Pagan and prevent the enemy from crossing the Irrawaddy at those places. Covering troops will also be sent to Pakokou to patrol Pakokou-Tilin Road. The unit should be in position by the 20 January.'

As is clear from this order, Major Dhillon's unit was supposed to prepare their defensive position by 20 January, whereas they actually received the copy of order on 29 January. This was due to the extremely bad system of inter communication. Inspite of his failing health, however, Major Dhillon at once took this task in hand. He had no mechanical transport of any kind and had to depend on the bullock carts hired from the Burmese to move the whole brigade; and the distance to be covered was over 80 miles. He left Myingyan during the first week of February with the advance parties of his battalion. On the way he heard that the British had already crossed the Irrawaddy; despite this he carried on, and on arrival there he found that although enemy patrol had reached Pakokou, they had not been successful in crossing the Irrawaddy, yet. Major Dhillon carried out a thorough reconnaissance of the area and allotted different areas to battalions. He allotted the area of Nyaungu to the No. 7 Battalion commanded by Lt. Hari Ram. The area of Pagan was allotted to the No. 9 Battalion, commanded by Lt. Chandra Bhan, and the No. 8 Battalion was kept in reserve in a village a few miles in the rear.

Fighting patrols were pushed across the Irrawaddy to keep contact with the enemy in the area of Pakokou. In the meantime, the main body of the brigade, which was being brought up by Major Jagir Singh began to arrive in their respective areas on the evening of 8 February 1945, and the digging commenced. Our troops had hardly been in position for a day when the enemy became active. Our patrols across the river were forced back and on the night of 9-10 February, a British patrol crossed the Irrawaddy into our area. They were all either killed or captured.

In the meantime, a whole British division, probably the 7th Indian Division, had arrived on the opposite bank of the river and lined up their heavy artillery in full view of our men. Our men were armed only with rifles, light automatics and a few medium machine guns.

On the morning of 10 February, the enemy started shelling our positions heavily. At night they attempted a crossing on a wide front, but were beaten back, with heavy losses, and for the next three days they made several attempts to cross, but everywhere our men held them and all their attempts were foiled.

On the night of 13-14 February, the enemy having considerably reinforced their artillery started a most determined attack. They subjected our defensive positions to a most intensive artillery barrage, and under the cover of it they tried to cross over in motorboats. A terrible battle raged throughout the night, and attack after attack by the British were beaten back. Fighting was particularly heavy on the Pagan front, where Capt. Chander Bhan had sited his machine guns in an excellent position. He allowed the enemy to come near his bank and then opened up with every available weapon. His opponents were British 'tommies' of the East Lancashire Regiment. His men fought with a vengeance. At least 20 boatful of enemy soldiers were sunk. The rest turned round and raced for safety to the opposite bank. Later on it was reliably learnt that the Commanding Officer, after his boat was sunk, had to swim back to his lines, leaving his trousers in the Irrawaddy.

On the morning of 14 February, as soon as it was daylight, enemy aeroplanes started an intensive bombing and machine gunning of our positions. At the same time the enemy's artillery on the opposite bank opened up an intensive barrage. Our men did not have even a 2" mortar to retaliate. They had to wait patiently for the enemy to come within rifle range before they could open fire. At about midday, a small Japanese outpost, which was on our right flank opposite Pakokou, was overpowered and the British forces secured a foothold on the east bank of the Irrawaddy and formed a bridgehead through which they pushed across large numbers of men. By this time due to continuous fighting, and the lack of spare parts, almost all our machine guns were out of action, and ammunition was almost completely exhausted.

The enemy, having lauded on the Japanese front, turned south and encircled our 7th Battalion. They also dropped a large number of men by parachutes behind our lines. Our men having used up all their ammunition resorted to bayonet charges, but eventually most of the men of the 7th Battalion were overpowered and had to surrender. But the battalion in reserve and the 9th Battalion, under Chander Bhan, continued to hold firmly to their positions. In the evening, Major Dhillon intended to rally all his men and counter attack the enemy to drive him across the river, but it was not possible to carry out the attack in daylight because of enemy planes and artillery.

The only means of intercommunication that Major Dhillon had with his Battalion Commander was through the runners. He did not even have a telephone to keep in touch with his unit. It was, therefore, almost impossible for him to keep control over his units and everything had to be left to the initiative of his unit commanders.

As soon as there was a lull in the aerial machine gunning and bombing, Major Dhillon himself went forward to contact his unit commanders to issue further instructions. By the evening of 14 February, most of the enemy division had crossed the Irrawaddy. Major Dhillon ordered his troops to fall back on Popa and Kyauk Padang and take up defensive positions there. Major Jagir Singh, the Regimental Second-in-Command to Major Dhillon rushed to Kyauk Padang and rallied all his men and made excellent arrangements, though under very adverse conditions, for local collection of rations and their supplies.

The next few days were spent by Major Dhillon in reorganizing his unit. On the evening of 21 February 1945, Major Mahboob Ahmad and I were sent by Netaji from Meiktila to inspect the Nehru Brigade and the No. 2 Infantry Regiment at Kyauk Padang and Popa, respectively.

On 23 February, a conference of regimental commanders was held at Popa and orders were issued by me allotting following tasks with the ultimate object of driving the British forces across the Irrawaddy.

1. No. 2 Infantry Regiment under Colonel P. K. Sahgal was to prepare Popa as a strong base and prepare for an offensive role.
2. No. 4 Regiment was ordered to carry out guerrilla warfare against the enemy along the road Kyauk Padang-Nyaungu in the vicinity of Taungzin.

No. 4 Guerrilla Regiment in spite of the heavy losses suffered by them took up this new role with great enthusiasm. Intensive guerrilla activities were started and the advance of the enemy force on Kyauk Padang was checked on this route.

On 27 February, a mechanized patrol of the enemy supported by tanks advanced on Kyauk Padang and reached Pozu where it encountered one of our patrols. Our men were armed only with rifles. They opened fire on enemy tanks knowing well that their rifles' fire would have no effect on them. To their great surprise, they saw that on encountering the fire, the enemy tanks turned round and went back.

By their constant and intensive activities, our units forced the enemy outposts to withdraw and by early March they were only eight miles from Nyaungu Bridge Road.

On 11 March, Major Dhillon attacked Taungzin, a locality which had, for past some time, been held by the enemy in force. But before our attack went home they had evacuated the place.

On 16 March, Capt. Khan Mohd. was ordered to go and raid a hill near Sade village. This hill was well-fortified by the enemy, estimated to be at least one battalion. With the help of a clever night march, Khan Mohd. reached the river bed just below the hill he was to attack. The hill was steep and rocky; he there upon left all the weak and barefooted soldiers at the foot of the hill to keep open their line of retreat, after they had raided the hill. He had quite a number of soldiers who had no footwear at all. They carried out all their duties in spite of it. In fact the soldiers of the Azad Hind Fauj never allowed the shortage of clothes, medicines and food to hamper their activities against the enemy. Khan Mohd's party crawled up to the hill as quietly as they could, but soon due to the noise of falling stones, their presence was detected and intensive firing from both sides commenced. Our men were not to be checked by this. They pushed on and got very close to the enemy post, who realizing that they were in grave peril of being annihilated put up an S.O.S. signal for reinforcements. Capt. Khan Mohd's force then fixed bayonets and charged into the enemy position, and a grim hand to hand fight started. In the meantime enemy reinforcement arrived. They counter attacked Sade HiU with about 400 men and encircled Capt. Khan Mohd's force attacking the post. Our men were caught between two rings of the enemy. They turned round and fought back this counter attack in a most determined manner, shouting 'Chalo Delhi' and 'Netaji ki Jai'. Capt. Khan Mohd's little force that had been left behind in the nullah to keep open the line of retreat could not contain itself any longer and shouting 'Bharat Mata ki Jai' and 'Netaji ki Jai' opened deadly barrage of fire on the enemy going uphill to counterattack Khan Mohd. The enemy was present in large numbers, crowded on the hill, and presented an easy target to our men. They suffered terrible losses. Our men in the Nulla, having finished their ammunition, advanced with fixed bayonets and charged into the enemy. The men who had been left behind because they had no boots, forgot all about the sharp splinters on the hill, and joined the rest in the attack. The fighting lasted from 03:00 hours to 05:00 hours when the remnants of the enemy escaped through our outer ring, leaving Sade Hill in our possession. It had been one of the grimmest battles in which the I.N.A. soldiers had been engaged and had acquitted themselves creditably. It was estimated and later confirmed from our Burmese informers that at least 200 soldiers of the enemy were killed in action.

Having completed his task of raiding Sade Hill, Khan Mohd. returned to his quarters. In that engagement we suffered seventeen casualties. This attack came as a very great shock to the enemy who thought they had dispensed the I.N.A. off in the battle of Nyaungu and Pagan.

The area in which we were operating was flat, open, waterless desert, with a few bushes here and there. Our troops fighting in that area had to be supplied with rations and water from Kyauk Padang, approximately 20 miles away. Since we did not have enough motor transport, water had to be supplied to the troops by bullock carts.

At this time the main strategy of the enemy on this front was to hold powerful bridgeheads at Pagan, Nyaungu, Pakokou and Myingyan and to push through powerful mechanized forces from Nyaungu via Pyinbin-Taungtha to Meiktila.

The Japanese forces in cooperation with the I.N.A. were powerfully counter attacking this thrust on Meiktila from all directions with the object of forcing the enemy across the Irrawaddy once again.

This new threat to their main base of Nyaungu by the I.N.A. caused a great deal of anxiety to the British commander, who decided to attack our troops in great force, on the day following Capt. Khan Mohd's attack on Sade Hill.

Battle of Taungzin, 17 March 1945.

On 17 March, one of our battalions was holding a defensive position in the vicinity of Taungzin. 'A' company commanded by Lt. Kartar Singh was in the vicinity of village Nalaing. 'B' company was commanded by 2/Lt. Gian Singh Bisht and was located N.E. of Taungzin. 'C' company was in battalion reserve.

At about 11:00 hours, enemy artillery from north-west direction started shelling our position very heavily. At that time a patrol from 'A' Company was out patrolling the area in front of our positions. This patrol was suddenly attacked by approximately one platoon of Gurkhas that had come up from Nyaungu direction in motor lorries.

Our patrol took up a defensive position and returned enemy's fire killing seven of them. The battalion commander on receiving information of this engagement sent forward another fighting patrol under Lt. Dittu Ram who contacted the first patrol and managed to hold up the enemy advance.

At about 12:30 hours, fifteen enemy tanks, eleven armoured cars and ten trucks advanced by the main road and started intensive shelling and machine gunning of our forward posts. Our men returned this fire with rifles and machine guns. This enemy column then divided itself into two halves, one went in the direction of 'A' company and the other towards the 'B' company which was holding a defensive position north-east of Taungzin under the command of 2nd Lt. Gian Singh Bisht.

The area which was held by this company was a flat stretch of land without any cover either from view or from fire. Near the position was a shallow dry pond near which three roads of great tactical importance met. Four miles north-west of this point was a hill 1423 ft. high behind which the enemy artillery was located, so as to cover the road junction and the area south of it; the occupation of which would have affected the entire plan of operations.

At a key point like this was placed the 'B' company of Gian Singh who was trained at the officer training school at Singapore. This company was only 98 strong. They had no machine guns or even light machine-guns. Rifles and offence mines were their only weapons of defence. His orders were to prevent the enemy from occupying that area at all costs.

He had been in that position for two days but the enemy had not dared to advance. On 17 March 1945, starting early in the morning, hostile fighter planes bombed and machine-gunned their positions until 11:00 hours. After this, the enemy's heavy artillery opened up heavy fire on his company position and under the cover of this fire advanced a column of motorized infantry. This column made its way straight towards the pond where the forward platoons of the company were in position. Armoured vehicles of the enemy rained shells and bullets on our trenches. Our men took cover and waited in their trenches for the infantry to disburse. Tanks and armoured cars like steel monsters creating hell with their fire power approached so close that they started charging on our trenches with the object of crushing our men. Two mines were thrown in their way, but unluckily they failed to burst.

There was no communication between this post and the Battalion Headquarters. When 2nd Lt. Gian Singh clearly understood that their rifle fire was no match to the enemy's mortar machine-gun, hand grenades and light automatic fire and that their staying in trenches meant certain death or captivity with no loss to the enemy, he ordered his men to charge. Leading the assault himself and shouting 'Netaji ki Jai', 'Inquilab Zindabad' and 'Azad Hindustan Zindabad,' Lt. Gian Singh led his men against the enemy infantry supported by the steel monster. All our men responded to his slogans which echoed above the enemy fire. Our men knew that they were charging into almost certain death but they had lost all fear. Their determination was the only support which these heroes had against the superior armament of the enemy. In the name of India and Indian independence they charged into enemy trucks. The enemy immediately debussed and fierce hand to hand fighting ensued which lasted for two hours, but our heroes would not give in. Forty of them sacrificed their lives after inflicting much heavier losses on the enemy. The enemy was so intimidated by their determination that they beat a hurried retreat.

Just then Lt. Gian Singh called forward his third platoon and was issuing orders when a bullet struck him in the head and he fell down never to rise again. His assistant then took over the command of the company and reorganized it.

Second Lt. Gian Singh Bisht used to tell his men that he would die with them. He fulfilled his promise and proved himself their true comrade both in life and death.

The enemy who had come towards the 'A' company started first by shelling the village, and then the tanks, armoured cars and motorized infantry approached 'A' company's position. The armoured fighting vehicles entered the village and opened fire. Our company also returned the fire. At about 18:00 hours, the enemy advanced with fixed bayonet deployed behind heavy tanks. Our soldiers set the village on fire to make an obstacle for the tank. Left without the protection of their tanks, the enemy soldiers had no guts to advance any further. As darkness fell, they retreated with three casualties, and Taungzin which had been the scene of very bitter fighting throughout the day was still in our hands. On 19 March 1945, I visited Colonel Dhillon at his headquarters at Khabok and met his battalion commanders Lt. Khan Mohd. and Capt. Mohd. Hussain. Inspite of the fact that they had been in two attacks, our troops were in excellent spirits. For the next week, extensive patrolling activity continued on both sides. Generally speaking, the enemy were most active during the day because of the support they received from their aeroplanes and tanks. Without this support, they felt helpless and at night they remained behind barbed wire defences. On the other hand, our men who had to remain under cover during the day were most active at night. It happened very often that some places in the battle area were in enemy hands during the day time and in ours at night. On 27 March, operation orders were issued to No. 2 Division to attack Pyinbin on the night of 30-31 March.

After successfully carrying out the role allotted to it, No. 4 Regt. (Nehru Brigade) was ordered to return to Popa. It arrived there on 5 April and the unit was given a new role to take over the defence on Meiktila-Kyauk Padang Road and at Popa. On 8 April, we received the information that the enemy, having occupied Meiktila, had advanced further and fighting was going on in the vicinity of Pyinmana. Another powerful British column had advanced from Meiktila on Kyauk-Padang Road and then turned south to occupy Natmau and Taundwingy. Thus two divisions of the enemy had gone approximately 150-200 miles in the rear of us. The situation became critical and the Japanese forces were ordered to retreat to Moulmein. No. 2 Division received orders to move to Magwe Minbu area, where No. 1 Infantry Regiment under Colonel S. M. Hussain was holding the area against enemy parachutists and Guerrillas.

Operation Order

1. *Information:* Unit No. 599 has been allotted new role and its responsibility will be as under: (a) Anti-Parachute work, (b) Guarding the 1.O.C. (c) Establishing law and order in areas where the I.N.A. troops are stationed. In connection with para (b) and (c) above, certain gangs of dacoits are looting and harassing the civil population and the supply line of the I.N.A. Our activities will mainly be against them.

2. *Intention:* Movement of formation of Unit No. 599: (a) Unit No. 603. In its present area of Magwe-Mainbu. Unit No. 606 on being relieved will re-join Unit No. 603 at Magwe. (b) Unit No. 747. In the area of Natmauk-Taungdwingyi. (c) Unit No. 801. In the area of Minhala

to Sinbaungwe. (d) H.Q. Unit No. 599 will move to a locality in Magwe area – Exact location will be intimated later.

3. *Method:* (a) Units will start moving independently from the evening of 10 April 1945. The move will be completed as soon as possible. All units will submit to these HQrs. a detailed programme of their move from this station. (b) Routes. (i) Marching columns of Unit No. 599-Unit No. 801, will use cart track running through the following villages: Kyauk Padaung-Ywala-Yez-on-Okshitton Wetmasut-Magwe. (ii) Unit No. 747 will use cart tract: Kyauk Padaung-Kyatkun-Sangon-Magyigon Yamun-Natmauk-Taungdwingyi.

4. *Admn.* (a) Rations. (i) All parties except the units going to Natmauk will carry enough rations for the journey, plus three days reserve. (ii) Units bound for Natmauk will carry a minimum of seven days' reserve rations. All rations that were issued as one month's reserve to units in this area will be returned to D.Q. M.G. (b) *Medical.* Medical Air Party Hospital closed here on 9 April 1945, patients and stores will be evacuated in accordance with the instructions issued separately by the A.D.M.S.

Eventually the unit left Popa on the night of 11-12 April 1945, and after breaking through two enemy encirclements arrived at Magwe on the morning of 19 April. At about 15:00 hours on the same day, enemy tanks broke through and unit was ordered to retreat to Prome. From Prome, it retreated to Taikyi, approximately thirty units north of Rangoon. Then finding the road blocked it turned east into the Pegu-Yomas. On 14 May, after all possible lines of withdrawal, we were blocked and the main body of the unit had to surrender to the British at Pegu. Full details of this trek of 500 miles from Popa-Pegu are given later in the book.

Activities of No. 2 Infantry Regiment

This regiment was raised in Singapore in December 1943 and Colonel Roderigues was appointed its commander. From there it was transferred to Ipoh and arrived at Rangoon early in December 1944.

On arrival in Rangoon, Colonel P. K. Sahgal was appointed its Commander in place of Colonel Roderigues who was appointed as General Staff Officer I to the Div HQs.

Early in February 1945, orders were issued to the regiment to proceed to Popa via Prome and Kyauk Padang. The role allotted to the Brigade was to prepare Popa Hill area as a firm base for Guerrilla operations against the enemy.

On 13 February, Colonel Sahgal left his headquarters in Rangoon for Popa. On the way up he called at the Headquarters of the Japanese Arakan Command (Saku Butai) and met General Iwakuro of Singapore fame. He was at that time working as the Chief of the General Staff to the Arakan command. Although he had been transferred from the Japanese Liaison Department after working for the I.N.A., after the crisis in the first I.N.A., he was still very much interested in its affairs. For purposes of operations, No. 2 Division of the I.N.A. was put under Command of Saku Butai. General Iwakuro – on being informed by Colonel Sahgal that I.N.A. had no artillery, anti-tank mines or anti-tank guns – promised to give full assistance to him.

From Saku Butai Headquarter, which was located in a jungle approximately 30 miles north of Rangoon on Prome Road, Colonel Sahgal proceeded to Yennawgyaung, and met General Yamamoto, who was commanding the Japanese Division operating in the area. He established close contact with them and sectors for operations were mutually decided upon.

It was here that Colonel Sahgal learnt that No. 4 Guerrilla Regiment (the Nehru Brigade) had been in action at Nyaungu and Pagan had been forced to fall back on Popa and Kyauk Padang. The situation had become very grave. Colonel Sahgal, therefore, decided to push on to Popa with his troops as fast as he could and to stem the enemy's advance on Popa and Kyauk Padang.

In the meantime, the enemy having crossed the Irrawaddy at Nyaungu and Pagan and Pakokou occupied Pyinbin, Taungtha and the outskirts of Meiktila. It was at this time that Netaji was nearly encircled by the British forces in Meiktila. Colonel Sahgal arrived at Popa on 18 February and immediately took in hand the preparation of the defences of Popa. His unit was arriving in small parties of approximately 200 men at a time.

In the meantime, he met Major G. S. Dhillon who had withdrawn for Nyaungu, and they pooled all their resources and decided to defend Popa and Kyauk Padang.

On 22 February, I (Colonel Shahnawaz Khan) arrived at Popa and took over the command of No. 2 Division and allotted tasks to the brigades as under:

1. No. 2 Infantry Regiment under Colonel Sahgal was to prepare Popa as a strong base for offensive operations against the enemy that had crossed the Irrawaddy. They were also ordered to carry out intensive patrol activity due north and north-east of Popa. Popa Hill area was the most important point in the plan for the defence of Burma. It was a small hilly platoon which had three important roads meeting on it. It was the only water source for an area of 20 miles all round. It was therefore a place of great strategic importance, the occupation of which would affect the entire plan of operation in this sector. It was ideally suited for defence. The preparation of defence works was taken in hand by No. 2 Regiment in real earnest. Arms were allotted to battalions as under:

a.   No. 1 Battalion area around Pyinbin-Popa Road.

b.   No. 2 Battalion – on area around Kyauk Padang-Popa Road.

c.   No. 3 Battalion – area around Taungtha Road.

In addition to this, No. 2 Battalion had to hold a defensive position approximately one mile east of Kyauk Padang on Kyauk Padang-Meiktila Road.

2.   No. 4 (the Nehru Brigade) Regt. under Major G. S. Dhillon was ordered to carry out guerrilla warfare against the enemy in the west of Kyauk Padang,

On the morning of 24 February, it was reported to Colonel Sahgal then officiating as divisional commander in the absence of Colonel Shahnawaz Khan, who had returned to Meiktila to report situation to Netaji that the enemy had broken through in Seiktin and was moving in the direction of Popa. Strong reconnaissance and fighting patrol were sent out and contact made with the enemy.

A few days later, one of our patrols commanded by S.O. Abdulla Khan, while reconnoitring the area in the vicinity of village Daungle, saw a mechanized patrol of the enemy coming towards Daungle village. He immediately decided to attack them. Dividing his little force of approximately twenty men in two parties, S.O. Abdulla Khan advanced on the enemy who opened fire on them. Our men took cover and returned the fire inflicting casualties on them. S.O. Abdulla Khan then by clever manoeuvring and by use of fire and movement tactics led the party close to the enemy and then charged, but the opponents had left already. That day the enemy left behind two dead soldiers and three Jeep cars. Our men also captured wireless sets, machine guns and large quantities of ammunition.

The next day, approximately one enemy battalion supported by tanks and artillery advanced on Daungle village and it looked as if they would attack Popa. Our men took up their posts and waited for the enemy to come. Strong fighting patrols were also sent out to harass the enemy's advances.

The enemy advanced on Daungle village and after intensive shelling occupied it. There were no I.N.A. troops there. They then set the village on fire and in the evening withdrew towards Pyinbin.

For the next few days, the No. 2 Regiment had no trouble from the enemy who thought it advisable to keep at a respectable distance from Popa.

On 14 March, the No. 2 Regiment was ordered to carry out a raid on Pyinbin. The raid party marched off from Popa at 23:00 hours. It was composed of two rifle companies under the command of Colonel Sahgal. Since there was no water in the area where they were to operate, they had to carry it on bullock carts. The situation of No. 2 Infantry Regiment was very unsatisfactory regarding arms and ammunition.

The unit was armed with three Dutch mortars and had only eighty rounds of ammunition for mortars with no hope of receiving any more supplies. Their medium machine guns were of two different types: some were of British make, others were Dutch. Each gun had only 400 rounds of ammunition with it, and there were no prospect of receiving a fresh supply. For our light automatics, we had a mixed assortment of Bren Guns and Lewis Guns. Every soldier carried 100 rounds of ammunition and there was no reserve of ammunition with the brigade. The unit had only enough ammunition to last it for two hours of continuous fighting.

Owing to the open nature of the country, the subunits had to be dispersed over large areas. We had no wireless or telephone intercommunications.

This raiding party having left Popa at 23:00 hours reached Setsetyo at 06:00 hours. It was occupied by a small outpost of the Japanese. The march was very heavy due to the sandy nature of the soil. Bullock carts carrying water could not reach the men. With the result that they had to buy water from the locals.

During the day our men hid themselves. Colonel Sahgal contacted the Japanese commander and learnt whatever he could of the enemy's disposition. As a result of the information received from our own patrols, Colonel Sahgal decided to attack Pyinbin on the night of the 15-16 March.

They started off from Setsetyo at 21:30 hours and reached a place called Meyne. Here the force was divided into two parts. One party was to make a faint attack from the right, whereas the main attack was to come a little later from the left. This show was entirely successful, and the enemy, feeling that he was in danger of being cut off and annihilated, left their trenches and retreated. Our men attacked their trenches later but found them empty. Only at one small post did they put up any resistance, but even this was eventually destroyed by Lt. Joginder Singh who threw hand grenades into it, killing approximately 8 men. In this operation, one platoon of the Japanese from Setsetyo was placed under direct command of Lt. Joginder Singh. We got one man killed and one wounded. After destroying various stores and huts in Pyinbin, one force returned to Setsetyo and on the morning of 17 March they returned to Popa.

At this time, extremely heavy fighting was going on at Meiktila between the British forces and the Japanese. Some I.N.A. units were also operating in that sector. The British force had occupied all the aerodromes and had cut off all the roads leading into Meiktila, from Mandalay, Rangoon, Thazi and Kyauk Padang. Since Meiktila was the nerve centre of the Japanese resistance in Burma, they were making supreme efforts to recapture it. A powerful counter offensive was launched against the British by the Japanese from Thazi, Pyay-bine, Myingyan and Kyauk Padang.

Around 20 March 1945, it was decided that it would be a great help to the Japanese attacking Meiktila if one of the forces could occupy Pyinbin, which was an important road junction and through which all supplies and reinforcements reached Meiktila. The enemy after our last raid on Pyinbin, had strengthened its defences very considerably, and it was believed that there was one battalion stationed there, and also large stores had been collected.

It was finally decided that the I.N.A. and the Japanese would launch a continued attack on Pyinbin and annihilate the garrison and destroy all the stores, and the following operation orders were issued for the attack:

a. The enemy: An enemy mechanized column estimated to be approximately one brigade that infiltrated into Meiktila late last month, was still there. It was being reinforced to form strong bridgeheads at Nyaungu and Pakokou The strength of the enemy at these bridgeheads was estimated to be approximately two brigades.

It was also learnt that the enemy had then occupied Pyinbin with ten tanks, ten armoured cars and approximately one battalion of Infantry. At Thedaw approximately 12 miles north-east of Pyinbin, enemy's reserves for Taungtha front were located. Strong detachment of the enemy were also known to be in the vicinity of Myingyan, Taungtha and Mahlaing.

b. Our own and Allied Troops: Powerful Japanese forces were fiercely attacking Meiktila and had managed to push the enemy out of the town to west side of the lake.

To our front one fresh Heidan had arrived at Seiktin 10 miles south-east of Pyinbin.

Khanjo Units were at Setsetyo, 4 miles south of Pyinbin. Further west on the Kyauk Padaung-Nayangu Road, one fresh battalion had taken over the defence of Taungzin and Mayaukye Negalaine from No. 459 Unit. The advance of Kantetsu on both sides of the Irrawaddy was progressing satisfactorily.

Intention: No. 531 Unit would attack, in cooperation with Khanjo, and annihilate the enemy garrison in Pyinbin on the night of 30-31 March.

3. *Method*: As a preliminary to the attack, units from their present locations would concentrate in the areas on dates shown below:

Unit	Place	Date
(a) No. 545 Unit	Seiktein	Night of 29-30 March
(b) 1. Khanjo Units	Oyin (2 miles S. E. Pyinbin.) Taungdaw (5 miles south of Pyinbin)	
(c) No. 450 Unit & Cross Roads 6 miles	Hosokawa Units S. W. of Pyinbin	

On the night of 30-31 March, Khanjo and No. 450 Unit would move forward from their concentration areas, carry out the assault on Pyinbin at 0100 hrs, and annihilate the enemy. No. 545 Unit would send forward strong detachment to cut off from the East Roads (I) Pyinbin – Tada; (II) Pyinbin – Thabyewa; (III) Pyinbin – Kama.

These detachments would be in position by 23:00 hours on the night of 30-31 March. During the attack on Pyinbin by No. 450 Unit and Khanjo, No. 545 unit would step in and annihilate any enemy that tried to escape from Pyinbin by these roads and also to stop any reinforcements from coming into Pyinbin from the East, and from the North-East No. 531 Unit Operation Order No. 2 would be in action. They would carry sufficient mines to effectively block all roads against enemy tanks. Heavy artillery would support the attack from the direction of Oyin.

Action after the attack: On the completion of the attack, all units of No. 531 Unit would fall back on their original starting lines before daybreak. During the day, the troops would be well-dispersed and every precaution would be taken against losses occurring from enemy aeroplanes and A. F. Vs.

4. Administration.

Supply routes for units would be as under:

(a) No. 450 Unit – Popaywa-Daungie-Cress Road (S. W. of Pyinbin).

(b) No. 545 Unit – Popaywa-Seiktein.

As many bullock carts as were necessary, were commandeered locally by the units and on the termination of the attack would be returned to the owners. All demands of the units including rations, water and other supplies would be submitted to D.Q.M.G. Popaywa, who would do his best to comply with them. A minimum of seven days' dry rations would be dumped in forward areas under unit arrangements. S.A.A.A. a very small reserve of 303 S.A.A. Ball was available with D.Q.M.G. The units were requested to exercise utmost economy in the use of ammunition, A/Tk. Mines. A very limited number were available. These were being sent with trained engineers to assist the units.

Medical: All casualties would be evacuated to Popaywa. A small quantity of bleaching powder for use in the cases where water could not be boiled was being supplied to the Units.

Intercommunication: No. 450 Unit. – No. 531 Unit would communicate through wireless Hosokawa with Unit. No. 545 Unit. – No. 531 Unit would communicate with Battle H.Q. 531 Unit would move from Popaywa to the vicinity of Seiktein on the night of 29-30 March. Main H.Q. 531 Unit would remain at Popaywa under the command of Major Ram Sarup.

Special Instructions to Units: (1) Attack on Pyinbin was to be more in the nature of a surprise guerrilla raid with the intention of causing as much damage to the enemy as possible and then clearing out of it. Commanders were supposed to use the troops very cautiously and avoid all unnecessary casualties. (2) Where possible some live prisoners would be brought back. (3) All papers, other documents and any unit distinguishing badges found in the enemy camp would be brought back.

Distribution:

No. 450 Unit	1	
No. 545 Unit	1	Shahnawaz Khan, Colonel.
No. 50 Unit	1	Commander No. 531 Unit.

Reconnaissance patrols were sent out, some of whom went behind the enemy lines, and brought back valuable information.

On 28 March, the Divisional Headquarters moved out into the battle area.

On the evening of 29 March, units of the No. 2 Brigade moved out into the area of operation to take up their positions in readiness to attack. Colonel Sahgal left Popa at 21:00 hours accompanied by reconnaissance parties of Brigade Headquarters and the No. 1 Battalion. The party was carried in one jeep and one truck, and was preceded by a motorcyclist. As the patrols reported that the area of Seiktin was clear of the enemy, Colonel Sahgal's idea was to proceed to Seiktin and Wellaung and he personally selected areas for companies.

That night as the troops were marching to the assembly area, I was going up and down the road in a Jeep car. At about 23:00 hours, when I was at Legy, I heard intensive machine-gun and rifle fire a few hundred yards ahead. Shortly afterwards, one officer came running to me and reported that the whole of Colonel Sahgal's party had been ambushed by the enemy as had walked straight into the trap laid for them. The enemy had opened fire on them from a range of about 30 yards, and it would have been a miracle how any one of them could have survived. There were fourteen bullet holes, in the car which was carrying Colonel Sahgal. By this time, the marching column of the No. 2 Company had also arrived and I decided to move forward and look for Colonel Sahgal. The officer who brought back the information did not know if he and his party had been killed or captured. A short while afterwards, Colonel Sahgal also arrived and explained the whole situation to me. We decided to push on and recapture our Jeep car and truck.

A counter attack was put in and all our vehicles were recovered, but the enemy had taken away all the papers and other documents including marked maps and operation orders.

By this time, it was very late and there was no time left to advance any further. It was, therefore, decided to fall back on Legy and take up a defensive position there.

Action at Kabyu

On 30 March, one of our companies, posted at Kabyu with the object of taking part in the raid on Pyinbin, was heavily attacked by enemy infantry and tanks. This company was commanded by an officer by the name of Capt. Bagri, who was commanding the No. 3 Battalion, but who had come up to personally command the company raiding Pyinbin. On his right flank was posted a Japanese Company. At about 10:00 hours, an enemy force comprising approximately 1,000 men and several tanks was seen advancing towards Kabyu from the direction of Pyinbin. Our men were entrenched in the middle of an absolutely open plain with practically no cover from ground or the air, and our only defence against those tanks were a few anti-tank mines which we had borrowed from the neighbouring Japanese unit and planted in a circle in front of our position. The futility of holding up the enemy on such a piece of ground was clear to every one of our soldiers. The enemy air force was also most active and since day break they had been bombing and machine gunning our positions. But despite this, men were determined to carry out the task allotted to them.

At first the enemy advanced on the Japanese front and one of their tanks were disabled by an anti-tank mine. This tremendously encouraged the Japanese soldiers. The enemy tank-column then turned towards our position. They were followed by the infantry which had been deployed in readiness for the battle. On approaching our position, another enemy tank ran into one mine-field and was knocked out. This cheered our soldiers a great deal and stopped the advance of enemy tanks. Enemy infantry, however, kept on advancing. They were the British troops. On seeing them coming so near, our men fixed their bayonets and shouting 'Jai Hind' and 'Netaji ki Jai' advanced 200 yards to meet the enemy. When the Japanese saw our soldiers charging, they too followed suite by advancing 600 yards.

The strength of this Japanese company was approximately 150 men. The enemy who numbered approximately 1,000 men opened up intensive machine gun and rifle fire on the Japanese and having pinned them to the ground, proceeded to encircle them. The Japanese lost nearly 60 per cent of their officers and men, and the remainder threatened with encirclement, turned round and ran back to their entrenched position leaving all their dead and wounded on the battlefield.

Capt. Bagri who was watching all this opened intensive fire on the enemy and inflicted severe losses on them. He then counter attacked from a flank and driving the British forces brought all the Japanese dead and wounded to their lines. In the evening, the Japanese Brigadier in the area came to thank me personally and to express his gratitude to the I.N.A. for saving the Japanese company and for bringing back their dead and wounded.

That night was fixed for our raid on Pyinbin, but this had to be postponed owing to the capture of our operation orders by the enemy. Also on the evening of 30 March, the Japanese artillery unit, which was to proceed to Oyin to give supporting fire to our troops attacking Pyinbin, was attacked by the enemy aircraft and all their guns and ammunition were destroyed.

The next day, Capt. Bagri was ordered to ball back on Gwedekkon and guard the left flank of the No. 1 Battalion holding a defensive position at Legy.

On the night of 30-31 March, the date fixed for the raid on Pyinbin, units of No. 4 Guerrilla Regiment (Nehru Brigade) and Khan Jo Butai, the Japanese Brigade, reached their respective areas and waited for the artillery to open fire from Oyin, but unfortunately due to enemy bombing earlier in the evening all our guns had been knocked out. Early in the morning, our units returned to their respective assembly areas and were ordered to wait for further orders to raid Pyinbin.

Intensive patrolling was then resorted to by both sides and our patrols from Legy often entered Seiktin and brought back information about the enemy's strength and disposition. On 2 April, at about 13:00 hours, the enemy machine-gunned and shelled our positions at Legy. We lost six men due to this shelling. On this day our units at Legy, where they were only partially entrenched due to the shortage of entrenching tools, were subjected to a most intensive machine-gunning and bombing by enemy aeroplanes. For two hours, fourteen enemy fighter-bombers bombed and machine-gunned our position. At the same time, enemy artillery kept up an intensive barrage of fire on our position throughout the day, and it was a miracle how we escaped more casualties. To reply to this artillery fire the heaviest weapons that we had were 3-inch mortars which were useless in the face of artillery. Most of our men faced all this very bravely, but there were a number of weak-minded soldiers who walked over to the enemy side. This naturally caused disappointment in our ranks. But now when I look back at it and think of the extremely heavy odds against which our men were fighting a battle, which they knew fully well they had already lost, I do not blame those who walked over to the enemy and changed sides.

At this time, the general situation of the fighting in Burma had taken a very critical turn for us and the Japanese.

Firstly, in the Shan States, the enemy had captured Kalaw and was advancing on Tangyi and Mochi mines with the object of outflanking the Japanese main defence at Toungoo.

Secondly, in the Central Sector, the enemy had occupied Meiktila and fighting was going on at Pyabwe.

Thirdly, further west, on the Meiktila-Kyaukpadang road, the enemy had advanced approximately 15 miles and a powerful column of mechanised infantry and tanks had moved down south and occupied Natmauk and Taundwingyi.

Fourthly, on the Popa front, one powerful division had arrived at Taungtha and was advancing along the Taurgtha-Popa Road.

Fifthly, on the Irrawaddy, the enemy had extended their bridgeheads at Nyaungu and Pakokou.

And, lastly, at Arakan front the enemy had captured Taungup and was advancing rapidly on Prome.

The Burmese Army, which had been raised and trained by the Japanese, left Rangoon in the middle of March under the command of General Aung Sang, with the object of holding up the enemy advance around Prome. On reaching Prome this army, approximately 7,000 strong, crossed over the Irrawaddy to the west in the area of Thayetmeyo. On reaching this area, where there were very few Japanese troops, this army declared itself independent of the control of the Burmese Government and declared war against the Japanese. They were then split up into small guerrilla bands and ordered to carry out guerrilla operations against the Japanese lines of communication from Rangoon to Prome, and from Rangoon to Toungoo. They carried out this duty in a most efficient manner and they made it impossible for the Japanese to supply their front line troops with rations and ammunition. This further aggravated the already critical position of the Japanese. These Burmese guerrillas dressed as ordinary civilians and lived in Burmese villages where they were given food and shelter by the local inhabitants.

The Burmese guerrillas were always on the lookout for small parties of the Japanese troops whom they annihilated whenever they had an opportunity. I would say that the unexpected collapse of the Japanese resistance in Burma was due more to the defection of the Burmese Army rather than to the might of the British forces. On the other hand, I feel that the Burmese had sufficient cause to resort to this course of turning round and fighting against their former allies. Ever since the occupation of Burma the Japanese had exploited the country in a most ruthless manner. It is true that they had declared Burma to be an independent country and had raised a Burmese Army, but in reality both these were unreal. The head of the Burmese state, Dr. Baw Maw and his ministers were weak-minded and selfish; hence, they easily submitted to the Japanese exploitation and Army because they came under the direct control of Japanese officers and were incapable of functioning independently. After three years of Japanese rule, which the Burmese themselves had helped to establish by fighting the British forces in 1942, the Burmese people found that they were better off under the British. Food was very scarce as all the rice and cattle were commandeered by the Japanese Army. There was a great shortage of cloth as well because Burma got most of its cloth-supply from India and Japan. There was much inflation. Money had lost all its value, and a chicken cost would as much as sixty rupees and an egg three rupees. Neither the Japanese nor the puppet Burmese Government took any interest in the welfare of the people. Practically no arrangements were made for the education of their children. On account of all these reasons, the people of Burma were very unhappy and dissatisfied with the Japanese occupation. All the beautiful cities and towns were being bombed to extinction by the British and American air forces. The Burmese were, therefore, anxious that the war which had brought so much unhappiness and devastation to Burma, should be terminated as soon as possible. Those very Burmese who had expected so much from the Japanese and had cooperated so enthusiastically with them now welcomed the return of the British forces to Burma. It was at this stage that General Aung Sang, a 32-year-old Burmese revolutionary, decided to revolt against the Japanese and end their control over the Burmese Army and the government. Together, with a few trusted officers and some Burmese priests who exercised considerable influence over the Burmese people, he made secret plans for the overthrow of Japanese rule. In the middle of March, when he left Rangoon as the head of a Burmese Army, he was given a rousing send-off both by the Burmese and Japanese. The Japanese military men and officers commanding Burmese units also accompanied them. On reaching Thayetmeyo, the first thing they did was to murder all the Japanese officers, and thereafter worked in small independent guerrilla bands attacking and destroying all lorries and railway trains supplying rations and ammunition to the front line-troops.

Encouraged by these successes, the majority of the local youth joined them and took every available opportunity of attacking Japanese soldiers with their '*dha*', a small Burmese sword, and snatching away their rifles.

The battle of Legy

It was in this unenviable situation that No. 2 Division of the Azad Hind Fauj was fighting and successfully holding up the advance of the enemy in Popa-Kyaukpadang sector. The enemy decided to use all available forces at his disposal to clear up this pocket of resistance, and an attack on our forces from three directions was planned. The plan was as follows.

(a) No. 2 British Division was to attack down from Taungtha *via* Wellaung-Seiktin-Popa.

(b) No. 7 British Division was to attack from Nyaungu to Kyaukpadang.

(c) No. 5 British Division was to attack from Meiktila-Kyaukpadang.

It was to meet the thrust of the No. 2 British Division at Popa and the No. 2 Infantry Regiment of the Azad Hind Fauj was posted at Legy.

On 1 April, an outpost located astride Seiktin-Wellaung sent the following reports about enemy movement: (i) At 11:30 hours, ten enemy tanks with 50 men were going towards Legy from Wellaung.

(ii) At 15:30 hours, eighteen lorries, two tanks, one armoured car, two motorcycles and two heavy guns were seen moving towards Legy from Wellaung. The lorries were carrying stores and soldiers.

(iii) At 16:00 hours, some more tanks were seen moving towards Legy. All the tanks in the above mentioned enemy force were medium and heavy Sherman and Churchill tanks. The whole of this force advanced as far as Seiktin and halted there.

A strong fighting patrol under S.O. Abdulla Khan was sent to Seiktin area. This patrol went forward and was engaged by enemy patrols sent from Sjiktin. It returned to Brigade Headquarters at 10:40 hours on the 2 April 1945. During the night of 1-2 April, there was practically no enemy activity on our front.

On 2 April, at 11:30 hours, approximately 2,000 enemy soldiers were seen digging in south of Seiktin, and at 13:10 hours, fourteen enemy planes heavily bombed and machine-gunned Legy for about two hours. The whole of the village was set on fire and all our rations, including water which had been brought up on bullock carts and lorries, were destroyed. As soon as this air attack was over, enemy artillery opened up a most intensive and harassing fire on our position. This fire continued till 21:00 hours.

From 15:00 to 17:00 hours, enemy patrol activity continued. At 17:00 hours, an enemy force consisting of 5 lorries, supported by tanks, moved from Seiktin towards Legy. The enemy, on reaching our front descended from their lorries and advanced towards our positions. When they came within range of our machine guns we opened fire on them. Some of the enemy were seen falling down and the remainder disappeared into the nullah. Tanks and lorries also turned about and raced towards Seiktin. This raised the morale of our men and they were all in good spirits. For the rest of the day there was no enemy activity. It was quite apparent that during the day the enemy had been reconnoitring and feeling our positions, and that a full scale attack was imminent the next day. Therefore, one company from the No. 3 Battalion was brought up from Popa and posted on the right flank of the No. 1 Battalion at Legy. This company was commanded by 2nd Lt. Kanwal Singh, a young officer who had been trained at the Officers Training School in Singapore. He was a Naik in the British Army when it surrendered in Singapore.

On 3 April 1945, a certain amount of alarm and despondency was observed among the officers and men owing to the desertion of some officers. Everybody appeared to think that the enemy had full information about our disposition and in front of their overwhelming weight, our case was hopeless. At this stage, Colonel Sahgal who was present at Legy, personally took over the direction of the battle. At 11:30 hours, an enemy force composed of 13 medium tanks, 30 light tanks, 16 lorries, 12 guns and 1,000 Infantry advanced in the front of our 'C' company which was on the left flank.

At 12:00 hours, enemy artillery opened intensive, harassing fire on our position.

At 13:00 hours, one enemy force consisting of two medium tanks, 30 armoured cars and 60 lorries was observed advancing towards Legy. This force halted at about 1,000 yards in front of our position and deployed.

At 13:30 hours, a small force of the enemy went round our right flank and attacked our 'B' echelon. This was a complete surprise to our men who were caught cooking food or carrying rations and water. The casualties on our side were very heavy. The enemy occupied this area but no information of this action was received in Headquarters until 19:00 hours.

At 13:45 hours, heavy shelling on the right flank followed by an attack by approximately one battalion on the position occupied by the company of 2nd Lt. Kanwal Singh. This time the enemy came very near our position and it was only after a very fierce battle at close quarters that the enemy was forced to retreat with extremely heavy casualties.

At 14:00 hours, approximately one platoon of the enemy that had infiltrated through our position had opened fire from our rear. This fire was returned and the enemy was dislocated from his position. By this time enemy artillery and mortars were shelling us from the front and our right, rear and left.

At 16:00 hours, enemy artillery opened rapid fire on our right flank, continued to fire for approximately ten minutes, during which period they must have fired at least 150 shells. This was followed by an attack by a fresh enemy battalion on Lt. Kanwal Singh's company. This company once again defended their positions most gallantly and drove the enemy back after inflicting heavy casualties on them.

During the entirety of this operation, 2nd Lt. Kanwal Singh, the company commander, and Hawildar Abdul Mannu, one of the platoon commanders, stood on top of two hills and personally directed the fire of their units. These two brave officers did not stir from their command post even when the small arms fire was concentrated on them. It was due mainly to the gallantry of these two officers that the repeated enemy attacks were beaten off.

By now it was apparent that the enemy was determined to make a breakthrough on our right flank. The 'C' company, which was on the left flank, was withdrawn and put in support of Lt. Kanwal Singh's company.

At 19:00 hours, we received a report about the enemy attack on our 'B' echelon and their occupation of that area. The 'C' company was accordingly ordered to counter attack and drive away the enemy from that area. The attack was launched at 21:00 hours by Lt. Ganga Singh and was completely successful. The enemy, after suffering severe losses, fled in disorder.

At 19:30 hours, heavy artillery fire was once again opened on our right flank, and Lt. Kanwal Singh's company was again attacked for the third time. Once again, the gallant company beat back the enemy attack. At the same time, an enemy force comprising approximately two companies and accompanied by tanks moved towards our left flank, in front of the 'B' company, and after an exchange of fire this force was also easily pushed back.

About this time Colonel Sahgal asked for more reinforcements and another company of 3rd Battalion under the command of Major B. S. Negi was sent forward to him.

On 4 April at about 03:00 hours, because we had been encircled by the enemy and our men, who had fought most gallantly against extremely heavy odds, were exhausted, orders were issued to Colonel Sahgal to fall back on Popa. This was done and they arrived at Popa at 07:00 hours.

On the same day, an order was issued to Colonel G. S. Dhillon to return with his unit to Popa, which he did with the Nehru Brigade on 5 April. I held a conference of the brigade commanders at which it was decided to allot the defence of Popa to the Nehru Brigade. The infantry regiment under Colonel Sahgal was ordered to reorganize itself and hold in readiness to take the offensive against the enemy.

On 7 April, our company at Kyauktaga, two miles North of Popa, was attacked by the enemy but the attack was successfully beaten back. On 8 April, I received orders that the No. 2 Division was to withdraw from Popa to the area of Magwe-Minbu-Yaunbuingyi where the No. 1 Infantry Regiment, under the command of Colonel S. M. Hussain had been operating since March 1945.

The new task allotted to units were the defence of their respective areas against the enemy parachutists and guarding the lines of communication.

Withdrawal from Popa

Units at Popa were ordered to start moving on 10 April and routes allotted to them for their withdrawal were:

Divisional Headquarters and No. 4 Regiment were to use a cart track running through the following villages Kyauk Padang-Ywalu-Yezon Okshitton-Wetmasut-Magwe.

No. 2 Infantry was to use the track Kyauk Padang-Kyatkun-Saigon-Magyigaon-Ywamun-Natmauk-Taundwingyi.

On 10 April, the area of our hospital and Divisional Headquarters were heavily bombed by 35 British bombers which dropped high explosive and incendiary bombs causing numerous casualties among our sick and wounded. This information must have been given to the British by the officers and men who had deserted to the British side. On the same day, the Divisional Headquarters came under heavy enemy artillery fire.

On 12 April, our forward company at Kyauktag was encircled by enemy tanks and infantry. This was the company commanded by Lt. Kanwal Singh who had put up such a magnificent fight at Legy. They fought on in spite of being completely cut off from the rest of the battalion. The British commander realizing the hopeless situation in which the company was placed, sent a note to Lt. Kanwal Singh to surrender. Kanwal Singh replied, 'Gentleman I still have some ammunition left. I do not come to you yet.' He fought on till all his ammunition was completely exhausted and he was then forced to surrender.

On the same day, the enemy, after a most intensive artillery shelling occupied Kyauk Padang and thus cut off our only line of retreat to Yennan, Gyaung and Magwe.

In the meantime, the enemy from Meiktila was heavily attacking our posts approximately 10 miles east of Kyauk Padang, and it was with the greatest of difficulty that they were holding to their position.

The main body of the division left Popa on 12-13 April at 02:00 hours. On the way to Kyauk Padang, we found the road blocked by enemy patrols. We were therefore obliged to abandon all our mechanical transport on the road and to attempt to break through the enemy encirclement. Capt. Khan Mohd. of the No. 4 Guerrilla Regiment was detailed as advance Guard Commander and ordered to create a gap through which the rest of the division could escape. To hold up the enemy's advance on the Popa-Taungtha Road the No. 3 Battalion under Capt. Bagri, was left behind at Popa to give time to the rest of the division to break through.

On 13 April, at 08:00 hours, the division had broken through the enemy's encirclement and arrived in the area of Indowakki. This was an open area with a few trees here and there. In this area, the whole of the division rested for the day and it was a miracle how we escaped from the observation of enemy aircraft, which were patrolling the area continuously. The same day Capt. Bagri's battalion at Popa having completed its task returned to Indowakki and joined its brigade.

On the evening of 13 April, in the vicinity of Indowakki, I gave final instructions to unit commanders. The previous night Colonel Sahgal had fallen down and had sprained his ankle. He had to be carried on a bullock cart, as also the rest of the sick and wounded of the division. From Indowakki we took different routes as already explained, but unfortunately the enemy had already occupied Natmauk and Taundungyi, and so Colonel Sahgal had to by-pass these places and make an attempt to reach Prome. On the way all his rations were exhausted and the enemy force was following close at his heels. In the initial stages of their journey, the No. 2 Regiment marched together in one column, but later on, after they arrived in the area of Natmauk, Col Sahgal decided to split up his force in two columns. This was considered essential on account of the difficulty of obtaining rations locally for such a large number of men, and also because there was danger of being spotted by British aeroplanes which were carrying out a very thorough search of the whole area. One column consisting of Brigade Headquarters No. 2 Battalion and No. 1 Battalion marched off under Colonel Sahgal. The second column, consisting of the No. 3 Battalion under Capt. Bagri, marched off on a parallel track a few circles apart. Both these columns managed to evade the enemy successfully and bypass Taundwingyi.

Heroic death of Captain Bagri

On about 20 April, when Capt. Bagri's column was approximately 20 miles south of Taundwingyi, they were overtaken and encircled by enemy tanks. At the time the battalion was dispersed in a small village in the middle of open paddy fields. Sentries reported to Capt. Bagri that enemy tanks in large numbers were approaching the village. His battalion was not prepared for this attack. They had not even had time to dig themselves in neither did they have any weapons to combat with those steel monsters. The choice before Capt. Bagri was either to surrender before the enemy or put up a hopeless fight and meet a glorious death. He called out to his men and explained them the situation. He said, 'We have been encircled by enemy tanks. We can now either surrender shamefully or meet a glorious death fighting like a true soldier.' He went on to say, 'I myself can never think of laying down my arms, before the cowardly British. I have decided to fight to the last.' So saying he led a party of 100 men into action against enemy tanks. With hand grenades and bottles filled with petrol, they charged into enemy vehicles and destroyed one tank and one armoured car. While charging into a second tank, Capt. Bagri was hit by a burst of machine gun fire and fell never to rise again. Most of the men who were following him were also killed.

British officers, who saw the valour of Capt. Bagri, were dumbfounded by his gallantry and his complete disregard for his personal safety. They wanted to know the reason why Capt. Bagri, in spite of realizing the impossible odds against him, charged into the enemy tanks, and met his death. The reason of course was a simple one, but rather difficult to understand for an Englishman. The true sons of India can be killed, but they can never be defeated. Bagri knew when he was charging into the enemy tanks that he was asking for certain death, but he was not afraid of it. He could never accept defeat. In this way died one of the bravest soldiers of the Azad Hind Fauj.

On 27 April, having successfully evaded the enemy at Taundwingyi, the second column under Colonel Sahgal arrived at a small village called Myew. This village was approximately two miles north of Allenmayo. Here they found that heavy fighting was going on in Allenmayo and gun fire was being exchanged by both sides. Colonel Sahgal then selected a place called Magi Gaon, approximately three miles to the east of the road, and ordered his units to take up a defensive position there. This area was well suited for a defensive position as it was surrounded on three sides by hills, and on the fourth side was a river bed. Stray piquets were posted on all the hills and the party rested there for the night. Next morning, a conference was called by Colonel Sahgal which was attended by all officers of the unit. He explained to them the military situation in Burma as a whole and particularly the situation on their part of the front. He told them that Allenmayo was already occupied by the enemy and that the main road to Prome had been blockaded by the enemy. He then pointed out to his men that there were three courses open to them. The first one was that they should fight their way through the enemy lines as they had done before and re-join the division at Prome; the second course was that they should all disguise themselves as civilians and infiltrate through the enemy lines; and the third was that they should all become prisoners of war. Having explained all this he left the final choice to the officers themselves. All the officers then requested that they should be given an hour's time to consider the matter. After one hour they all reassembled and informed Colonel Sahgal that they had decided unanimously in favour of becoming P.O.Ws. After this, Colonel Sahgal wrote a letter to the commander of the Allied troops communicating his decision to surrender his forces to the British as prisoners of war. He then ordered all the officers to return to their units and inform their men of this decision. He also ordered all the pickets to withdraw into the village.

At about 13:00 hours, information was received that some Gurkha troops were advancing on the village. Colonel Sahgal told his men to keep clear and not to get excited and fire on the enemy. He then went forward and met the commander of the Gurkha troops, and arranged for the surrender of his forces. They were then taken to Magwe jail.

Retreat of Divisional Headquarters No. 4 Regiment

On the night of 13 April 1945, having issued final instructions to Brigade Commanders at Indowakki, the Divisional Commander Colonel Shahnawaz Khan marched off with his force to Magwe, which was 100 miles to the south. The next morning they arrived at a village called Eino and spent the day in a Burmese temple. Troops had marched the whole night through a sandy area and were very tired indeed. At this time, the enemy was converging on them from all sides, and all the main roads and highways were in their hands. Colonel Shahnawaz, therefore, selected jungle routes to bypass the enemy that had gone ahead of them. The offensive against the oil-fields area was also well on the way and it looked very doubtful if this party would be able to go through the enemy lines and reach Magwe. However, despite all these difficulties our men kept on marching. Their rations were exhausted and they had to live on whatever they could buy locally from the village.

On 18 April, at 04:00 hours, this party, having successfully evaded the enemy, arrived at Magwe. Here they were met by Colonel S. M. Hussain who was the commander of the No. 1 Infantry Regiment which had been allotted the defence of Magwe, Minwu Taundwingyi area. Troops that arrived with the Divisional Commander were dispersed in the Magwe area while Colonel Hussain explained the local military situation of his area to the Divisional Commander. He revealed that Taundwingyi, which had been defended by the No. 1 Battalion under Commander Major B. S. Rawat, had been occupied by the enemy and that fierce counter attacks to recapture it were being launched by the I.N.A. and the Japanese. On the Magwe front he explained that on the previous evening some enemy tanks had attacked out posts approximately 12 east of Magwe and on being fired at, these tanks withdrew towards Tonangi.

It was quite evident from this that the situation was developing fast, and that an attack on Magwe was to be expected either the next day or the day after. Major Man Singh, the commander of the No. 2 Battalion defending Magwe, was then detailed to take forward three companies to reinforce the outposts which had been attacked the previous day. All the sick people and valuable stores were sent across the river to Mimbo under the command of Lt. Col Roderigues.

Here I would like to explain that the No. 1 Infantry Regiment which was composed of perhaps the best trained troops in the I.N.A. had lost all its heavy arms and equipment including three mortars and machine guns during the transit from Malaya to Burma. Inspite of our best efforts to make good this deficiency, we were unable to obtain a fresh supply. It was, therefore, only with rifles and light machine-guns that we had to defend an absolutely open area like a desert against the enemy tanks. They did not have any anti-tank mines or guns.

On the following day, the enemy dropped parachute troops in the vicinity of our outposts. They were immediately engaged by our troops and were forced to retreat. The same day some more troops from Popa arrived at Magwe. They had been marching continuously for the last seven days. On account of enemy air activity, they could move only at night. During the day they had to disperse and take shelter from hostile aircraft. During these marches the men had very little sleep. It was, therefore, in a very tired and exhausted condition that our men arrived at Magwe. The first essential, therefore, was to give them a little rest to recoup and reorganize their units.

At about 15:00 hours, enemy tanks and lorries broke through the line of our outposts and came into Magwe by complete surprise. We had no means of intercommunication other than a runner with our out posts. It was, therefore, not possible for them to have warned us of the approach of enemy tank columns. There were very few troops in Magwe, hence no organized resistance could be put up. Lt. Col. G. S. Dhillon and Major Chandra Bhan of the No. 4 Regiment rallied a few men and formed a line of defence and held up the enemy for some hours and enabled the remnants in Magwe to withdraw to their next destination. They were subjected to intensive artillery shelling and serial bombardment, but they tenaciously hung on to their positions until all their comrades had been evacuated from Magwe. Some of our troops were, however, forced to surrender in Magwe, and Colonel Hussain, the commander of the No. 1 Infantry Regiment was unfortunately one of them. Having completed their task, Colonel G. S. Dhillon and Major Chandra Bhan fell back on Kama where fresh orders were issued by the Divisional Commander to the No. 2 Division to withdraw to Prome. During the night of the 19-20 April, all the remnants of the No. 2 Division crossed over by local boats to the west bank of the Irrawaddy. Information was sent to Colonel Roderigues at Minbu to withdraw with the No. 3 Battalion of the 1st Infantry Regiment to Prome. Unfortunately, information could not reach Man Singh who was holding the outpost position with the No. 2 Battalion. The following day he was forced to surrender to the British forces in Magwe.

When we crossed over to the west bank of the Irrawaddy, we found that the enemy had occupied Migyaungye and Minhla from Taundwingyi side. We were, therefore, obliged to move further west, and by using jungle routes we tried to reach Prome. On 28 April, we arrived at a village called Minde, approximately 10 miles north-west of Kama. During the night, with the help of the Burmese troops who had rebelled against the Japanese, we crossed over at Kama to the east bank of the Irrawaddy. At that time heavy fighting was going on at Allenmayo and the enemy was trying to capture Prome as early as possible.

All along our retreat from Kyauk Padang to Prome the Burmese Army which had rebelled against the Japanese and had occupied all the area, particularly the area west of the Irrawaddy from Minbu to Prome. They behaved in most friendly manner with the I.N.A. They had established their own government in 42 villages west of Prome. In this area, there were practically no Japanese troops and any small party of Japanese that tried to escape from British encirclement was cut off and slaughtered by the Burmese guerrilla forces. The villagers were working in complete cooperation with the Burmese rebel army, which had now adopted the name of 'People's National Army', and had declared war upon the fascist powers. General Aung Sang, the commander of these forces, had his headquarters in the area of Thayetmeyo. They established a very effective parallel government in the area. In each village they stationed a few soldiers under an officer. These officers or NCOS lived in the villages dressed as ordinary villagers and no one ever betrayed their presence or their plans to any foreigner. In fact, they were given shelter, food and protection by the villagers. These men controlled everything in the village and without their cooperation it was not possible to purchase anything from the villagers, nor was it possible to hire any bullock cart, the only form of transport available in these areas. This group of men were specially trained in the duties of administration and intelligence work. They obtained with the help of the local villagers all information regarding the movement of the enemy in that region. Sentries were posted in all villages to give warning of the approach of enemy troops. Each village had a special type of drum made out of a hollowed tree trunk to give warning of the approach of enemy troops. These drums were very effective and its sound carried a long way. As soon as these drums were beaten all the villagers, including women and children would run away into previously prepared shelters in the jungles. Here in these shelters they had stored away all their corn. All their cattle were also hidden away in those jungles with the result that whenever Japanese forces arrived they found the villages completely deserted and without any rations. This was a great handicap to the Japanese forces which lived mainly on that country.

Cooperative with this intelligence group were the actual fighting guerrillas who remained hidden in jungles in groups of 40 or 50, fully armed with the most modern Japanese arms and always on the alert. It was the task of these fighting groups to annihilate any Japanese force whose presence was reported to them by the intelligence groups. These guerrilla forces were an absolute terror to the Japanese forces, and on whom they inflicted extremely heavy casualties at that time. There was a great scarcity of cloth in Burma, and Burmese guerrilla forces would attack Japanese supply dumps and clothing depots, or ambush their motor convoys and trains carrying such stores, and would distribute the loot to the villagers. By this action of theirs and by their just and fair administration they won the sympathy and cooperation of all the villagers.

While at Popa and Magwe in March 1945, the I.N.A. was requested by the Japanese to take action against Burmese guerrillas. But we refused to fight the Burmese on the ground that our fight was only for the liberation of India and against the British who dominated it. We were not the Japanese Army or under the control of the Japanese Army, and as such, we were not prepared to fight the Burmese, who, after all, were also fighting for their liberation. These reports had reached General Aung Sang who had issued similar instructions to his troops to help the I.N.A. in every possible way and never to fight against them.

As is well known, the British, while they were ruling Burma before 1942, had generated bitter feelings between the Burmese and the Indians. During the Japanese advance into Burma in April 1942, when a number of Indians tried to escape to India, thousands were slaughtered in cold blood by the Burmese. It is said that as many as 50,000 were murdered in this way. During the time when Netaji was in Burma, he managed to establish most friendly relation with the people of Burma and they began to look upon him as a leader not only of the Indian people but also of the Burmese and other nationals of East Asia. This change in the Burmese attitude towards Indians must, therefore, seem, amazing, and the only explanation for this change was the personality of Netaji Subhas Chandra Bose. Had it not been for the cooperation of the Burmese forces it would not have been possible for the main body of the No. 2 Division to reach Prome and later Pegu.

On the morning of 1 May, after getting all the troops to the east bank of the Irrawaddy opposite Kama, I crossed over with the last party which included all officers of my Divisional Headquarters: Colonel Roderigues, Major Ram Sarup, Major Mehar Dass and Major A. B. Singh. Colonel Dhillon, who was suffering from an acute attack of appendicitis, was also in this party. In the morning, we reached a village approximately five miles due north of Prome. Here I received the information that Prome had been evacuated and set on fire by the Japanese. It was also intimated to me that Toungoo had been occupied by the British, that Rangoon had been evacuated by the Japanese and the Indian National Army and that all the I.N.A. troops left in Burma had been ordered by Netaji to surrender to the British. I was, however, not prepared to accept these orders and was determined to continue fighting and to try and reach Netaji, who it was rumoured, was, at that time, in Moulmein. The situation was, therefore, even worse than I had expected and I realized that the trek to Moulmein would be difficult and that the sick and wounded would not be able to face it. I, therefore, decided to collect all the sick and wounded personnel in an Indian village called Kalabasthi and left them there under the charge of Colonel Roderigues and Major Ranganathan. These two officers realizing that they would receive very hard treatment from the British, very sportingly volunteered to stay behind and look after the sick and wounded. They had been ordered to surrender to the British when they arrived at Prome.

With the rest personnel, I left Prome on the night of 1st May. At that time enemy was heavily shelling the town and there were no troops to stop their advance. It was a heartbreaking sight when we had to leave the sick behind at Prome. Most of them despite being in an extremely poor state of health wished to accompany the division. The very idea of having to surrender to the British was revolting to them; but eventually they had to stay behind under orders as I did not wish to have the story of the Imphal withdrawal repeated.

South of Prome was still clear of the enemy, and we, therefore, followed the main Rangoon-Prome Road. The Japanese were retreating in a great hurry. They were using every available vehicle to evacuate their men. We had no transport at all and our men kept marching day and night to avoid being overtaken by the enemy forces. The Japanese, as usual, left us in the lurch and ran as fast as they could. Having no wireless sets we were dependent entirely on them for giving us information about the general situation around us.

On 5 May at 07:00 hours, we reached a village two miles south of Okpo. From here the Japanese forces went east into the Pegu Yomas. We decided to march on to Letpadan.

On 7 May, our party arrived at a place called Taikchi at about midnight. This place was approximately 30 miles north of Rangoon. Here we found that the British forces, having occupied Rangoon, were marching north with the object of capturing us. Here, we were trapped in the encirclement again.

I decided to leave the main road and strike east into the Pegu Yomas with the object of infiltrating through the enemy lines, crossing the Sittang River and re-joining our own forces at Moulmein or Bangkok.

For about one week we travelled right across the Pegu Yomas through the thickest jungles, and on 12 May reached the village of Niata, approximately 20 miles to the west of Pegu. Here I found that the enemy had captured Pegu about a fortnight earlier, and that fighting was going on at Waki.

I also learnt that Germany had surrendered unconditionally to the Allies, and that owing to intensive aerial bombardment, Japan was also on the verge of collapse. I decided to spend the day in that village and sent a patrol to the next village to get full information regarding enemy dispositions. The patrol returned the next day and brought back all the facts. It was quite clear that we were completely trapped and the British forces were closing in on us from all sides.

There was also a large number of Japanese troops, approximately 50,000 in number, trapped in a similar manner.

We were being bombed and shelled continuously, rations were exhausted, and all the villagers had fled into jungles. The Japanese were eating up everything: pigs, buffaloes, cows, dogs and monkeys. The situation was extremely grave and everything appeared grim for us.

I realized that everything was over for the rest of us, and I did not see any point in sacrificing any more men under those circumstances. Our rations were finished, we had very little ammunition left, and the monsoons had started. On 13 May, at about 19:00 hours, we left the village of Niata and halted in a thick jungle to spend the night. There, in that tropical forest, at the time of setting sun, I gave my last lecture as divisional commander to my men – the gallant men who had stood by me through terrible ordeals and privations.

I thanked them for the glorious manner in which they had fought for India's Independence, and for the fortitude with which they had faced all hardships. I explained to them how on account of the change in world situation and, owing to the invention of the atom bomb and collapse of Germany, the struggle which we had waged for nearly two years, had become hopeless, and that it was by no means the end of their struggle for the achievement of their final goal – the liberation of India. We had to change our tactics alone. The struggle for Indian Independence had to go on, whether we had any allies or not. I told them that the best course for them was to surrender to the Allies and go into India. Those who survived must start the struggle again for Indian Independence from inside India.

I told them that as far as I was concerned I could not induce myself to surrender to the British, and that I had made up my mind to make a suicidal attack on the British forces and end my life that way. I then asked for 50 volunteers who would come with me prepared for the suicidal attack. The 300 men and all officers came forward. I explained to them that we had very little money left, with which we could buy rations and that 50 was the maximum number that I required. Colonel Dhillon then selected men out of the 300 volunteers. I then bid farewell to the rest and gave them orders to surrender. I detailed Major Jagir Singh and Major A. B. Singh to go with the party. It was perhaps the most painful day in my life to have to depart from the comrades who had stood by me through all kinds of hardships. I saw some of those gallant soldiers sobbing like children, those soldiers who had stood up unflinchingly to the most violent attacks of the enemy. Some of those who had volunteered to come with me, but who had not been selected, loaded their rifles, and with one shout of 'Jai Hind' began to shoot themselves. In this way six of them took their own lives. In the end I collected them again and talked to them. I told that if there was one more case of suicide, I, too, would shoot myself. This put an end to further suicides.

That night we all spent together and the following day I marched off the party under Major A. B. Singh and Jagir Singh to go and report to the British. When they had left, I, with my party of 50 men, which included Colonel Dhillon, Major Mehar Dass and some other officers, marched off into the heart of the Pegu-Yoma, mountains. There we proposed to make a base and carry put suicidal guerrilla attacks on the enemy. On the evening of 14 May, we reached a small village called Loga where we spent the night. By now heavy rains had set in, and we were obliged to take shelter in a village at night. All the villages were full of British spies and where ever we went our movements were reported to the British and as we were dependent for our rations upon local villagers, we could not disappear into jungles.

In the meantime, the British, having consolidated their position, were closing in on us. We found it difficult on account of the attitude of the local inhabitants to obtain information regarding the enemy to enable us to attack them successfully. This state of affair continued for the next few days. During this period, I was trying to get myself killed as I did not wish to be captured alive by the British. It was also my desire to inflict the maximum losses on the enemy before I died.

Eventually, on the night of the 17 May, at about 11, on a bright moon lit night we arrived in the vicinity of a village, Sitpinzeix. I halted the party a few hundred yards outside the village and myself with three men went forward to reconnoitre the village for spending the night there.

As I reached the entrance to the village, someone shouted in Hindustani, 'Tum kon ho?' 'Who are you?' I replied that we were Indians. They again shouted, 'Tum kon ho?' I shouted back, 'Tum Kon Ho' and I told them that we were the men of the Indian National Army thinking that they were probably our own men who had refused to go and surrender to the British. As soon as they knew that we were men of the I.N.A. I heard a British officer shout 'Rapid Fire'. On this order from a range of approximately 15 yards, intensive rifle and machine-gun fire was opened on us. All three of my companions who were on my right, left, and one in front were killed outright, and a leather hand bag which contained my diaries, and was produced at the time of my trial in the court martial in the Red Fort, was shot out of my hand. I remained untouched through some miracle. I walked back to my party and brought them up, attacked this British position and forced them to abandon it.

Since our route was blocked, I decided to go back a few hundred yards and took up a defensive position.

The following morning, I took the party to a place which was only 500 yards away from the main British artillery position, with the object of making our last charge at them and getting killed. When we reached there we found that we were completely surrounded on all sides by British troops. I then called a meeting of all my men and told them that there were three ways by which we could choose our death. The first, and perhaps the easiest one, was to commit suicide by shooting ourselves. I did not favour this method as it was a cowardly death. The second method was to charge into the enemy guns, and either destroy them or get destroyed ourselves. This I explained to my men was glorious death, perhaps the ideal death a soldier could wish for. And the third method was to allow ourselves to be captured by the British and to be shot by them. In my own mind I had no doubt whatsoever, what the British would do if they captured me alive. The advantage of this I told my men was that we would probably be taken to India, court martialled, and then shot. There was a faint ray of hope that we might have an opportunity of telling the full facts about our movement to our countrymen, and then, of course, there was a hope that our graves may be on Indian soil.

I left the final choice to my officers and men. Colonel Dhillon then spoke. He said we must rule out the first method, that of committing suicide. The second, he said, while it was a glorious method of dying would end there. The third one, he said, was the best, firstly because if we had to die, it was better to let the British do the dirty work of shootings, and this he said, 'Would leave the roots of hatred against the British in the minds of our relative and countrymen, who may one day feel it their duty to avenge our deaths.' He, therefore, favoured the last course and majority supported him.

Consequently, we were captured by the men of an Indian battalion and taken to the Battalion Headquarters, where we were treated kindly. We were than taken to the Brigade Divisional Headquarters and eventually to a jail at Pegu.

While I was at the British Military Headquarters, several Indian and English officers and other ranks gathered round me. One senior British officer talked to me in a very arrogant manner. He asked me certain questions to which I replied in an equally arrogant manner. Here is the exact conversation as it took place:

B.O.:   What were you fighting for?
Reply: We were fighting for the Independence of our country.
B.O.:   Why did you surrender then?
Reply: You should not ask me this question, you know the reason very well. The British are experts in surrendering. What happened to you at Dunkirk and Singapore?

This irritated him very much. He then asked again.
B.O.:   What would you do if you were taken to India and released?
Reply: I will continue the struggle for India's freedom.
B.O.:   How much pay were the Japanese giving you?
Reply: The Japanese were not giving me any pay. Our Netaji was giving us pay. My pay as a Divisional Commander was rupees 250 per month, and its actual buying value was equivalent to the price of chickens.
B.O.:   Where did your Netaji get his money from?
Reply: It was donated by Indian civilians by voluntary contributions.

At this, he was infuriated and banging his foot on the ground said, 'I hope they will shoot you,' and then went away. This conversation between us spread like wildfire among the Indian troops who had been led to believe that the I.N.A. was a Japanese army. When I was in custody, large numbers of them would come to me to know all about the I.N.A., and when they were told the full facts about the I.N.A. they used to feel very sorry, and said that they had been misled by the British propaganda, and that had they known the full facts earlier they would have also joined the I.N.A.

The next day, I was taken to the interrogation centre where I stayed for about twenty days. There I was treated very well. The officer commanding was an Irishman.

From Pegu, I was sent under escort to Rangoon and then flown to Calcutta. There I was in charge of British Military Police. From Calcutta, I was brought to Delhi under an armed escort of four Gurkha officers and men. This journey was very interesting. Before my departure from Calcutta at the police lock up, the officer in charge of my escort was called up and given full instructions. He was told, 'The person you are escorting is a very dangerous and a great enemy of the British Government. If you are slack he will snatch your Tommy gun and shoot you or escape from the compartment. If he escapes, you will be either shot or imprisoned. So, be on the alert and shoot at the least suspicion.'

The Gurkha officer then sprang to attention and said that he would do exactly as he had been told. I was then taken in a closed van to the station and there I was put in a first class compartment reserved for us. Outside the compartment written in big block letters was, 'Dangerous Prisoner. No one allowed in.' The Gurkha guards were as alert as they had been asked to be. As soon as the train moved I lay down on a separate berth. The Gurkha Subedar then distributed his three men so as to form a ring round me. He then asked them to load their Tommy guns and put the safety catches forward. Whenever I happened to move my leg or arm, all the four guns were turned on me, and I am really surprised why with all this nervousness one of the guns did not go off.

This state of affairs continued throughout the first day and night. The following morning, after he had carefully watched me, the Subedar came to the conclusion that I was a normal human being. During all this time, they had not spoken even one word to me. The Subedar then came to me and asked who I was and what crime I had committed. I told him that I was an officer of the Indian National Army, who had gone to Malaya to fight for the British, but later when the I.N.A. was raised I joined it to fight for India's Independence.

He could not understand all this, and asked me to explain the reasons which had compelled me, who was a well-paid officer, to join the I.N.A. and fight against the British Sarkar. This officer, incidentally, had been fighting against my unit at the Chin Hill, and he had his own ideas about the I.N.A.

I asked him if it was a fact that in actual fighting the Indian and Gurkha troops were always in the forefront, and the Tommies always in rear. He agreed. I then asked him if his soldiers, the Gurkhas and the British Tommy received the same pay. He replied in the negative; and said that the tommy received at least four times as much pay as an Indian or Gurkha sepoy. I then asked him the reason for this. I told him that when it is the question of facing the bullets of the enemy they were in the forefront, why then should the Tommy receive more pay than the Indian sepoy?

He began to think very hard and in the end he said, 'Sahib, it is an injustice.' I explained to him that it was against this injustice in the difference in pay, rations, pensions, accommodation and travelling facilities, and the rude behaviour of the British officers with the Indian soldiers, that the I.N.A. had fought the British.

He again began to ponder deeply and eventually said, 'If this was that the I.N.A. fought for, they did very well.'

He then asked me who our commander-in-chief was. I showed him a photograph of Netaji. He looked at it with great admiration, and said, 'Oh, then even Indians can become commander-in-chief.'

He then opened out his heart to me. He said it was the British who were making such indiscrimination between the Indian and British sepoys. He told me that the Americans had raised a battalion of Burma-born Gurkhas, and that they were paying the same salary to Gurkhas as to their own white soldiers.

On hearing all this, his attitude changed immediately. He ordered his men to unload their guns and apologized for his officious behaviour on the previous day.

I have merely mentioned this incident to show how the minds of Indians as a whole, and of soldiers in particular, had been poisoned against the I.N.A. and how quickly that false propaganda was exposed and its effects nullified.

On the evening of 14 June 1945, I reached Delhi and was taken straight to the Red Fort. I was interrogated for about one month and then tried by a court martial, the details of which I would not like to repeat as these are well known to the Indian people.

I will now turn to the fate of the other two divisions of the I.N.A. First, the No. 1 Division which was at Pyinmana and most of the personnel of which were in hospital.

As already stated before, the regiment was formed out of the remnants of this division and was placed under the command of Colonel Thakur Singh. The regiment fought gallantly until it was overtaken by tanks and armoured columns, and all routes of its withdrawal were blocked by the enemy. Toungoo and Pegu were occupied. Colonel Thakur Singh then decided to strike east into the mountains, cross Siltang and reach Papun in Siam Thailand. This trek across huge mountains without any maps or guides and almost no rations was a most remarkable feet. From Papun, our men marched to Moulmein and then to Bangkok.

Most of the soldiers were men of the Subhas Brigade, which had reached Kohima. These soldiers had started marching in February 1944, and since then were on the move the whole time. During this period they must have covered over 3,000 miles on foot, on extremely poor rations and without any kind of transport. This remarkable trek and the spirit of our soldiers was admired even by our opponents.

While crossing huge tropical mountains, our men were continuously harassed by enemy guerrilla groups. They were also extremely short of rations and had to live on leaves and jungle grass for several days. They were eventually persuaded to lay down their will, when the British forces arrived at Bangkok in September 1945. The rest of the No. 1 Division surrendered at Zeyawadi.

CHAPTER EIGHT

NETAJI'S DEPARTURE FROM RANGOON

In the middle of April 1945, Japanese resistance on the line of Toungoo collapsed very unexpectedly, and the enemy advanced rapidly. The Japanese approached Netaji and asked him to be prepared to leave Rangoon. At first, he refused to do so and told them that he would stay behind at Rangoon and fight to the last.

Eventually, he was persuaded by all senior officers to go back to Bangkok. The Japanese placed a special plane at his disposal, but he refused to go by air. There were a large number of the Rani of Jhansi girls in Rangoon. Netaji knew that if he went by plane, they might be left behind. He, therefore, told the Japanese that he would not leave Rangoon until all girls of the Rani of Jhansi Regiment were evacuated first. The Japanese promised that they would arrange a railway train for the Rani of Jhansi girls from Rangoon to Waw on the evening of 23 April. But, unfortunately for us, the train was bombed and the railway engine destroyed in the afternoon. In the meantime, the enemy was pressing extremely hard and was very close to Pegu. Once Pegu was captured, it would have meant that no troops could be evacuated to Thailand. All the Japanese left Rangoon on 23 April, but Netaji refused to move until the Rani of Jhansi girls were evacuated first. In this grave situation, he was very calm indeed. He looked into every minor detail and himself issued instructions to all commanders.

He made arrangements for sending all the Rani of Jhansi girls who lived in Burma to their homes. All those who were from Malaya and Thailand were to accompany him. Before he left, he issued a Special Order of the Day thanking the Burmese people for their help and cooperation extended to him and to his government.

He sent another message to the Indians living in Burma and to the soldiers of the Azad Hind Fauj thanking them for their kindness and for the great sacrifices they had made. With what wonderful dignity and grace he left Rangoon!

To my Indian and Burmese friends in Burma!

Brothers and Sisters! I am leaving Burma with a very heavy heart. We have lost the first round of our fight for Independence. But we have lost only the first round. There are many more rounds to fight. In spite of our losing the first round, I see no reason for losing heart.

You, my countrymen in Burma, have done your duty to your Motherland in a way that has evoked the admiration of the world. You have given liberally your men, money and material. You set the finest example of total mobilization. But the odds against us were overwhelming and we have temporarily lost the battle in Burma.

The spirit of selfless sacrifice which you have shown, particularly since I shifted my Headquarters to Burma, is something that I shall never forget so long as I live.

I have the fullest confidence that that spirit can never be crushed. For the sake of India's Freedom, I beseech you to keep up that spirit, I beseech you to hold your heads erect, and wait for that blessed Day when once again you will have an opportunity of waging the War for India's Independence.

When the history of India's Last War of Independence comes to be written, Indians in Burma will have an honoured place in that history.

I do not leave Burma of my own free will. I would have preferred to stay on here and shared with you the sorrow of temporary defeat. But on the pressing advice of my Ministers and high-ranking officers, I have to leave Burma in order to continue the struggle for India's liberation. Being a born optimist, my unshakable faith in India's early emancipation remains unimpaired and I appeal to you to cherish the same optimism.

I have always said that the darkest hour precedes the dawn.

We are now passing through the darkest hour; therefore, the dawn is not far off. INDIA SHALL BE FREE.

I cannot conclude this message without publicly acknowledging once again my heart-felt gratitude to the Government and people of Burma for all the help that I have received at their hands in carrying on this struggle. The day will come when free India will repay that debt of gratitude in a generous manner.

* * *

Brave Officers and Men of the Azad Hind Fauj!

It is with a heavy heart that I am leaving Burma – the scene of the many heroic battles that you have fought since February 1944, and are still fighting. In Imphal and Burma, we have lost the first round in our Fight for Independence. But it is only the first round. We have many more rounds to fight. I am a born optimist and I shall not admit defeat under any circumstances. Your brave deeds in the battle against the enemy on the plains of Imphal, the hills and jungles of Arakan and the oilfield area and other localities in Burma will live in the history of our struggle for Independence for all time.

Comrades! At this critical hour, I have only one word of command to give you, and that is that if you have to go down temporarily, then go down as heroes; go down upholding the highest code of honour and discipline. The future generation of Indians who will be born, not as slaves but as free men, because of your colossal sacrifice, will bless your names and proudly proclaim to the world that you, their forbearers, fought and lost the battle in Manipur, Assam and Burma, but through temporary failure you paved the way to ultimate success and glory.

My unshakable faith in India's liberation remains unimpaired. I am leaving in your safe hands your National Tricolour, our National honour, and the best traditions of Indian warrior. I have no doubt whatsoever that you, the vanguard of India's Army of Liberation, will sacrifice everything, even life itself, to uphold India's National honour, so that your comrades who will continue the fight elsewhere may have before them your shining example to inspire them at all time.

If I had my own way, I would have preferred to stay with you in adversity and shared with you the sorrow of temporary defeat. But on the advice of my minister and high-ranking officers, I have to leave Burma in order to continue the struggle for emancipation. Knowing my countrymen in East Asia and inside India, I can assure you that they will continue the fight under all circumstances and that all your suffering and sacrifices will not be in vain. So far I am concerned, I shall steadfastly adhere to the pledge that I took on the 21st of October, 1943, to do all in my power to serve the interests of 38 crores of my countrymen and fight for their liberation. I appeal to you, in conclusion, to cherish the same optimism as myself and to believe, like myself that the darkest hour always precedes the dawn. India shall be free and before long.

May God bless you.
INQUILAB ZINDABAD! AZAD HIND ZINDABAD!
JAI HIND!
(Sd.) SUBHAS CHANDRA BOSE.
Supreme Commander,
AZAD HIND FAUJ

Dated: 24 April, 1945.

The following evening, 24 April, his convoy of 15 lorries carrying the Rani of Jhansi girls, and six cars carrying his Headquarter staff, left Rangoon for Bangkok at 22:00 hours. Six hundred men of the 'Janbaz' were ordered to march to Bangkok under Major P. S. Raturi. All the rest of the troops, totalling approximately 5,000, were left behind in Rangoon under the command of Major General A. D. Loganathan. The duty allotted to these men was to look after and protect the life, honour and property of Indian civilians residing in Rangoon. This was considered very necessary, owing to the rebellion of the Burmese army and withdrawal of all Japanese military and police forces. There was no law and order in Rangoon. On such occasions, it was the habit of Burmese dacoits to loot and rape Indian civilians. It was to prevent this that Netaji left behind a powerful force of the I.N.A.

in Rangoon to maintain law and order. This duty our men carried out very creditably, especially units commanded by Lt. Col. Jivvan Singh, and won the everlasting gratitude of the Burmese and Indian civilians alike.

On the morning of 25 April, at about 06:00 hours, his convoy reached a small village north of Pegu on the Rangoon-Moulmein road. It was a very hazardous night journey that Netaji had gone through. All the Japanese had gone and Burmese guerrillas were most active on this road and were shooting up all transport. Fortunately, Netaji's convoy got through without and mishap. He always seemed to have plenty of luck. On the following day, the British occupied Pegu, had he not gone through that night, he would probably have been either killed or captured there.

The rest of this eventful journey is described vividly in the diary of the Commander of the Rani of Jhansi detachment, Lt. Miss Janaki Thevers. It reads:

25 April: On the previous night, Netaji had no rest. He personally allotted lorries and seats to everyone, and gave instructions for the order of march. Throughout our journey, he has been checking up all the lorries in the convoy… Today, he is up again early in the morning, allotting dispersal areas to the lorries, and to all the troops. He is wonderful. He goes into every minor detail himself. Having done this, Netaji went for a cup of tea… Through sleeplessness his eyes are red but he looks quite fit. After this, Netaji sends food to all areas and then personally visited each area. He is very reckless today. Numerous enemy fighting planes are hovering above us, but he does not seem to take notice of them. I am accompanying Netaji wherever he goes… must look after him… We reach Colonel Mallick's area, where Netaji sits down to have a little rest, then starts shaving… suddenly three enemy fighter planes arrived and started circling above the trees under which we were resting. All of us took cover. Netaji continued to shave and refused to enter the trench. Luckily, the planes did not spot us and went away without firing at us. After this, Netaji decided to visit another area where our girls were resting. As we were going through the open paddy fields, six enemy fighter planes arrived. I told Netaji to be down and take cover, but unfortunately there was no cover. I was terribly nervous, not on account of the fear of enemy planes, but because of Netaji's safety. On seeing the enemy planes Netaji sat down, lighted a cigarette and started smoking. The planes missed us; why is it that he is always having miraculous escapes? I think he is charmed against danger. Nothing can happen to our Netaji until India is free. It is nearly 16:00 hours now. Netaji had a little rest and when he woke up he took out a map and studied it carefully. He called up a staff officer, and ordered him to send a motorcyclist to meet the Janbaz unit and to warn them to leave the road and come by the railway line, as there was danger of enemy tanks breaking through. This order comes just in time. I heard from Colonel Raturi that a few minutes after they had left the road, enemy tanks came charging down it. Our men had just been saved. Did Netaji have a premonition? At about 18:00 hours, we received orders to prepare to move. Netaji is going from place to place. It is raining very heavily. He is thoroughly drenched. At last our convoy is on the road. There are hundreds of other Japanese lorries, all racing to Waw to get across the Sittang River before being caught up by British tanks. The road is in a terrible condition. Netaji's car skidded and went into a ditch about 8 feet deep, but thank God, he is unhurt. We have to leave that car there.

26 April: At last we reached Waw at about 02:00 hours on 26 April. There is no bridge over the Waw River, we have to cross it by ferries. The Japanese are using all the ferries themselves. We have one ferry allotted to us. The Japanese General Isoda, who is attached to Netaji's staff, came and suggested to Netaji to cross over first, the rest, he said, would follow afterwards. Netaji told him, 'Go to hell, I will not cross over till all the girls have gone across first,' was Netaji's reply. Colonel Mallick and Major Swami went and reconnoitred the river. They found that at one place it was only six feet deep. I ordered all the girls to march to that place and swim across. They did so carrying their rifles with them. Netaji is directing ferrying of lorries across the river. All the girls are across the river, although some of them were nearly drowned, but thanks to Colonel Mallick's height, he saved them. It is nearly day light now… we are getting very worried about Netaji. He is still on the other side of the river. Enemy planes are expected any moment. At last, Netaji has come by the last ferry. He has been working throughout the night and has managed to get across six lorries. Others must remain on the other side of the river for the day, because no movement, not even of individuals, is possible during daytime owing to enemy planes. Netaji has left full instructions with the officer in charge of the convoy.

26 April: We have prepared some tea for Netaji. When he arrived we asked him to have a little rest and a cup of tea, but for Netaji there is no rest. He had a very hurried cup of tea and went personally to see that all the lorries are properly concealed and camouflaged. Today, Netaji again allotted dispersal areas to all units. He is indefatigable. Rani of Jhansi have been allotted a small village where they will spend the day. This village is situated near the river and it looks very dangerous. Enemy planes are sure to search it. There are no trenches either. All the villagers have deserted. Anyhow, we have to take our chance, luckily there are plenty of trees in the village. We can take shelter under these, as long as the planes do not spot us we may be saved. At about 15:00 hours, six British fighter planes arrived and started hovering over our area. We all took shelter behind tree trunks. General Chatterji tried to make Netaji take cover in a small shell hole, on this, Netaji became very angry. He told General Chatterji, 'How can I get inside a trench when the girls have no shelter?' Netaji just kept standing and smoking a cigarette. Netaji's cool and calm manner under most adverse conditions inspires all of us. Enemy planes attacked our area for half an hour. Five of our lorries were burnt. We have very little transport left with us… It was a terrible machine gunning that we experienced today. Bullets were whizzing past our heads… It was just a miracle how Netaji, in spite of not taking any cover, could escape without even a scratch.

27 April: Our convoy started off soon after midnight but unfortunately we could not make much progress as, due to heavy rain and mud, all our transport got stuck in the mud. Netaji left the convoy in charge of Colonel Chopra and with the Rani of Jhansi he marched off on foot to cover the last ten miles to the Sittang River. The enemy, we are told, is hot on our heels. Once we get across the Sittang River, we will be safe for the time being. Powerful Japanese forces are taking up defensive position on the east bank of the river. We crossed the river just before day break. Our convoy also arrived at Sittang ferry early in the morning. Today Netaji's headquarters were again bombed and machine gunned, and Lt. Nazir Ahmed, who was taking cover in a trench next to Netaji, was killed.

We could only get one lorry and Netaji's car across the ferry, all the rest have been abandoned. There are thousands of Japanese lorries that have been left there too. Enemy planes are burning all these.

From now on, we have to march on foot. Roads are nearby knee deep in mud which is being continuously churned up by heavy traffic… My girls are wonderful, each one of them is carrying her own pack, containing all their belongings, rations and ration looking tins, rifles, ammunition and hand grenades... We are taking no chances, there are plenty of enemy guerrilla troops in the area, we are prepared to fight them any time. Each girl is carrying as much as 35 lbs. in her pack. Netaji is marching at the head of the column, also carrying his own pack. We marched throughout that night and covered 10 miles.

28 April: In the morning we reached a village and took cover there for the day. The Janbaz unit has also arrived... We are now nearly 1,000 strong. In the evening we marched again and covered 15 miles at night... Going is very heavy indeed, we are becoming night birds, we do all our marching at night and rest during the daytime, and thanks to the excellent night training given by our instructors, we now feel no inconvenience in marching at night.

29 April: Today as we were resting, I asked Netaji to take off his heavy boots to give rest to his feet and to give me his socks for washing. As he took off his boots and sock, I was shocked to see that his feet were a mass of blisters. Netaji's car is following us, but he never thinks of using it, we all persuaded him to go by car, but he would not hear of it. In the evening, we start marching again. Netaji, as usual, is at the head of the column and in spite of his blisters we again covered 15 miles tonight. The Japanese General accompanying Netaji requested him to go by car. Netaji refused. All the Japanese then got into their cars and drove off to Moulmein. Tonight we had to cross several streams by ferries. The Janbaz unit could not cross over today. They are on the far side of Bilin. Netaji has decided to wait for them. In the evening General Isoda of the Liaison Department returned from Moulmein with some lorries and told Netaji that he and the Rani of Jhansi should go by motor lorries and the Janbaz unit would follow-on foot.

Netaji was annoyed with the Japanese. He feels that they are trying to bluff him, and once he leaves any troops behind they might find themselves in difficulties, especially in crossing ferries under Japanese control. There are thousands of Japanese also retreating with us, and it is only because Netaji is with us that we have a priority in crossing over.

The Japanese General again approached Netaji and requested him to go by car.

Netaji was furious; he turned round to him and said, 'Do you think I am Be Maw of Burma that I will leave my men and run for safety I have told you repeatedly that I will not go unless my men have gone ahead.' On this the Japanese General quietly walked away. Poor devils, they hate walking, but they too, have to walk when Netaji is walking. That night we walked another 15 miles and on the morning of 30 April, we reached a small village on the out skirts of Moulmein.

1 May: On the following morning, we arrived in Moulmein. During the last six days that we have been on the move, Netaji has hardly slept for more than two hours a day. We were marching at night and by day everyone except Netaji rested. He spent the whole day looking after our comfort.

On arrival in Moulmein, there is no rest for Netaji, he is working like one inspired. He is arranging for our food and accommodation. It was excellent food after six days of semi-starvation, but we were so tired that none of us could eat anything.

Tonight, Netaji has arranged for all girls to be evacuated by train from Moulmein to Bangkok. He has detailed General Chatterji and Colonel S. A. Mallick to accompany us.

He, himself, is staying behind in Moulmein to arrange for the transportation of the Janbaz Unit. We are allotted a few good wagons and are packed in those like sardines, anyhow it is better than marching in mud. Our train left Moulmein late at night.

2 May: At about 01:00 hours, after covering approximately 20 miles our train halted and we were told that a bridge had been blown up by American bombers. They are a terrible nuisance. It is with the sheer weight of metal that they are winning this war. General Chatterji has gone to talk to some Japanese to obtain more information. He returned after a tedious business to extract any type of information from the Japanese. They do not understand our language and we do not understand theirs. Our Japanese interpreter has been left behind with Netaji at Moulmein. I understand that we have to march another 16 miles to reach the next railway station. We started off at about 02:00 hours. On the way Colonel Mallick managed to hire three bullock carts. He is such a resourceful officer. We put all our packs on bullock carts. It is such a relief. My shoulders are aching, the leather straps have cut into my shoulders, without the pack we can march any distance. We marched all night and in the morning reached the railway station.

3 May: We spent the day in the vicinity of the station. British and American planes seem to be everywhere. Even this little station they did not spare, but the Japanese are very clever too. Long before day-break they disengaged all the wagons from the railway engines from each other and dispersed them one by one all over the railway lines, so as to appear damaged by enemy planes.

They are extremely short of rolling-stock particularly railway engines. They have commandeered, almost all the railway engine from Malaya and Siam. They hide their railway engines with great care.

In some places, they have made tunnels in mountains for hiding them. In other places, they have constructed bamboo shelters over the railway line. There are several of these shelters and the railway engine is always being changed from one to the other. These bamboo shelters are very well camouflaged and from top they appear as if there is no tunnel, they resemble railway lines, but in spite of this British planes always seem to spot and destroy them.

On the evening of 3 May, we entrained again and before we reached Bangkok, three days later, we had to go through several such transhipments, as the railway line and bridges were very badly smashed up by enemy bombers. On our way we were visited twice by Netaji. He is travelling by car, and is constantly in touch with the 'Janbaz' Unit and with us. We reached Bangkok on the morning of 7 May. Netaji had arrived the day before us, and had already made excellent arrangements for our accommodation, clothing, rations, milk and fruit. The following day 'Janbaz' units also arrived. They had to march very long distances. In fact, they have been on the march since early January 1944. They are mostly men of the 1st Battalion of the Subhas Brigade, which had operated under Major P. S. Raturi, in the Kaladan Valley. Most of them are suffering from malaria and are very weak. Within a very brief space of time through excellent food we are all fit again.

20 May: We have received information that 1,000 men of the 'X' Regiment, under the command of Colonel Thakur Singh, are making their way across huge mountains and virgin forests to Bangkok via Papun and Moulmein. We had not expected this as the enemy tank columns had broken through and had overtaken the 'X' Regiment in the area of Pyinmana. But our men had achieved what appeared the impossible to most soldiers. There was no accommodation or any arrangement for their rations. For four days Netaji worked day and night nearly 20 hours a day hiring houses, visiting each area, allotting accommodation within those four days with the cooperation of the Indian Independence League and through the strenuous efforts of Netaji's staff, officers camps were in good order to accommodate the 'X' Regiment.

27 May: The 'X' Regiment has arrived. They are in a terrible condition – almost semi-starved. They have had to march over 1,000 miles to meet Netaji. Since they left Pyinmana early in March, they had been on the move the whole time. Netaji had made excellent arrangements for their clothing and feeding. Every man and woman of the force that arrived from Burma is getting a pound of milk and fresh fruits daily, men are regaining their strength very rapidly.

Early in June Netaji left Bangkok for Malaya on a tour of inspection of the No. 3 Division which was under the command of Colonel G. R. Nagar. Soon afterwards, rumours were heard that the Japanese were negotiating terms of surrender. On 11 August, news of the official surrender of the Japanese was announced to the world.'

During this period, June to August 1945, Netaji was occupied with an extensive inspection tour of all I.N.A. units which were dispersed throughout Malaya. In July they celebrated Netaji week throughout Malaya and Siam. During this week to commemorate the heroic deeds of the Azad Hind Fauj, Netaji laid the foundation stone of the war memorial to its *shaheeds*. This magnificent memorial was completed late in August 1945. Colonel C. J. Stracey, who was a Staff Officer to Major–General M. Z. Kiani, worked day and night over this memorial and it was chiefly due to his efforts that this memorial was completed before the British forces bombed Singapore. As is well known to everyone that the British who claim to be guardians of modern civilization, put dynamite under this sacred memorial to the martyrs of the Azad Hind Fauj and blasted it. They were frightened that the loyalty of the soldiers of the British India Army would be affected by this. Their intention was to eliminate even the memory of those people who have sacrificed their lives so generously for the cause of Indian Independence. They realized that the memorial was a monument, the very sight of which would shatter the false propaganda which the British had created in the minds of the British Indian soldiers. But the memories of those 'Shaheeds' were not to be forgotten by the Indians so easily. The Azad Hind Fauj was under detention, but the local civilians went and placed every day fresh wreaths of flowers on the heap of brick and mortar which had once been the glorious memorial to the Azad Hind Fauj. The British posted sentries over it to stop people doing this. Still the practice continued. Indian sentries had not the heart to stop people from doing this. Many of them were punished and sentenced to long terms of imprisonment. When Pandit Jawaharlal Nehru visited Malaya in April 1946 he also went to pay homage to the martyrs of the Azad Hind Fauj and placed a floral wreath on the spot where the memorial had stood. He was accompanied by the British Commander-in-Chief, Lord Louis Mountbatten and it is believed he also paid homage to this memorial... What a hypocrisy!

At about the same time when Simla negotiations were going on Netaji broadcast, several times his views on Lord Wavell's offer.

On 18 June 1945, he broadcasted:

> Sisters and brothers! I listened with great attention to the speech which the Viceroy of India, Lord Wavell, broadcast on June 14, from New Delhi conveying the offer of the British Government to India. That was the offer to bring which Lord Wavell made a long pilgrimage to London.
>
> At such a juncture, it would neither be untimely nor out of place to inform my countrymen at home as to how Indians in East Asia have reacted to the British Government's offer. First of all we found out, as the Viceroy has himself confessed, that the only motive of the British Government is to mobilize India's support in the war against Japan. The British people are war-weary and after the termination of the war in Europe they badly need rest, and as such, they want others to fight their battles while

they themselves reap the fruits of victory. But the British Indian troops, too, are war-weary, and after the recent successes of the Anglo-Americans in Burma they also desire rest and relaxation. It is, therefore, vital for the British to make the Indian people pour out their money and shed their blood for the preservation of the British Empire. While the fighting was going on inside India and along the Indo-Burma border, the British could bluff the British Indian Army with the preaching that it was their duty to fight for the defence of India. The British could also bluff them later on by preaching that the Burma campaign was merely a continuation of the campaign for the defence of India.

But now, that the British want India's blood and money for campaigns beyond Burma and for the campaigns in the Pacific, a new scheme must be found in order to obtain India's support for such campaigns. That is why the British Government has now put forward this new offer which is in reality Sir Stafford Cripps' old offer in a slightly altered garb.

In deciding what reply we Indians should give, we will have to consider what we stand to gain by fighting Britain's war against Japan. It is one thing for Britain to forcibly exploit India for her war of aggression but it is quite a different thing for Indian nationalists to voluntarily fight Britain's war. To cooperate in Britain's war effort at this stage will mean that we have completely nullified our moral struggle against the British. It will mean political suicide on the part of the Indian National Congress and for us Indians as well.

At an earlier stage of the war British propagandists and their Indian trumpeteers could possibly bluff and bamboozle the Indian people that India's defence was at stake as the Japanese were then knocking at India's gates. But now with the change in the war situation in East Asia, no Indian can have the slightest interest in fighting Britain's war against Japan. It is, therefore, crystal clear that any acceptance of Lord Wavell's offer will be tantamount to a voluntary shedding of precious Indian blood and draining our resources in fighting Britain's imperialistic war. But what would India gain in return? Nothing except a few jobs on Viceroy's Executive Council.

We cannot even argue that by accepting the offer we shall be reaching the 'goal of self-Government', which Lord Wavell and the British Government want us to believe. India does not care any longer for self-government within the British Empire, and India will never be content with anything less than complete independence. But even if any Indian is prepared to accept self-government he would have a much better chance of achieving that objective by continuing the resistance now than by accepting the present offer. The moment we accept the offer it will be inferred by the British Government that we are prepared to compromise by taking something very much less than even self-government. I have no doubt in my mind that the acceptance of this offer will seriously jeopardize all chances of securing even self-government in future, not to speak of complete independence. In short, by accepting the offer we shall gain nothing but we shall lose a lot, and it is Britain that will profit by our lack of strength.

Under normal circumstances, there would not be even a ten to one chance for any Indian nationalist to be enamoured of the present offer, but the British are cunning politicians and they have chosen the proper psychological moment for aiming this offer at India. British politicians are hoping that the Indian people are now overawed by recent Anglo-American victories. The Indian people may, therefore, feel that we stand no chance of achieving independence during the course of the present war and might as well make the best of a bad bargain and take whatever is being offered by the British. This is going to be the attitude of pessimists and moderate politicians like Sri Rajagopalachari, but this attitude is entirely mistaken and unjustified, and will inevitably result in putting back the clock of freedom by many years.

I shall refer to the merits of the British proposal. On close and careful analysis it will be found that the present proposal is in essence and in substance identical with that of Sir Stafford Cripps', offered to us in 1942. Three more seats on the Viceroy's Executive Council have been offered to us this time, for example, those of Home, Finance and External Affairs; for these and other portfolios the persons will be appointed by the Viceroy and will be responsible to him and not to the representatives of the people. On the other hand, the most important portfolio, that of the War Member, has been reserved for a Britisher namely, the C-in-C. While the present offer is the old offer of Sir Stafford Cripps appearing in a slightly altered form, there are other obnoxious features which render the offer totally unacceptable. In his speech the Viceroy has clearly indicated that he regards the Congress as one among many parties as has been the traditional policy of the British Government. This attitude was indignantly repudiated by Mahatma Gandhi at the Round Table Conference in London in 1931 when, as representative of the Congress, he represented the Indian people. If the Congress accepts the offer now it will repudiate once for all what it has consistently maintained, namely, that it represents the people of India; and it will accept what the British Government has repeatedly held, namely, that the Congress is one among many parties in India. I cannot, for the slightest moment, imagine how any Indian nationalist can think of accepting this offer.

There is another mischievous feature in Lord Waveil's offer. He has ordered the release of the member of the Working Committee of the Congress, but has maintained that unless his offer is accepted, all those who participated in the rising of 1942 will have to remain in custody. There is, nowhere, mentioned in his speech that even if his offer is accepted, those who were imprisoned in the year 1939 and 1942 will be set free. It is a well-established convention in all democratic centuries that a constitutional change is heralded by an amnesty for all political prisoners. In the case of India, however, this convention has been given the go-by.

The British Government has been telling us that no constitutional changes can be introduced during the course of the war though we have seen that throughout the world far reaching political changes are being carried out. Here in East Asia, we have seen quite a different state of affairs. Right in the midst of the war, several independent governments have been set up and power has been handed over to people. So, you see that this British plea is completely hollow and it is intended to delay and deny the Indian demand. If Britain really wants to set up a responsible government, she should lose no time in declaring India a self-governing nation and hand over power to the people's representatives.

Sisters and brothers in India! You have suffered long and suffered much from the political persecution and economic exploitation of British capitalism. Let us suffer a little longer. We have to resist British imperialism by all the moral and material means at our disposal, and above all, let us keep the flag of independence flying. By continuing our fight against imperialism, and by refusing to compromise over independence we shall be able to keep burning the question of India's freedom before the bar of world opinion. That is the way to freedom. On the other hand, by accepting the offer we will be humiliating ourselves and losing the moral sympathy of the world.

It may be that some of you are asking what is the best way for achieving the liberation of India. To that my answer is perfectly clear. Firstly, from outside India we shall carry on the armed struggle for our freedom to the last man and to the last round. Secondly, there are numerous friends of India abroad who advocate our cause before the bar of world opinion and in all international conference. And, lastly, my countrymen, you too must be prepared to launch a revolution at the opportune moment which will spread like the wild fire of the prairies and may even be supported by the British Indian forces.

Sisters and brothers! In conclusion, I appeal to you not to give up hope. I repeat that the forces that are now working inside India and outside are irresistible. There is no earthly power that can stop the Indian people from achieving their goal of freedom. With patience and determination we shall achieve our goal. The Viceroy has asked for your goodwill and co-operation. Tell him that your goodwill and cooperation has been reserved for India's struggle for liberty and for none else.

On 19 June 1945, he broadcasted:

Sisters and brothers in India! Yesterday I spoke in a general way about Lord Wavell's offer and what our reaction to it should be. Today I want to speak to you again on the same subject.

British and American news agencies have been giving detailed reports of the daily developments inside India. With the help of these reports it is possible to form a correct picture of what is going on inside our country. I would, beg you to consider first of all what the inevitable results of accepting Wavell's offer will be, because the Congress leaders will have to take the responsibility of sending at least half-a-million Indian troops to fight Britain's imperialist war, not on the Indo-Burma border of inside Burma, but in the regions beyond Burma and the Pacific. With all due respect I would like to ask Mahatma Gandhi, Maulana Abul Kalam Azad, Pandit Jawaharlal Nehru, Sardar Vallabhbhai Patel and other leaders whether they will take the responsibility of fighting Britain's imperialistic war in the Far East and of sacrificing half-a-million Indian lives for the same.

There are definite reasons as to why the British Government is unable to obtain from Britain itself the necessary fighting men needed for the future campaigns in the Far East. First of all, the British have suffered tremendous losses during the war on many fronts over a period of five years and nine months. As a result, the British people are war-weary and British troops are not willing to face another long campaign which will have to be fought under conditions much harder than in Europe. Secondly, unlike the First World War, this war has well-nigh brought about the financial bankruptcy of Britain. Owing to the pressure of war and the colossal demand for war material British industries had to switch over almost entirely to war production. This was not the case with American industries. The result was that during the war Britain has been fast losing her pre-war markets and these markets were steadily going into the hands of American industry. If this process goes on for a long time during this war then Britain, in spite of an Allied victory, will lose the greater portion of her pre-war foreign trade and will be economically ruined. Owing to this reason, British leaders find it imperative to release their factory workers from the fighting forces and war services as soon as possible and thereby restart peace-time industries. It is absolutely impossible for British to do both things at the same time, namely, to fight another long campaign in the Far East and to restart her peace-time industries.

I have no doubt in my mind that under normal circumstances nobody belonging to the Congress would have even looked at Lord Wavell's offer. In order to give their consideration to that offer, Congress men will have to give a go-by to the fundamental principles and beliefs of the Indian National Congress. The Congress stands for complete independence. Lord Wavell's offer, as has been rightly pointed out by Mahatma Gandhi, does not even mention the word 'independence.' Secondly, the Congress stands for non-participation in and resistance to Britain's imperialist war. Thirdly, the Congress is still pledged to the 'Quit India' resolution adopted three years ago, and the national slogan for the Indian people since then has been 'Do or Die' in the fight for India's freedom. No Congressman can, consistent with his principles, therefore look at Lord Wavell's offer not to speak of giving consideration to it. Nevertheless, the fact that so many Congressmen and leaders are actually considering the British offer it is because a wave of defeatism has swept over India since the Anglo-American successes in Europe and in Burma. In a fit of pessimism and defeatism, some Congressmen are forgetting their life-long principles and are now reconsidering the offer which they rejected in 1942.

What I want to tell my countrymen at home clearly and frankly is that the pessimism and defeatism which seems to have overtaken them is altogether unjustified. Whether one considers the international political situation or war situation, there is no cause for pessimism or despondency. The war in East Asia, whatever its ultimate result may be, is going to be a long and bitter one. The whole world knows that there is no real unity in the camp of the so-called

United Nations. The war aims of Soviet Russia are quite different from those of the Anglo-American Powers and the conflict between the Soviet and the Anglo-American is growing from day-to-day. Both sides have of late been tiring to patch up their differences in Europe, but that is because they are preparing for a showdown in the Far East. Since the collapse of Germany in Europe, Soviet Russia has been taking an increasing interest in the affairs of Asia. Had it not been for this, M. Molotov, the Soviet Foreign Minister, would not have declared at San Francisco that the day was not far off when the voice of Free India will be heard in the world.

While the war in the East will be going on, surprising developments are bound to take place in the domain of international affairs. Some of these developments will not be favourable to our enemies, and they will afford India further opportunities for achieving her independence. Syria and the Lebanon, in spite of the Allied victory in Europe, are fully utilizing the international situation for achieving their independence. By using England and the United States of America against French imperialism, Syria and the Lebanon are setting an example to India as to how India can utilize the present international situation for winning her freedom. There is no doubt that if today Syria and the Lebanon are using Britain and America against France, the day is not far off when other Arab States will use other friendly powers against Britain. British politicians realize this, and they realize also that India will utilize the support of friendly powers for winning her independence, and some of these friendly powers may come from inside the camp of the United Nations. During the course of this war, India has become a live issue in world politics, and there is no doubt that in all international conferences in future the Indian issue will be raised. British politicians, therefore, want to prevent India remaining an international issue any longer, and want to convert India into a domestic issue of the British Empire. Let us not forget that the moment there is a compromise between nationalist India and Britain, India will become a domestic issue of the Britain Empire, and it will then be impossible for foreign powers such as Soviet Russia to intervene on behalf of Indian independence.

Inspite of the recent military successes of our enemies, India has been making rapid progress towards her goal of independence. In addition to what the Indian people have been doing at home, two distinct forces have been working for India's independence. Firstly, those who have been fighting with arms against India's enemies, and secondly, those who have been advocating India's independence before the bar of world opinion. Those who have hitherto been fighting with arms against India's enemies shall go on fighting in future. So far as the Indian National Army is concerned, it will go on fighting to the last man and to the last round. Similarly, those who have made India an international issue and who have been advocating on India's behalf before the world will also go on doing so. The forces working outside India, coupled with the resistance inside India, are irresistible. If you, my countrymen at home, cannot fight British imperialism with arms, then at least keep up moral resistance to our enemy by refusing to compromise with him or to fight his imperialist war.

In this connection, I want to make an honest appeal to Mahatma Gandhi, to the President and members of the Congress Working Committee, and to the millions of Congressmen and Congress women who stand behind them that they should not judge the international situation wrongly at this critical moment. A mistake in appearing the international situation is likely to lead to a wrong step in Indian politics. India is not beaten. We have not fallen yet.

The present international situation is not unfavourable to us. On the contrary, it is much to our advantage and will become more so in the days to come. Why then should we think of a compromise now, why then should we accept the offer which we deliberately rejected three years ago?

I speak now as an ordinary member of the Congress, who throughout his whole public life has faithfully served the Congress and the cause of India's independence. Even if you, my sisters and brothers at home, feel that our allies will be ultimately defeated and that the Anglo-Americans will ultimately emerge triumphant, there is still no reason to despair so far as India is concerned. No matter what happens in world politics in future, India is bound to win. India's star is definitely in the ascendant. Do not try to drag it down by a wrong step at this juncture. We have suffered long and have suffered much. Let us suffer a little more, a little longer. But, by all means let us stick to our guns till the end of this war. Sisters and brothers at home, don't you understand why Lord Wavell is in such a beastly hurry? Don't you understand why he has rejected the suggestion of Mr Jinnah to postpone the Simla Conference? To us, outside India, the matter is very simple and very clear. The general election in Britain takes place on July 5. The Conservative Party wants to prevent India becoming an election issue. That is why Wavell's offer was flung upon us one month before the general elections in England. Nobody knows what the result of the general election may be. But everybody knows that whether the Labour Party gets a clear majority or not, it will, in any case, emerge much stronger in Parliament after July 5. The Conservative Party is afraid that if the Labour Party comes to power and if in the meantime the Indian problem is not settled, the Labour Party is bound to make another attempt to solve the Indian question. Personally, I do not believe in bargaining, because, for me there can be no compromise over India's independence. But if you are keen on bargaining, and if you are determined to compromise over India's independence, then I beg you not to commit yourselves before July 5. I do not know what was in the mind of Mr Jinnah when he asked for the postponement of the Simla Conference, but if he intended to avoid playing his trump card before July 5, then I must express my admiration for his political sagacity and farsightedness. I can make a clear prediction that Lord Wavell will move heaven and earth to arrive at a decision before July 5, if he succeeds, it will be a feather in the cap of the Conservative Party and will help considerably to swell the votes of the Conservative Party's candidates at the election. Moreover, if Lord Wavell succeeds in arriving at an agreement with the Congress before July 5, and if thereafter the Labour Party comes to power, then the Conservative Party will be able to prevent the Labour Cabinet reopening the Indian issue.

It is not my intention to say that I believe in bargaining with the Labour Party. Far from it. My own plan is clear, and that is to go on fighting with the Azad Hind Fauj to the last man and to the last drop of our blood. But if you are not prepared to go that way because you regard it as a perilous adventure, and if you are determined on bargaining with the British Government, then I should say that the time for bargaining is after July 5. If you do not come to an agreement with Lord Wavell before July 5, then you will help to swell the votes of the Labour Party's candidates at the general elections. We won't forget that both the Cripps offer and the Wavell offer have been made under the auspices of a predominantly Tory Cabinet. The Labour Party has, on both occasions, been a minority party, and the initiative and responsibility did not rest with the Labour leaders. If Lord Wavell fails in his endeavour, it is inevitable that the British public would like to give the Labour Cabinet another chance to tackle the Indian issue. Therefore, to sum up, if you believe in bargaining, then break with Lord Wavell and reject his offer. It will undoubtedly aid the Labour Party to come into office. After that the Labour Party will certainly take the initiative in reopening the Indian issue, hoping that it will succeed where the Conservative Party had failed. Remember, my conviction is that if there is any other Cabinet after July 5, that Cabinet will consider it as a matter of duty and necessity to solve a problem which has remained unsolved for a long time. Therefore, with the Labour Cabinet you can strike a bargain which will be much more advantageous to India than a bargain with Lord Wavell dictated by the Conservatives.

Sisters and brothers at home, I shall address you again tomorrow at about this time. Today before I close, I should like to say one thing more. You are now violently condemning the Viceroy and you are criticizing him for giving an equal number of seats in the Executive Council to caste Hindus and to Muslims. But why don't you go deeper into the question and find out the idea behind it? So far not one single Indian leader has done so, judging from the reports that are now before me. I regret that the members of the Hindu Mahasabha have taken what appears to be their own peculiar line. Our objection should not be to Muslims getting a majority of seats on the Executive Council. The moot question is what type of Muslims come into the Executive Council? If we have Muslims of the type of Maulana Abul Kalam Azad, Asaf Ali and Rafi Ahmed Kidwai the destiny of India will be safe. And I personally believe that it is only right to give all the freedom to such patriots. There is no difference between a patriotic Muslim and a patriotic Hindu. The British intention in the present case is to give all the Muslim seats to the nominees of the Muslim League. Seats reserved for the caste Hindus should all be given to the Congress. For the remaining seats the Viceroy will appoint his own nominee, who will act according to the Viceroy's directions.

Consequently, with the Muslim League acting in full cooperation with the British Government, the Congress Party in the Executive Council will become a permanent minority. Thus, by a clever stratagem the Viceroy will not only continue to rule India arbitrarily as he has done until now, but he will continue to do so in future with the help of the Congress.

Now the question arises as to whether the Muslim League members in the Executive Council will cooperate with the Viceroy. Personally, I am absolutely certain that they will do so because the Viceroy has agreed to give them a weightage in his Executive Council. If the Muslim League cooperates with the British Government in its war effort, then the British purpose of exploiting Indian manpower and resources for fighting Britain's imperialist war will be easily fulfilled.

I have no doubt in my mind that in the offer of Lord Wavell there is a secret understanding, either explicit or implicit, between the Muslim League and the British Government. But it is Mr Jinnah and his colleagues who will outwit Wavell. In the Executive Council the Muslim League Party will carry out Britain's war policy in order to realize their plan of Pakistan as a reward for the Muslim League's cooperation in Britain's war effort. The Congress Party, if it accepts this offer, will become a permanent minority in the Executive Council. Nevertheless, she will have to carry out Britain's war policy as part of the compromise. After cooperation of the Congress has been secured by the British Government through this clever stratagem the

British will try to get the Congress to agree to bring about the vivisection of India, namely, Pakistan. In the meantime, the Congress will have committed political suicide by accepting a position in which it will have admitted that it is not the representative of the Indian people, but only one party among several parties in India.

In conclusion, I want to say that though I do not agree with the line of approach of the members of the Hindu Mahasabha and of the anti-Pakistan front, I feel very strongly that they have done a great service to India by giving an outspoken expression of their opposition to Lord Wavell's plan. In fact, I should go one step further and say that at this critical juncture it is the duty of all right-thinking and patriotic Indians, particularly of all progressive Congressmen, to start a raging and tearing campaign all over the country against Lord Wavell's offer. Mahatma Gandhi has always been responsive to public opinion as a leader should be. By declining to represent the Congress officially at the Simla Conference, he has done the right thing and he kept himself free to adopt the line which he thinks is right and in accordance with the wishes of the people and in the true interests of India. I have no doubt in my mind that public opinion, and in particular, the opinion among the rank and file of the Congress, should oppose this plan without delay. Mahatma Gandhi will not fail to take notice of it and he will then advise the Congress to reject the unwanted offer. Sisters and brothers, the destiny of India now lies in your hands; be up doing and see to it that Lord Wavell's offer goes the same way as the Cripps' offer of 1942.

On 20 June 1945, Netaji broadcasted:

Sisters and brothers in India! I am going to speak to you today as I would have done if I had been with you at this critical juncture. I shall speak to you as one who has been with the Congress and has served the Congress with loyalty and devotion since 1921, through fair weather and foul. You remember very well, I hope, what political developments took place in India after September 1939 when the war broke out in Europe. At that time, the British Government wanted to use the Congress ministries in the Provinces for the prosecution of the war, but the Congress refused to cooperate in the war effort, and for two reasons: firstly, because India's national demand for independence had not been conceded by the British Government, and, secondly, because Britain's war was an imperialist war, in which India had no interest. At that time, there was no question of Congress ministries. Since the Congress decided not to cooperate in Britain's war in 1939, the Congress ministries resigned, although it was very clear to every Congressman that if these ministries had remained in office they could have done a lot of good to the Indian people in other matters. After the resignation of the Congress ministries the Congress gradually once again resumed the fight for freedom. The climax came in 1942 when the 'Quit India' Resolution was passed, and when the people were given a new slogan in their renewed struggle for liberty; the slogan of 'Do or Die.'

Now in the year of grace, 1945, we are confronted with Lord Wavell's offer. We are told that if the Congress agrees on wholehearted participation in the coming campaign in the Far East, then the Congress can get two things now plus a promise of self-government for the future. These two things are: firstly, some jobs on the Viceroy's Executive Council, and, secondly, the restoration of the Congress Ministries in the Provinces.

From the reports coming from India, it appears that some Congressmen are very favourably disposed towards

Lord Wavell's offer, which means that they are satisfied with the promise of self-government, not independence mind you, provided the Congress ministries in the Provinces are restored and a few jobs in the Viceroy's Executive Council are made available to Congressmen. But all these alluring offers have been before the Congress for a long time. First of all, the British have all along promised us self-government. Secondly, in the Provinces there were eight ministries under our control in 1939, and it is we, who decided that they should resign. Thirdly, jobs in the Viceroy's Executive Council have always been open to Congressmen who were prepared to sell themselves.

There are two new conditions in Lord Wavell's offer. Firstly, the number of jobs on the Viceroy's Executive Council has been increased. Secondly, there is the explicit condition that acceptance of the offer will mean their pledge of wholehearted participation in the coming campaign in the Far East. This was not the case when the Congress ministries tendered their resignation in 1939. The Congress ministries, if they had so desired, could have accepted the offer after 1939, without giving a clear pledge of wholehearted participation in Britain's war.

To those who are now eager to accept Lord Wavell's offer, I should like to put a few questions in order to clarify the issue before us. (i) What has happened to our goal of independence, to which there is not even a partial reference in Lord Wavell's offer? (ii) Does *Purna Swaraj* mean only Indianization of the Viceroy's Council, or does it mean complete independence and a total severance of the British connection? (iii) Why did the Congress ministries resign in 1939? (iv) What has happened to our slogan, 'Do or Die'? (v) Why did we condemn Congressmen like Shri Aney and Dr Khare for accepting jobs on the Viceroy's Executive Council?

Lord Wavell's proposal may best be described in the words of the late Vithalbhai Patel, as '*Swaraj* for the Viceroy,' but not even *swaraj* for the Executive Council. As to the Department of External Affairs being handed over to an Indian member, I feel that it will prove to be an eye-wash, because the affairs of Indian States, as well as those relating to tribal and frontier affairs, will be outside the jurisdiction of this member. Though there is no question of collective responsibility or majority rule in the new Executive Council and though the Viceroy and Governor-General will remain the same autocrat as before, he has to nevertheless hide his autocracy in the new Executive Council through an ingenious political device or strategy. This stratagem consists in providing for a permanent majority in the Executive Council which will stand by the Viceroy in all circumstances.

Sisters and brothers at home! At this critical hour, the destiny of India lies in your hands. Now is your time for starting the 'Quit India' campaign all over the country and thereby making it impossible for anyone to arrive at a compromise. Jai Hind.'

On 21 June 1945, Netaji said:
Sisters and brothers in India! During the last three days, I have been speaking to you from a broader point of view, both national and international, and I have also been considering the Indian problem in its proper setting, that is, against the international background.

I have no doubt in my mind that public opinion in India, and in particular the Congress organization, has moved much further in a revolutionary direction since the beginning of the present war in 1939. Consequently, if a plenary session of the Congress were held today or even a full meeting of an All-India Congress Committee,

Lord Wavell's offer would be rejected by an overwhelming majority. The British Government and Lord Wavell know the Indian situation and they realize that if the British offer had been left to the verdict of Congressmen in general or even to the All-India Congress Committee, then there would not be the slightest chance of its acceptance. They have, therefore, created a situation in which only the members of the Congress Working Committee will decide about Lord Wavell's offer on behalf of the Congress. According to the Congress constitution, the Working Committee cannot make a final decision on behalf of the Congress on such an all important issue.

I am, however, prepared to admit that if the Congress Working Committee had represented all sections of the Congress or if there had been a real emergency, there might have been some moral, though not legal, justification for the Congress Working Committee to handle this all-important issue on its sole responsibility. But it is well known that the Left Wing of the Congress, which is quite influential, is not represented on the Working Committee at all. And, nobody can maintain that there is such an emergency in the country that the Working Committee is obliged to make a momentous decision behind the back of the All-India Congress Committee and of the rank and file of the Congress. I can understand that the British Government, to achieve its own ends, has manoeuvred in such a way that Lord Wavell's offer has been placed not before the All-India Congress Committee or a plenary session of the Congress, but only before the Congress Working Committee, but I cannot understand why members of the Working Committee are walking into the trap cleverly laid by Lord Wavell. Apart from the provision of the Congress constitution, according to which the Working Committee is a mere executive body and not its deliberative or law-making body, from the purely moral point of view it is wrong and unfair for the Working Committee to dispose of a matter which will affect the entire future of the Congress and India for several decades. Even at this late hour, I honestly and humbly appeal to Mahatma Gandhi not to make a decision behind the back of the Congress. I make this appeal particularly because by accepting the Wavell offer we shall be receding from the progress already made and nullifying the fundamental principles and resolutions of the Congress, and we shall be undoing the work and sacrifices of the Congress over a long period.

If Indians at home do not give up resistance to British imperialism, nothing can prevent the attainment of India's independence by the end of this war. By a combination of resistance inside India, armed struggle in East Asia and the adoption of a realistic policy in the international field, India will certainly emerge as an independent nation by the time this war ends. But, for the achievement of our liberation internal struggle against the British has to be guaranteed. Armed struggle in East Asia, I am in a position to guarantee. I can also give this assurance that if resistance to British imperialism is kept up inside India, then India will remain an international issue, and diplomacy in the international field will be able to help our cause considerably. For the present, the British do not have much to worry about trouble inside India, but they are nevertheless afraid of two things. They are afraid that if moral resistance inside India continues, India will remain an international issue. They are also afraid that if the Indian people remain hostile to the British, it will be impossible for them to obtain adequate help from India in men and resources for the coming campaign in the Far East. The British know that without India's help in a large measure and in particular without the help of India's manpower they cannot win the war in the Far East. Lord

Wavell's offer is calculated to kill two birds with one stone: Firstly, the offer is a bait to guarantee India's wholehearted participation in Britain's imperialist war; secondly, it will convert the India issue into a domestic issue of the British Empire and thereby bring about a withdrawal of all help to India by the United Nations including Soviet Russia.

Before the members of the Working Committee decide to accept Lord Wavell's offer they should be prepared to sacrifice half-a- million Indian lives for Britain's imperialist war in the Far East. I have envisaged what the Congress stands to lose if it were to accept Lord Wavell's offer. Consequently, before deciding to accept the offer, members of the Working Committee will have to calculate carefully what they will gain thereby and whether that gain will compensate in adequate measure what we shall lose. It stands to reason that if what we gain is much less than what we lose, we should reject that offer as we rejected Sir Stafford Cripps' offer in 1942. There may be Congressmen who think that what we are thinking of doing now, we shall have to do that in the long run. This view is entirely erroneous. I have already remarked in a previous talk that even if the worst happens and India fails to obtain her freedom during the course of the present war, then we shall have another opportunity as soon as the present war comes to an end.

The change-over from war to peace is a period of unrest. During this period of unrest even a victorious power is at a disadvantage because it needs rest and relaxation. That is why the revolutions of Ireland and Turkey after the First World War revolutions, which failed during the war period, attained complete success after the termination of the war.

On reading a report which is before me today, I find that the Congress President, Maulana Abul Kalam Azad, said; 'If the present negotiations fail the Congress will wait till the end of the war before launching a further attempt.' I cannot agree with the Congress President that we should not renew the struggle at home while the war is on, but I agree with him that at the end of the war, if India still happens to be enslaved, Indians will again have another opportunity of launching a large-scale offensive against British imperialism, and I have no doubt in my mind that in that post-war campaign the demobilized members of present British-Indian Army will play a very important role.

In the Executive Council the chief position will be held by the British War Member, namely, the Commander-in-Chief. What the War Member will demand the Viceroy will certainly endorse. Consequently, next to the Viceroy the War Member will be all-powerful. So long as the Viceroy and the C-in-C act in concert they will be able to control all the departments. The other Executive Councillors will not be able to object because they will be illegally bound by their responsibility to the Viceroy and they will be morally bound by their pledge of wholehearted participation in the war. The Department of External Affairs, which is to be run by an Indian, will prove to be an eye-wash because foreign affairs will be excluded from its jurisdiction. The Member in charge of this Department will become like the Indian Defence Member of the Viceroy's Council who is in charge of Army canteens.

I have pointed out what we shall lose by accepting the offer. I shall now say something as to what more we shall lose if the Congress cooperates with the British Government for a period of time. Firstly, the independence movement as well as the freedom mentality of the Indian people will suffer a serious setback. And, lastly, by compromising with British imperialism the Congress will forfeit the sympathy of freedom-loving men and women all over the world and will lose the support of those friendly Powers like Soviet Russia who have full sympathy for our cause and willing to lend us active help.

Whatever the other objections to the Viceroy's offer may be, the single objection, namely, the communal implications of it, is enough to condemn that offer and render it totally unacceptable to any nationalist party. The Congress is a national institution representing Indians of all religious faiths and it has fought hard and suffered much to maintain its national character, it will commit veritable suicide if at this stage of its career the Congress were to renounce its national character and accept a communal label. Likewise, it will stultify itself once and for all if it gives up its role as a representative of Indian Nationalism and if it accepts the position of one party among many parties in India.

In conclusion, let me remind once again, as I said yesterday, that in this fateful hour the destiny of India lies in your hands and the responsibility is exclusively that of the Indian people and not of the Congress Working Committee. Therefore, carry on a raging and tearing campaign against this sinister offer and see that this offer is consigned to the scrap-heap before July 5, 1945.

* * *

Netaji's broadcast on 22 June 1945 was as follows:
Sisters and brothers in India! Latest news reaching us from India is to the effect that the Congress Working Committee decided last night to accept Lord Wavell's invitation to participate in the Simla Conference. To those who are acquainted with the present attitude of the Indian National Congress, this news has not come as a surprise. Referring to the opinion inside the Congress Working

Committee, the political correspondent of the Associated Press of India has reported as follows: 'The opinion among the Congress leaders about the Viceroy's proposal divides itself into three groups. The first party is led by Mr Gandhi and Sardar Vallabhbhai, who take strong exception to the use of the term 'Caste Hindus' in the Viceroy's broadcast. The middle group is led by Mr Nehru and Maulana Azad who, not being satisfied with the quantum of power contemplated to be transferred, take the view that the scheme can be given a fair trial as an interim measure, provided there is sufficient possibility of advancing India's demand for national independence and to improve the lot of the poor. The third group, led by Mr Rajagopalachari and Mr Bhulabhai Desai, feel that the terms of reference of the Simla Conference are so wide and elastic that all fears of the Congress are groundless. They advocate that the Congress should accept the proposal without picking holes in it and give it a fair trial and thus demonstrate the determination of the Congress to get on with the business.

I cannot judge from this distance if the analysis of the political correspondent of the Associated Press of India is correct or not, but I would not be surprised if it is. In fact this analysis conforms with what I said yesterday about the political character of the present Congress Working Committee. It appears that the Radical Democratic Party on this question is not supported by any member of the Congress Working Committee. The argument seems to be that even while agreeing to accept the invitation to the Simla Conference, the Working Committee has not committed itself in any way. But this argument cannot seriously be accepted because the offer as it stands and the implications of its acceptance are clear. Everybody who attends this Conference will have to accept the policy of wholehearted participation in the coming campaign in East

Asia, and the Congress will have to repudiate the policy it laid down regarding participation in the war when the Congress ministries resigned office in 1939. Moreover, everybody attending this Conference will have to accept the present constitutional position of the Viceroy and Governor-General in the Executive Council and will have to accept the humiliating position of functioning as mere advisors and not responsible ministers. Lord Wavell has made no secret of this and in fact he has made it quite clear that it is he who will appoint the members of the Executive Council. So, the members of the Executive Council will be responsible not to the Legislature but to him, and there is no question of majority rule or of collective responsibility in the Executive Council. Consequently, everybody who attends the Simla Conference will have to give up the demand for independence. They will have to give up also the usual demand for a National Government at the Centre, responsible to the Legislature, and will have to be content with Indianization of the Executive Council functioning within the framework of the 1935 Act. Presently, there can be no doubt whatsoever that acceptance of the invitation to the Simla Conference after all this will amount to giving up the fundamental principles and policies of the Indian National Congress, including the 'Quit India' resolution for which so many of our brethren and comrades are still rotting in prisons. Moreover, it is very unfortunate and painful that not a single member of the Congress Working Committee has put forward the demand for the release of all political prisoners, prior to negotiating with the British Government, although many of them have issued statements dealing with certain points in Lord Wavell's offer.

I said in my talk yesterday that the Working Committee is an executive body and is not constitutionally empowered to decide the destiny of so many million people and to commit the country to a course of action which is contrary to the fundamental ideals and policy of the Congress. Since the Working Committee does not represent all sections within the Congress and since there is no agreement on this question inside the country, there is no moral – not to speak of legal – justification for the Working Committee to deliberate on such vital issues behind the back of the All-India Congress Committee and the Congress as a whole. There is also no justification for the Working Committee to accept on its own responsibility the invitation to the Simla Conference especially when the whole offer is contrary to the fundamental principles and policy of the Congress.

I beg and implore Mahatma Gandhi and the Working Committee, even at this late hour, to pause and ponder over this great responsibility which they are taking upon themselves by ignoring the All-India Congress Committee and the Congress on such a momentous occasion. I fail to understand why the Working Committee should act in such an unfair manner. That Lord Wavell and the British Government know that the Indian people are overawed by the recent military successes of the Anglo-Americans and that the Indian people are at last beginning to realize that the Anglo-Americans are bound to win this war, Lord Wavell and the British Government want to exploit this psychological moment and strike while the iron is hot. They are afraid that after a few months the whole world will realize that despite the collapse of Germany and the overthrow of Japan in the Far East is not an easy proposition. Secondly, Lord Wavell and the British Government must somehow bamboozle these leaders and secure at least 500,000 Indian troops and vast quantities of military supplies for Britain's imperialist war in the Far East. Thirdly, Lord Wavell and the British Government must come to some agreement with the Indian leaders before July 5, when the general elections in England will commence. All these three motives afford sufficient explanation as to why Lord Wavell and the British Government are in a beastly hurry. But that is no reason why the Congress Working Committee should fall into their trap. In this connection, I would like to repeat what I said previously as to why Lord Wavell is moving heaven and earth in order to come to an agreement with the Indian leaders before July 5.

Now I want my countrymen to understand that the Conservative Party will do everything possible to prevent the Indian issue being brought up before an international conference. Ultimately, there is no doubt whatsoever that if Lord Wavell's offer is turned down by us, as I hope it will be, there will be another opportunity for bargaining with the British Government after the general elections, no matter which party secures the majority on the 5th of July. The fact that a long and bitter campaign in the Far East lies ahead of the British Government is an additional guarantee that British will have to placate India.

I want to make it clear before I proceed further that there is no question of bargaining except that the British quit India. But, since there are so many Indians at home who are thinking in terms of a compromise with British imperialism, it is their duty to consider when and how to make this bargain. On this point I am quite sure, that the best time for bargaining is after July 5, and though there is very little hope of the Labour Party recognizing India's independence it would be possible to strike a better bargain with that party. A compromise with the British Government on the issue of Lord Wavell's offer can be justified only on two conditions. First, if there had been no chance of winning independence. Secondly, if this had been the last chance for arriving at a compromise with the British Government. As to the first condition, I may say that in spite of the recent successes of the Anglo-Americans, India has now a better chance of achieving her independence than ever before. As to the second condition, I will repeat that no matter which party in Britain is called upon to form a Cabinet, India will get another chance and a better chance of bargaining with the British Government after July 5.

In my view there are three factors, the immediate effects of which will help India to win her independence by the end of this war. They are (i) resistance to British imperialism inside India; (ii) armed struggle against the British outside India; and (iii) diplomacy in the international field. Even moral resistance inside India will be enough. India must remain an international issue, and our diplomacy in the international field should be directed towards mobilizing support for Indian independence. India must take the assistance – moral and material – of those nations which are fighting Britain and are, therefore, her enemies. So far as armed struggle is concerned, in spite of our recent reverses in Burma the main forces of the Azad Hind Fauj will not give up the struggle. We shall continue fighting, and we shall fight to the last man and to the last round. We in East Asia can take a much more objective view of the war situation than our countrymen at home, who are easily misled by British propaganda, and have begun to believe in an exaggerated view of the strength of the Anglo-American powers. If our countrymen at home believe in our word, they should accept our reading of the war situation and change the policy of the Congress in accordance with this.

Those Congressmen who are thinking of accepting Lord Wavell's offer should look ahead and prepare themselves for the day when they will have to provide half-a-million Indian troops as canon- fodder for Britain's imperialist war in East Asia, and they should also be prepared for fighting their own countrymen in the Azad Hind Fauj, who are prepared to fight the British wherever they happen to meet them. Even if these Congressmen are not ashamed to take up arms against their brothers and sisters in the Azad Hind Fauj, they should at least refuse to provide half a million Indian lives as cannon fodder for the perpetuation of the British Empire. To those who doubt that India can achieve her independence by the end of this war, I should like to say that India will never get another opportunity like this for fighting for her freedom.

* * *

Netaji broadcast over the Provisional Government of Azad Hind Radio, Singapore, on June 23, 1945:

Sisters and brothers in India! Yesterday I told you that in any case it is wrong according to the Congress constitution and also morally unfair for the Congress Working Committee, which is an exclusive body, to exceed its powers and make decisions on behalf of the All-India Congress Committee or the Congress. I should have added, it is also unwise and impolitic for the Working Committee to do so. To an outside observer it appears as if the Working Committee was acting with indecent haste. I feel constrained to say that as compared with Mahatma Gandhi and the Working Committee, Mr Jinnah acted wisely and cautiously. He declared, according to the report before me that he could not advise the representatives of the Muslim League to attend the Simla Conference until after his interview with Lord Wavell on the 24th. Whatever Mr Jinnah's inner motives might have been, he did not show any anxiety to jump at the offer made by Lord Wavell. Mr Jinnah took another prudent and cautious step in asking Lord Wavell to postpone the conference.

I have said that unless Mahatma Gandhi is exceedingly careful he might be outmanoeuvred by the Viceroy and Mr Jinnah into a position in which the Congress will nominate the members of the Executive Council for only those seats which have been reserved by the Viceroy for the caste Hindus. In other words, there is very danger that Mahatma Gandhi might be manoeuvred into a position in which he will make a hasty admission that the word 'Congress' is synonymous with the word 'Caste Hindus'. That would be the political death of the Indian National Congress, from which it will be impossible for the Congress to retrieve itself.

This danger could be avoided if the Congress representative to the Simla Conference submit a panel of names concerning all the seats, barring that of the Commander-in-Chief. Will the Congress representatives do so? I am glad to find that the Working Committee has been thinking along these lines. But it is not enough to think. Congress representatives will have to insist that the Viceroy give up altogether the religious and communal basis for the composition of the Executive Council, and adopt a political and national basis instead. We must not forget what the difficulties before us are. I have always been of the view that as in a peace conference, so also in a political roundtable conference, it is only belligerent parties who are entitled to participate. That the British have now agreed to the partial Indianization of the Executive Council as a stepping stone to other far-reaching changes is not because of Mr Jinnah and the Muslim League, but because of the Congress which has consistently fought the British Government with all the means at its disposal.

Here in East Asia, we are going to have a celebration on July 4. The 4th of July is known all over the world as the day of American Independence, in East Asia it is the day on which the Indian Independence League in East Asia was imbued with new light and commenced a new phase in its career. Celebrations on July 4, which will be held all over East Asia wherever there are Indians will be in the nature of a referendum. We shall call upon Indians in East Asia on that day to give their verdict on Lord Wavell's offer, and if that verdict be one of condemnation to renew then and there our determination to continue the armed struggle for India's freedom under all circumstances, even if the Congress Working Committee were to accept Lord Wavell's offer.

Our task in East Asia is a two-fold one. Firstly, to continue the armed struggle which we launched on the 4th February 1943; secondly, to agitate for Indian independence in the international field and to utilize every conflict within the camp of the so-called United Nations, and in particular the conflict between the Soviet Union and the Anglo-Americans. For our fight in East Asia, Malaya is our base. So long as the British are kept out of Malaya, our work for India's independence will continue uninterrupted. Therefore, if at any time the British try to land in Malaya, we will fight with all the strength that we have.

When the history of Indian independence is finally written, Indians in Malaya will have a glorious place in that history. The contribution of Indians in Malaya for India's struggle for freedom in men, money and material has been great. India will always remain grateful for the same. In particular, Malaya has been the birth-place of the Azad Hind Fauj and of the Provisional Government of Azad Hind. Malaya has contributed a large number of young men who have fought bravely and died for India's freedom, and Malaya has made the largest contribution to the ranks of the 'Rani of Jhansi Regiment'. Indians in Malaya must maintain the brilliant record that they have already set up.

It is from Malaya that the call for total mobilization first went out.

Today I want to appeal to you for more men, more money and more material. After our most recent reverses in Burma your responsibility has become greater. Knowing what you have done in the past, I have no doubt that you will do even more in the future. I only want you to keep up your faith in the justice of our cause. So long as you keep up this faith you will also keep up your optimism and your confidence in final victory.

'Jai Hind.'

Netaji's broadcast from Singapore on 26 June 1945 was as follows:

India is now facing a political crisis, and if a wrong step is taken, we might suffer a setback in our march towards independence. I cannot tell you how worried I feel today, because on the one hand, independence is within sight, while on the other if a wrong step is taken that independence may recede into the distance.

If our countrymen at home cannot take up arms, and if they cannot even continue civil disobedience against Britain's war effort, let them at least keep up their moral resistance to British Imperialism and refuse to come to any compromise. We shall continue to assert India's right to freedom with arms, and so long as we do so no power on earth can prevent India remaining an international issue, provided you do not let us down by compromising with the British Government.

I understand that some of the leaders at home are furious with me for opposing their plans for a compromise with the British Government. They are also furious with me for pointing out the blunders of the Congress Working

Committee and the Congress; and they are furious with me for pointing out that the Congress Working Committee does not represent national opinion in the Congress or in the country. These imperialist leaders are abusing me for taking the help of the Japanese. I am not ashamed of taking the help of Japan. My cooperation with Japan is on the basis that Japan recognizes India's complete independence, and it has already granted formal recognition to the 'Provisional Government of Azad Hind' or Free India. But those who now want to cooperate with the British Government and fight Britain's imperialist war are prepared to accept the position of subordinates responsible to Britain's Viceroy in India. If leaders cooperate with the British Government on the basis that Britain grants formal recognition to the Government of Free India that would be a different matter. Moreover, Japan has given us the arms with which to organize an army of our own with which we can fight British imperialism which is our sole enemy. This army, the Azad Hind Fauj, has been trained by Indian instructors using the Indian language. This army carries India's national flag, and its slogans are India's national slogans. The army has its own Indian officers and its own officers' training schools run entirely by Indians. And, in the field of battle this army fights under its own Indian commanders some of whom have now reached the rank of Generals. If this army is called a 'puppet army', then it is the British Indian Army that should be called 'puppet army', because it is fighting Britain's Imperialist war under British officers. Am I to believe that in an army of 2,500,000 only a microscopic number of Indians are found fit to obtain the highest honour in the British army, namely, the Victoria Cross? Not one single Indian has yet been found fit to hold the rank of General.

Comrades! I have said that I am not ashamed to seek the help of Japan. I can go forward and say that if the almighty British Empire can go down on its knees in order to obtain the help of the United States of America, there is no reason why we, an enslaved and disarmed nation, should not take help from our friends. Today we are taking the help of Japan, tomorrow we shall not hesitate to get help from any other Power if that be possible, and if that be desirable in the interests of India. Nobody will be more happy than myself if we could achieve India's independence without foreign help of any sort. But I have yet to find one single instance, in modern history, where an enslaved nation has achieved its liberation without foreign help of any sort.

In August, when the Japanese had decided to lay down their arms, Netaji informed the Japanese General in Singapore that they must give no undertaking to the British on behalf of the I.N.A., as it was an entirely independent army. General Itagaki, the Japanese commander, told Netaji that he could not promise anything as the policy and orders for him would be laid down by Marshal Count Terauchi, who was the commander of all the Japanese forces in South-East Asia. Netaji, therefore, left Singapore on 16 August by plane and arrived at Bangkok the same evening. In Singapore, he left Major-General Kiani in command of all the troops in Malaya.

On the evening of 16 August, Netaji visited all camps and delivered short farewell speeches to each unit. Last of all, he visited the S. S. Group and delivered a short speech. He then personally declared the officers and men with awards which they had won for their gallant deeds on the battlefield. He then shook hands with all the officers. From the men there were thunderous shouts of 'Chalo Delhi' 'Inquilab Zindabad'. 'Azad Hind Zindabad' and 'Netaji Zindabad'. Tears rolled down Netaji's eyes; no leader could have expected greater devotion and loyalty from his men.

At night, he called all senior officers to his bungalow for a buffet dinner and gave them full instructions regarding the course they were to follow should anything happen to him. The following morning, accompanied by some of his selected staff officers, he left, for Saigon to meet Field Marshal Count Terauchi to settle full details of the surrender of the I.N.A. But, Count Terauchi informed him that he was not in a position to decide anything about it as the orders would come from Tokyo. Netaji, therefore, left Saigon on the following day accompanied by Colonel Habibur Rehman. It is stated by Colonel Rehman that when their aeroplane took off from Formosa aerodrome *en route* to Tokyo it was suddenly hit by something and there was a big bang. He is of the opinion that it was probably a vulture that had hit one of the propellers. This was at a height of 300 feet above the ground. The plane suddenly crashed on the side of a hill which was near the aerodrome and caught fire. He then leaped out of the plane and pulled Netaji out of burning mass. Colonel Rehman was himself very badly hurt and his hands and face still bear marks of those burns. According to him, when Netaji was brought out he had two serious injuries on his head. He was also very badly hurt, but he was conscious for half an hour after which he became unconscious. They were then both taken to the same hospital and according to Colonel Rehman, Netaji died six hours later. Colonel Rehman then tried to bring back his body to Singapore, but owing to air transport difficulty, this could not be arranged. Netaji was cremated, and Colonel Rehman says that he was present at the cremation ceremony and he has safely stored Netaji's ashes at a home in Tokyo. When the British forces landed at Singapore and Bangkok, the Azad Hind Fauj at these places under the command of Major General Kiani and Major General Bhonsle, surrendered as an independent force to the British. Thus closed in tragic fashion a glorious chapter in the history of India's struggle for freedom, which was started by Netaji Subhas Chandra Bose.

Back to India

One thing we all found on arrival in India, and that was that the people inside the country knew very little about the real worth and activities of the I.N.A. British propaganda had been too powerful and despite four I.N.A. broadcasting stations at Saigon, Bangkok, Singapore and Rangoon working day and night to explain the truth about the I.N.A., the Indian people still believed that the I.N.A. was just a puppet army of the Japanese.

All the I.N.A. officers were more upset and worried about this than their fate before the British Court Martial. Some of our leaders were still referring to us as 'misguided soldiers of India.' It was at this time that Pandit Jawaharlal Nehru, on release from jail, exposed the full facts to the Indian people and won the everlasting gratitude of the I.N.A. for saving their prestige and honour.

We can also never forget the services rendered to the I.N.A. by late Sri Bhulabhai Desai. I still remember vividly the first interview three of us. He said, 'Gentlemen, I have come to defend you, but much more important than the defence of your persons, is the defence of the honour and prestige of Netaji and the I.N.A. If your lives can be saved with honour we will try and save you, otherwise it would be better for you all to die and save the honour of your leader and the organization to which you belonged.' In saying so, he took the very words out of our mouth. This was precisely what every I.N.A. officer and man had wanted.

At the time Mr Bhulabhai was in a very poor state of health. His doctor warned him, 'Mr Desai, you are working too hard. If you continue like this, you will kill yourself.' Bhulabhai replied, 'Doctor, don't worry. Even if I have to die.' I am going to save these three young men.' With indomitable spirit and determination, he fought out his case, and won the last 'Great Victory' of his life. We were released and Bhulabhai was perhaps the happiest man in India.

In March 1946, when I went to see him in Bombay, he was on his deathbed. He was moved to see me. He said, 'I do not mind dying now. I have seen you alive, and my last advice to you is to continue the struggle for which you have suffered so much, and I am sure in the end Netaji will triumph, and India will be free. Jai Hind,' and he closed his eyes.

IMPORTANT PERSONALITIES IN THE INDEPENDENCE MOVEMENT

1. Major General J. K. Bhonsle

This officer originally belonged to the 5th Marhatta Light Infantry in the British India Army. He had graduated from the Royal Military College, Sandhurst in 1929. At the time of the fall of Singapore, he was commanding 5th Battalion 18th Royal Garhwal Rifles and held the rank of Lt. Colonel. He was intensely patriotic, and was one of the first to join the I.N.A.

In the first I.N.A., he commanded the Field Force which consisted of:

Three Infantry battalions. One Heavy Gun Battalion. One Armoured Fighting Vehicles Battalion and other Artillery units.

During the period of the crisis, he was of the opinion that the I.N.A. should not be dissolved, as it was a unique opportunity that the Indians outside India had of doing some service to their motherland.

On the recognition of the I.N.A., he was very deservingly appointed as the Director of Military Bureau. He was at the helm of affairs of the I.N.A. from February, 1943 – August, 1943, when Netaji took over the direct command of the I.N.A. as the Supreme Commander. During this period General Bhonsle commanded the army magnificently. He was a very fine organizer and a brilliant strategist.

On Netaji Subhas Chandra Bose's arrival, the post of the Director of Military Bureau was abolished and he was appointed as the Chief of Staff to the Supreme Commander, and as such he was second in command to Netaji.

When Netaji moved to Burma in early 1944, General Bhonsle was left behind to manage the affairs in Malaya. When Netaji flew to Tokyo in August 1945, General Bhonsle was left as the in charge of the main I.N.A. Headquarters at Bangkok, where he was captured by the British forces. He was a minister in the Provisional Government of the Azad Hind and a member of the 'War Council'. He was a descendent of Shivaji and was related to the Gaekwar of Baroda.

2. Major General A. C. Chatterji

Major General Chatterji is an old I.M.S. officer and at the time of the fall of Singapore he had approximately 26 years' service to his credit. Before going out to Malaya, he was the Director of Public Health in Bengal.

At the time of the fall of Singapore, he was the senior most Indian Medical Officer and undertook to look after the medical arrangements for the prisoners of war. In addition to this duty, he also acted as one of the advisors to General Mohan Singh.

He was one of the most ardent and sincere workers in the movement from the very start. He organized numerous meetings and gave several propaganda lectures to troops, and it was due to his activities that a large number of officers and men joined the I.N.A.

He was one of the closest associates of Mr Ras Behari Bose and during the crisis in the I.N.A., he was against its disbandment by General Mohan Singh. On the recognition of the I.N.A., he was appointed General Secretary to the I.I.L. under Mr R. B. Bose. On arrival of Netaji Subhas Chandra Bose, he was put in charge of the Publicity and Propaganda (E & C Department).

During the operations in 1944, he was appointed Governor Designate of the liberated areas and he was to be the first Governor of Manipur area. In June 1944, he visited the front line troops and the areas liberated by them where he was slightly wounded by enemy shell fire. On return to Rangoon in November 1944, he accompanied Netaji on his visit to Tokyo from where they all returned in January 1945. Early in January 1945, he was appointed as the Foreign Minister to the Provisional Government of Azad Hind.

He was in the party which was accompanying Netaji to Tokyo on his last trip in August 1946, but owing to the difficulty of air transport, he with the rest of his party had to be left behind in Saigon, where they were all later captured by the British forces.

In the I.N.A., he was one of the most trusted officers of Netaji, and was perhaps the most experienced. He was a passionate lover of his country and an untiring worker. He was a great organizer under whom it was a pleasure to work with.

3. Major General M. Z. Kiani

This officer originally belonged to the 1st Battalion 14th Punjab Regiment. He was commissioned from the Indian Military Academy in 1935, where he won the Sword of Honour and the Gold Medal Prize for being the most outstanding cadet of the term.

During the Malayan Campaign, he served as a staff officer-in-charge operation to General Heathe, Commander of Third India Corps. At the time of surrender of Singapore, he was the Battalion Second in Command.

He joined the I.N.A. from the very beginning, and was responsible, as the Chief of General Staff, for organizing the first I.N.A. under General Mohan Singh.

During the crisis in the I.N.A. he agreed with General Mohan Singh to disband it. But later on being assured that Netaji Subhas Chandra Bose would be coming to take over command of the I.N.A., he decided to remain in it.

After the recognition, he was appointed Army Commander under General Bhonsle – the Director of Military Bureau.

On the arrival of Netaji, he took command of No. 1 Division which was sent to fight in Burma early in 1944. He had under him three brigades –

No. 1 Guerrilla Brigade (the Subhas Brigade) under Major General Shahnawaz Khan.

No. 2 Guerrilla Brigade (the Gandhi Brigade) under Colonel I. J. Kiani.

No. 3 Guerrilla Brigade (the Azad Brigade) under Colonel Gulzara Singh.

It was this division that fought in the Arakan, Haka-Falam, Tamu, Palel and Kohima during the operations in 1944.

On return from the front in October 1944, he was appointed General Secretary to the War Council and accompanied Netaji to Tokyo in 1944. At the time of the surrender of the I.N.A. he was in command of troops in Singapore.

During the operations, General Kiani proved himself to be the most capable commander in the field; but it was really as a Staff Officer that he made a name for himself. He was generally looked upon as the best staff officer in the I.N.A.

4. Major General A. D. Loganathan

This officer belonged to the Indian Medical service and at the time of the fall of Singapore had approximately 25 years of service to his credit. He was, at that time, commanding No. 19 Indian Hospital and held the rank of a Lt. Colonel. After the surrender he was one of the very first officers to join in the Indian Independence Movement and also to create an active propaganda to motivate others to do the same. In the first I.N.A. under General Mohan Singh, he was the Director of Medical Services. He was also one of the delegates to the Bangkok Conference.

During the crisis in the I.N.A., he was not in favour of General Mohan Singh disbanding the I.N.A. He was a member of the Administrative Committee that was formed during the period of the crisis from December 1942 to March 1943, and was largely responsible for creating that atmosphere among the officers which later enabled Mr Rash Behari Bose to reorganize the I.N.A. He was also a member of the Executive Committee which was constituted by Mr Rash Behari Bose to consider the appointment of various officers to important military posts in the I.N.A.

In the second I.N.A., under the Director of Military Bureau General Bhonsle, he worked as the Chief Administrator in the I.N.A. Supreme Command and was responsible for looking after the general administration and discipline of the I.N.A.

On the arrival of Netaji Subhas Chandra Bose in Singapore and the establishment of the Provisional Government of the Azad Hind, he was appointed one of its ministers. In February 1944, he was sent as High Commissioner of the Andamans and Nicobar Islands, which being part of Indian territory, were ceded by the Japanese to the Provisional Government of the Azad Hind and were renamed *Sheed* and *Swaraj* Islands. He returned to Singapore in September 1944 on account of ill-health.

Early in 1945, he arrived at Rangoon to submit his report to Netaji Subhas Chandra Bose. At the time of the surrender of the I.N.A. in Burma, he volunteered to remain behind in command of the I.N.A.

He was greatly respected by all officers and popularly known as 'Uncle' by all the officers in the I.N.A. He was a passionate lover of his country and despite his failing health an untiring worker. He had a very pleasant disposition which endeared him to all his subordinates.

5. Major General Aziz Ahmad

This officer belonged to the 1st Kapurthala Infantry and at the time of the fall of Singapore was commanding the State Forces and held the rank of a Major. He is one of those officers who originally did not believe in the sincerity of the Japanese and in the idea of forming an I.N.A. but later, he changed his mind and volunteered to join the I.N.A. in May 1942. In doing so he believed that he would be better able to serve his men and protect them from Japanese exploitation by being in the I.N.A. He was a member of the Bangkok Conference and in the first I.N.A., he raised and commanded the Nehru Brigade. During the crisis in the I.N.A., he was one of the staunchest officers who supported General Mohan Singh in his idea of dissolving the I.N.A.

After the arrest of General Mohan Singh, he was called for an interview by General Iwakuro and Mr Rash Behari Bose and offered the command of the Indian National Army which he refused. But on being assured that Netaji Subhas Chandra Bose would be coming in the near future to take over the command of the I.N.A., he decided to continue. On the re-organization of the I.N.A. under the D.M.B., General Bhonsle, he continued to command the Nehru Brigade. On the arrival of Netaji and the establishment of the Provisional

Government of the Azad Hind, he was appointed a Minister of State.

He arrived in Burma with his Brigade in May 1944, but had to return to Malaya to take over the command of No. 2 Division which was newly raised. He returned to Rangoon in early October 1944, with advance parties of No. 2 Division, which by this time had started moving to Burma. In November 1944, he was elected a member of the War Council and during the absence of Netaji Subhas Chandra Bose on his visit to Tokyo from November to December 1944, he officiated as Supreme Commander.

Early in 1945, when the main body of No. 2 Division had concentrated in Rangoon and was preparing to advance to the front line, he was unluckily injured in a bombing raid and admitted to the hospital with a serious head injury and I (Major General Shahnawaz) had to take over the command of No. 2 Division. On his recovery in April 1945, he was given the command of No. 1 Division, which was at that time concentrated at Zeyawadi. Most of the personnel of this Division which had been in action around Imphal in 1944, were sick men and were very poorly armed; hence they equipped; hence they were in no position to offer any resistance to the British armoured forces when they arrived at Zeyawadi. He surrendered with the whole of his Division at the end of April 1945 in Zeyawadi.

Major General Aziz Ahmad was one of the most trusted officers of Netaji Subhas Chandra Bose to whom he was intensely devoted. He was always willing to sacrifice his all for the achievement of his ideal – the liberation of his country. He had excellent military knowledge in handling large formations and was always well known for his skill in training the troops under his command. He was also an excellent speaker and could move masses.

6. Major General G. R. Nagar

This officer belonged to the R.I.A.S.C. and at the time of the fall of Singapore held the rank of a Lt. Colonel. Soon after the surrender, he was given command of Bidadari prisoner of the war camp which accommodated approximately 15,000 Indian prisoners of war.

In April 1942, he was sent to Saigon to work at the Broadcasting Station there. Most of the people in India must be familiar with his broadcasts and commentaries under the name of Major Mirza. He returned from Saigon in July 1943. Around the middle of 1944, when No. 3 Division was raised, he was appointed its Commander. During the campaign in 1945, he was given the role of defending the western coastline of Malaya in the vicinity of Alorstar, Serambag and Ipoh. Under orders from the Supreme Command, he surrendered with his division in Malaya on arrival of the British forces there. Major General Nagar participated in the freedom movement with lot of enthusiasm.

7. Major General Allagappan

This officer belonged to the Indian Medical service and at the time of the fall of Singapore was commanding 27th I.G.H. and was holding the rank of Lt. Colonel. He was regarded as one of the best surgeons in the British Army. After the surrender, he volunteered to join the I.N.A. from the very beginning. On the organization of the first I.N.A. his services were loaned to the Indian Independence League. He worked with the I.I.L. from May 1942 till July 1943 when he was recalled by Netaji and appointed in-charge of the Enlightenment and Culture Department of the Indian National Army. He surrendered in Singapore with the rest of the I.N.A. Troops. Major General Allagappan was an excellent surgeon and held strong nationalistic views.

8. Colonel A. Q. Gilani

This officer belonged to the 1st Battalion Bahawalpore State Infantry and at the time of the fall of Singapore he held the rank of Lt. Colonel. He played a prominent part in helping General Mohan Singh to raise the first I.N.A. and was generally regarded as the leader of the Muslim community.

Colonel Gilani went to Bangkok conference as a delegate and was elected a member of the 'Council of Action' under the Presidentship of Mr Rash Behari Bose. He resigned from the council during the crisis, and proceeded to Penang where he took over command of a school for training the I.N.A. propagandists' infiltration into India.

Later, towards the end of 1943, he was recalled to Singapore and made in charge of Recruiting and Training department of the Indian Independence League. He was captured in Singapore by the British forces when they reoccupied it.

9. Colonel N. S. Bhagat

This officer belonged to the Indian Engineers, and at the time of the fall of Singapore was commanding a Field Company of Bombay Sappers and Miners.

He was one of those officers who opposed the formation of an I.N.A. which might be exploited by the Japanese. On account of his uncompromising attitude on this issue, he was sent out from Singapore to Borneo in March 1942.

On the return of delegates from Bangkok conference, he was recalled to Singapore in September 1942. Realizing that an I.N.A. was going to be formed whether he was in it or not, he decided to join it, with the object of preventing it from being exploited by the Japanese.

During the crisis, he perhaps played the most prominent part in inducing General Mohan Singh to stick to his demands, and if necessary to even dissolve the I.N.A.

On the arrest of General Mohan Singh, he resigned from the I.N.A. and in spite of being offered high posts, he refused to re-join, until the arrival of Netaji Subhas Chandra Bose.

After an interview with Netaji, Colonel Bhagat decided to re-join the I.N.A. in July 1943, and from then on worked for the cause. In the reorganized Headquarters of the I.N.A. Supreme Command under Netaji, he worked as the Chief Administrator and was elected one of its ministers on establishment of the Provisional Government of the Azad Hind.

Early in 1944, when No. 2 Division was raised he was appointed its commander. He organized and commanded the division very efficiently. In May 1944, however, owing to certain differences of opinion with General Bhonsle and Colonel Bhagat, he had to be removed from the command of No. 2 Division, which was taken over by Colonel Ahmad.

After his removal, he was sent to Taungyi, a hill station in Shan States and kept separate from the rest of the I.N.A. Early in 1945, he was transferred to Zeyawadi where on arrival of the British forces, he reported to them.

During the time that Colonel Bhagat was holding appointment in the I.N.A., he always worked very sincerely. He was looked upon as one of the most efficient and popular officers in the I.N.A. He was very strong-headed and straightforward, and was always known for his anti-Japanese views. He was an ardent nationalist.

During the first I.N.A. trial, he was approached by British authorities to give evidence against my other two colleagues, Colonel Sahgal and Dhillon, and me and give statements against Netaji, but he refused and consequently he was asked to resign from the Indian Army.

10. Colonel Elisan Qadir

This officer belonged to 5/2 Punjab Regiment and was adjutant to his battalion during the early part of Malayan Campaign.

He was commissioned from the Indian Military Academy in 1935 and at the time of the fall of Singapore he had approximately eight years of service, and was holding the rank of a Captain.

He was captured in January 1942, in the vicinity of Kuala Lumpur and was sent by Capt. Mohan Singh to take charge of the Radio Broadcasting station at Saigon.

People in India must be quite familiar with English and Hindustani broadcasts which were sent from Saigon. All these broadcasts were arranged and controlled entirely by Colonel Qadir.

When a crisis arose between General Mohan Singh and the Japanese, he returned from Saigon in order to attempt to persuade General Mohan Singh not to disband the I.N.A. In the second I.N.A. under the Director of Military Bureau General Bhonsle, he was made in-charge of the training of civil volunteers. On the establishment of the Provisional Govt. of the Azad Hind, he was appointed one of its ministers. He moved with the headquarters, when Netaji transferred it from Singapore to Rangoon. In Rangoon, he raised and organized the 'Azad Hind Dal' which was an organization of civilians especially trained to administer liberated territories. He moved to Maymyo with his Dal in April 1944.

On the failure of Manipur Campaign, he returned to Rangoon in October 1944. He was also a member of the War Council. He was captured by the British forces at Pegu in April 1945. Colonel Qadir had very good knowledge of the political problems of India. He was a good organizer and a brilliant schemer. He was the son of Sir Abdul Qadir of Lahore.

11. Colonel S. M. Hussain

He belonged to the 4/19th Hyderabad Regiment and at the time of the fall of Singapore held the rank of a Captain.

In the first I.N.A. he acted as a staff officer to General Bhonsle, who was commanding the Hind Field Force.

In the second I.N.A. he was given the command of the 1st Infantry Regiment. He arrived in Rangoon with the advance parties of the regiment in October 1944, but owing to all heavy arms and equipment being sunk in the sea transit, his unit could not leave Rangoon till February 1945. He arrived at the front in March 1945 and took over the defence of Magwe-Taundwingy area which is adjacent to the Burma oil fields area. He surrendered to the British forces at Magwe in April 1945. He was also a member of the Cabinet of the Provisional Government.

12. Colonel Habibur Rehman

This officer belonged to 1st Battalion 14th Punjab Regiment and was the adjutant of the battalion when it went into action at Jitra in December 1941. He was commissioned from the Indian Military Academy in 1936 and at the time of surrender held the rank of a Captain.

He was captured by the Japanese in the vicinity of Kuala Lumpur. He never at any time completely trusted the Japanese. He was always of the opinion that the only way to secure India's freedom was to organize a powerful army in East Asia, and then fight whoever dared to try to dominate India.

He was a member of the delegation that went to Bangkok Conference. In the first I.N.A. he was the Adjutant General in the I.N.A. Headquarters. After the crisis, he was appointed commandant of the Officers' Training School, and it was here that he made a name for himself. In a very brief space of time of three months, he was able to infuse great national spirit in the cadets, and equipped them with the necessary military knowledge. After graduation, these cadets went straight to the front line and took command of platoons and, in some cases, companies and gave excellent account of themselves wherever they went and won even the praise of their adversaries. It was at this institution that he taught them the famous motto *'Jeena Hai To Marna Seekho'*, and his cadets always lived up to this motto.

In May 1944, Netaji appointed him Assistant Chief of Staff and ordered him to report at his headquarters in Rangoon, where his services were urgently required as Netaji was moving up to the front line and he wanted someone reliable to take charge of Military affairs in Rangoon.

In November 1944, Colonel Rehman accompanied Netaji to Tokyo and returned with him to Rangoon in January 1945.

In March 1945 he was sent to take over command of all I.N.A. troops in Singapore and relieve General Bhonsle who was required in Rangoon. In August 1945, he was also the only I.N.A. officer accompanying Netaji on his last and hazardous air trip to Tokyo. He was in the same plane which was carrying Netaji and crashed at Formosa.

Colonel Rehman was the fortunate person to have the honour of bringing back Netaji's last message to his countrymen, 'Tell all my countrymen that Subhas fought for India's independence till the last breath of his life.'

Colonel Rehman was one of Netaji's most trusted officers. He is cool, calm and solid as a rock, a devoted follower of his Netaji and a most selfless worker for Indian independence.

13. Colonel S. A. Malik (Sardar-e-Jang)

This officer belonged to the Bahawalpore State Forces and at the time of the fall of Singapore, held the rank of a Captain.

He was a staunch supporter of the I.N.A. movement from the very start, and went to Bangkok conference as a delegate. On the formation of the I.N.A., he was given the command of the Intelligence group, in Singapore which he commanded efficiently and trained the personnel with remarkable skill. In early September 1943, he left Singapore for Burma. His group was one of the first I.N.A. units to go into action during the Manipur operations. He was the first Indian officer to hoist the Indian national flag on the Indian soil in 1944, in the region around Bishanpore. During the operation, he was made the Commander of all liberated areas to carry out the administration of those territories. He commanded his unit with rare skill and distinguished himself for which he was awarded the much honoured medal, 'Sardar-e-Jang.'

He returned to Rangoon in October 1944 to recoup his health. He was again sent to the front in February 1945. While in Mandalay, his force surrendered to the British, but he managed to break through and returned to Rangoon. On 24 April 1945, he was in the party that accompanied Netaji on his trek from Rangoon to Bangkok. He was captured by the British forces, with the main forces of the I.N.A. at Bangkok. Colonel Malik was a happy-go lucky type of officer, who took delight in running into danger. He was intensely patriotic and a great admirer of Netaji.

CHAPTER TEN

RANI OF JHANSI REGIMENT

Soon after his arrival in Singapore, Netaji – who from his past experience in India had fully realized the worth of securing the cooperation of Indian women in the fight for India's liberation – expressed a desire to raise a special fighting unit of Indian women to be known as 'Rani of Jhansi Regiment'. Accordingly, on 12 July, the women's section of the Indian Independence League convened a mass meeting of Indian women. The meeting was addressed by Netaji. Some of the Indian women had walked 10 to 12 miles to the meeting place. There was a great enthusiasm amongst the women who were always as anxious and willing as men to sacrifice themselves for the sake of Indian Independence.

Netaji addressed them in the following words:

Sisters, you all know, as well as I do, the part our women at home have played in the Freedom Movement, especially during the last 22 years, since the year 1921, when the Congress was reborn under the leadership of Mahatma Gandhi. It is not only in connection with the Congress movement of Civil Disobedience, but also in connection with the secret revolutionary movement, that our sisters have played a noble part… In fact, it will be no exaggeration for me to say that there is no sphere of public activity, there is no department of national endeavour, in which Indian women have not gladly and bravely shared, along with our men, the burden of national struggle. Whether it is touring from village to village without food and drink, whether it is lecturing at one meeting after another, whether it is carrying the freedom-message from door to door, whether it is running election campaigns or whether it is leading processions along public streets in defiance of official orders in spite of lathi charges by the inhuman British Police, or whether it is facing bravely imprisonment and persecution, insult and humiliation, nowhere have our women been found wanting. Our brave sisters have also played a prominent part in the secret revolutionary movement. They have shown that when the need arises they could, like their brothers, shoot very well… If today I express my fullest confidence in you, it is because I know what our women are capable of, and therefore I say without the slightest exaggeration, that there is no suffering, which our sisters are not capable of enduring.

History teaches us that every empire has its fall just as it has its rise. And the time has come for the British Empire to disappear from the face of this world. We see with our own eyes how that empire has disappeared from this part of the world. It shall disappear from another part of the world, from India, as well…

If there is anyone either here or elsewhere who thinks that it is an unwomanly act to shoulder a rifle, I would ask her to turn to the pages of our history. What had our brave women done in past? What did the brave Rani of Jhansi do in the revolution of 1857, India's First War of Independence. It was this queen who with drawn sword on horseback led her men to battle. Through our ill-luck she fell, she failed, and India failed. But we have to continue and complete the work which the Great Rani undertook in 1857...

Therefore in the last and final War of Independence we want not one Rani of Jhansi, but thousands and thousands of Ranis of Jhansi. It is not the number of rifles you may carry or the number of shots you may fire which is important. Equally important is the moral effect of your brave example...

Concluding his speech, Netaji asked for recruits for the Rani of Jhansi Regiment and the Red Cross unit. A very large number of women immediately volunteered their services and a training camp was set up for them in Singapore. Amongst the 600 volunteers that joined this regiment at Singapore there were young girls as well as elderly women mostly from very good and respectable families. Among them were Hindu, Muslim and Sikh girls; girls who came from every nook and corner of India. In that training camp there were no luxuries. They had to undergo very strenuous military training which included the use of machine guns, Tommy guns, hand grenades, rifles and bayonets. They were also put through a very strenuous course of physical training. General lectures on India's social and economic life were also delivered to them. In the camp they had to live on very simple food. Rice, fish and vegetables were the only part of the diet they had. For sleeping at night they did not have soft and comfortable beds. They slept on hard wooden floor with only one blanket underneath.

The rules and regulations in the camp were very strict, no visitors were allowed, and relatives were permitted to meet them only once a week. From morning till late in the evening they were busy with the training. Dr Lakshmi Swaminathan, a young, energetic and outstandingly brave lady was selected by Netaji to be their commander.

Within a very brief period of six months, they had mastered all their training and were every bit as well trained and disciplined as any soldier of the Azad Hind Fauj. They were particularly good in bayonet-fighting and all of them were always eager to use their bayonets against the British forces.

Early in 1944, when other units of the Azad Hind Fauj were moving to Burma for an assault on Imphal, the girls of the Rani of Jhansi Regiment submitted an application written in their own blood to Netaji informing him that they were as anxious as any male member of the Azad Hind Fauj to proceed to the front and to lay down their lives for the liberation of their country. In this letter they requested Netaji to give them an early opportunity. Netaji conceded to their request and Rani of Jhansi Regiment was moved from Singapore to Rangoon where a second camp for training of women volunteers was started in early 1944. The strength of the regiment now had reached to a 1,000 volunteers; thousands more were on the waiting list, but due to various administrative difficulties they could not be taken in.

When the Azad Hind Fauj began its assault on Imphal, detachments of the Rani of Jhansi Regiment were moved to Maymyo. There were two sections, one was the operational section, the primary role of which was to take part in actual fighting; and the other was the missing section. Nevertheless, every girl in the Rani of Jhansi Regiment was trained to fight as well as to work as a nurse in a hospital. Reference to the excellent work that the nursing section of the Rani of Jhansi

Regiment did at Maymyo has already been made in this book elsewhere. Hence, I will not repeat it here.

As regards the fighting section, it was Netaji's intention that these girls should take part in actual fighting after the capture of Imphal. It was also his intention if and when Calcutta was captured, the Rani of Jhansi Regiment would be at the head of the Azad Hind Fauj in the triumphant entry into Calcutta. Although due to our failure in capturing Imphal, the Rani of Jhansi Regiment never actually had an opportunity to fight. I am certain that had they been given an opportunity they would have distinguished themselves. All of them were as brave as tigresses and as hard as nails. In the final stages of their training they had to march 15 to 20 miles a day twice weekly, carrying their packs weighing at least 40 lbs. of rifles and ammunition. Every morning during the physical training period, they used to run at a fast pace of two miles at a stretch. On one occasion in October 1944, a ceremonial parade of the Azad Hind Fauj in Rangoon was held. There were approximately 3,000 soldiers on parade. The Rani of Jhansi Regiment was on the right and was the leading unit. All the Japanese generals, Burmese ministers and other prominent citizens of Rangoon had come to witness the parade. Netaji was standing and talking from a dais and all the troops were lined up in front of him in the middle of a big open parade ground.

After Netaji finished his speech, orders were given to troops to march past and give salute to Netaji. As the Rani of Jhansi Regiment started marching there was an air-raid alarm. Japanese fighters took off from an aerodrome nearby. The British bombers and fighter planes were coming to raid Rangoon. In a few moments, they arrived and a fierce machine-gun battle started just above us. All the visitors including the Japanese generals realizing the grave danger ran away for safety and took shelter in trenches nearby. Netaji stood on the dais, calm and unmoved, like a statue. The Rani of Jhansi Regiment girls kept marching past him in perfect steps in a manner as if nothing had happened. All of a sudden, the enemy planes swooped very low on the area where this parade was being held. One of them flying at a tree top height approximately 50' off the ground, passed within 100 yards of Netaji. The anti-aircraft guns opened fire on this plane. The shells hit one of our gallant soldiers marching past Netaji and blew off her head. She died instantaneously. There was no panic at all. Others kept marching on in perfect steps. Had the enemy plane which had as many as six machine guns in it opened fire, both Netaji and all the members of the Rani of Jhansi Regiment would probably have been killed.

On another occasion, when some members of the Rani of Jhansi Regiment were being evacuated from Rangoon to Bangkok early in December 1944, their train was attacked by the British guerrillas. Our girls immediately opened fire on the enemy and forced them to retreat. In this fight, two of them got killed and two injured; but they had inflicted much greater loss on the enemy.

The determination and fortitude with which they faced the rigours on closely followed up withdrawal from Rangoon to Bangkok in the middle of monsoon season has been described in full detail elsewhere. During this withdrawal, they covered over 200 miles on foot carrying all their arms and equipment. The achievements of the Rani of Jhansi Regiment have proved beyond doubt that there is nothing that our women cannot do, and that if they are given an opportunity they are as good if not superior to the women of any country in the world.

Before the surrender, Netaji personally ascertained that each girl was sent back safely to her parents.

CHAPTER ELEVEN

SUBHAS BRIGADE

Soon after taking direct command of the I.N.A., Netaji called a conference of all senior officers at his Military Headquarters in Singapore. The following officers were present:

1. Major General J. K. Bhonsle
2. Major General M. Z. Kiani
3. Major General Aziz Ahmed
4. Major General Shahnawaz
5. Colonel I. J. Kiani
6. Colonel Gulzara Singh
7. Colonel Habib-ur-Rehman
8. Colonel P. K. Sahgal

At the conference, Netaji revealed the discussions he had with Field Martial Terauchi, Commander-in-Chief of all the Japanese forces in South-East Asia, regarding the employment of the Indian National Army in the coming operation.

Netaji stated that Count Terauchi had told him that the Japanese did not think that the I.N.A. would be able to fight as well as Japanese soldiers as it had been defeated in battle of Malaya and consequently its soldiers were demoralized.

Secondly, he said that the I.N.A. which had once been a part of the British Indian Army was used to fighting under British system of administration in which ample supply of luxurious rations was considered a necessity, whereas in the Japanese Army the case was just the reverse. In fighting they had to undergo great hardships and live on very meagre rations. The I.N.A., he said, would not be able to stand up to these hardships.

Lastly, he said that the I.N.A. was an army composed of soldiers who were once British mercenaries, and had no political education or political feeling and as such they would not be able to resist the temptation of deserting over to the British side where they were better prospects of getting good rations and pay, and of meeting their families whom they had not seen for several years.

He, therefore, suggested to Netaji that the main force of the Indian National Army should be left behind in Singapore as they would not be required for fighting. The Japanese soldiers, he said, would do all the fighting and liberate India. And all that the Japanese solicited was the personal cooperation of Netaji to enlist the goodwill and sympathy of the Indian people. He also suggested the use of a small number of the I.N.A. soldiers belonging to the special services and intelligence groups for purposes of infiltration and propaganda in the front line with the object of lowering the morale of the British Indian Army.

Netaji's reply to Terauchi was short and decisive. He said: 'Any liberation of India secured through Japanese sacrifices is to me worse than slavery.' He told Terauchi that the Manipur Campaign was a Battle for Indian independence and as such it was against the national honour of India that the soldiers of the I.N.A. should stay behind while the Japanese advanced into Indian territory. Netaji insisted that in the coming struggle, the I.N.A. soldiers must form a spearhead of the advance into India so that the first drop of blood to be shed on the sacred soil of India would be that of a soldier of the I.N.A. He maintained that the Indians must make their utmost endeavour to secure Indian independence entirely by themselves and then, if, in spite of their maximum efforts and sacrifices they were still unable to achieve it, then and then only would they ask for Japanese assistance. The Japanese Commander-in-Chief agreed to this, but requested Netaji to send only one selected brigade into action as a test case, and if it proved that it could really fight and bear the hardships as well as the Japanese troops then the rest of the I.N.A. would also be sent into action.

Having explained this, Netaji asked all officers to express their opinions on the subject, and it was eventually decided that a new brigade known as No. 1 Guerrilla Regiment should be raised by selecting best soldiers from other three brigades, the Gandhi, Azad and Nehru. This brigade was to go into action first and if it proved satisfactory the I.N.A. would follow suit.

I was selected its Commander with Col. Thakur Singh as the Regimental Second-in-Command, and Col. Mahboob Ahmad as the Regimental Adjutant.

The regiment was raised at Taiping in September 1943 and the soldiers themselves gave it the name of Subhas Brigade. Netaji did not approve of it as he was against the idea of giving the name of living persons to I.N.A. brigades. He repeatedly issued instructions that no one should call it that but the soldiers found it hard to obey the orders.

On arrival at Taiping, the brigade was properly reorganized with Major P. S. Raturi, Major Ram Singh and Major Padam Singh in command of first, second and third battalions, respectively. Orders were issued that the Brigade must be prepared to move into action within two months. This brigade, like the other three brigades of No. 1 Division, was armed with medium machine guns, light machine-guns, rifles and hand grenades.

The I.N.A. guerrilla brigades had no artillery or mortar-covering fire support nor did they have any wireless or telephonic communications. Machine guns were deficient of belts and magazines. There were no optical or other instruments and no spare parts for machine guns were available, nor was there any animal or mechanical transport available for carrying these weapons across the country.

Medical arrangements within the brigade were very inadequate. There were only five medical officers to look after the 3,000 men. They had to be split up to form advance and base regimental hospitals. Doctors had particularly no surgical instruments and very little medicine. There was also a great shortage of clothing and boots. Some of the soldiers had to do jungle war-fare training barefooted in the most impenetrable and poisonous insects-infected tropical forests of Malaya.

It was under these circumstances that No. 1 Guerrilla Brigade had to be prepared to proceed to Burma to take part in the operations within a short period of two months. Thanks to the efforts of Col. M. Z. Kiani, Divisional Commander and Lt. Colonel. N. N. Khosla, the Quarter Master Adjutant. The deficiency of arms, equipment and clothing was made up to some extent by withdrawing those items from other brigades.

The Japanese, however, gave no assistance. Netaji worked like one inspired. He collected large sums of money from civilians who contributed voluntarily and bought whatever was available in the market to make up the deficiency of the I.N.A. He always maintained that it was our fight and we must not depend too much on Japanese assistance.

Most intensive military as well as spiritual training of the soldiers was started. In military training, special attention was paid to jungle warfare. In his special talks to the troops, Netaji talked very frankly to them and told them exactly in clear and concise terms the hardships they would have to endure. He advised all those who were not prepared for all these to stay behind, but the soldiers with one voice exclaimed, 'Netaji, give us a chance and we will prove to the whole world that the so called "Indian mercenary soldiers" can fight as gallantly for the liberation of their country as any other soldier in the world.' Netaji also told the soldiers of the Azad Hind Fauj that never at any time were they to accept any orders, racial superiority, any other form of domination by the Japanese. He told them that they were Indians and that they should always feel proud to be Indians, who were as good as any other citizens of in the world.

The Japanese, he said, by helping us to wage war against the British were doing no special favour to us. He explained that as long as the British held India and used it as a base of operations against Japan, the Japanese Empire in East Asia could never be secure and that in their own interests it was imperative for the Japanese to help the I.N.A. drive the British out of India. Furthermore, in a free India, Japan was likely to gain a great deal commercially and economically through a free exchange of goods.

But he always warned his soldiers that where the question of the independence of their country was concerned, they were to trust no one, not even their allies, the Japanese, and that the surest guarantee against betrayal was their own armed might which must be increased hundred-folds as they advanced into India. His instructions on this subject were implicit. He said if ever you find the Japanese trying to establish any type of control ever India, turn round and fight them as vigorously as you will fight the British.

He warned his soldiers that they were an army of starving millions and as such they must do away with all luxuries and prepare to fight and starve like their brothers in Bengal. 'You are the saviours of Indian masses.' He commanded, 'There must be no looting or raping. Anyone seeing an Indian or a Japanese committing this crime must shoot him at sight.' He trained his soldiers to respect Indian women like their own mothers and sisters.

He talked to his men as a man to a man, and whenever an occasion rose, his men stood up and fought like valiant soldiers. He trusted his soldiers and they trusted and loved him and for him thousands laid down their lives without a flinch. As reported already in a speech at Singapore on 4 July, he told all the officers and men of the I.N.A. that one who had decided to fight for India's liberation must know that he was *fakir*. He had no guns, no tanks, no aeroplanes with which to equip his army, nor did he have unlimited sums of money or treasures to keep his soldiers in luxury. He told them:

On the march to Delhi, I can promise you only thirst, hunger, forced marches and in the end death. Give me blood – the price of "Liberty" – and I promise you the independence of your country.

All the soldiers with one voice replied, 'Netaji, if we can free India by shedding our blood, we promise that we will make such sacrifices that our blood shall flow in streams on the plains of Manipur.' In the actual fighting that followed in April and May 1944, they lived up to their promise and shed their blood most generously; 4,000 of them were killed and as they had promised streams of their blood flowed on the plains of Manipur, and in those streams of blood of the soldiers of the Indian National Army, the blood of Hindus, Muslims, Sikhs and Christians intermingled and flowed freely for one cause – a great, free and united India.

It was under such a leader and for such a great cause that the soldiers of the Subhas, Gandhi, Azad and Nehru Brigades together with their other comrades of the Intelligence and Bahadur groups decided to face the formidable forces massed by the British on the Indo-Burma border. Full details of actual fighting that took place occur elsewhere in the book.

ARRIVAL OF NETAJI IN SINGAPORE

The news of the exact time of the arrival of Netaji was kept a close secret. Only officers of the I.N.A. and leading Indian civilians were told about it.

On 2 July 1943, at about 11:00 hours, all the leading Indian civilians, Japanese embassy and military staff and senior officers of the I.N.A. assembled at the civil airport to receive him. A Guard of Honour composed of the selected men of the Indian National Army was also present there. At about midday, a twin-engine Japanese plane arrived and landed at the airport and halted where we were all waiting for him. After a few seconds which seemed like hours, the door of the plane was opened and Netaji stepped out followed by his secretary, Mr Abid Hasan.

Mr Rash Behari Bose, Col. Yamamoto, and Mr Senda of the Japanese Liaison Department were also in the same plane and had accompanied Netaji from Tokyo.

On alighting from the plane, Netaji came straight to us and one by one shook hands and had a few words with every one of us. I was thrilled, it was the first time in my life that I saw him. I had expected so much from him and watched every movement of his with great interest. He was dressed in a light brown civilian suit and was wearing a Gandhi cap. After meeting us he proceeded to inspect the Guard of Honour and then to his official residence.

In the meantime, the news of his arrival had spread like wild fire and every man, woman and child turned out to welcome him. It was a breathtaking display of love and admiration. A sea of humanity – Indians, Chinese, Malayans and Japanese – jostled and got themselves crushed for a look at the great revolutionary.

With his upright and erect carriage, his head held high, proudly unbending, giving his enchanting smile, Netaji captured all hearts. We felt confident that here was a leader who could be trusted to take us along to our goal.

The next day, 3 July 1943, Netaji met the leaders of the A.H.F. and League workers from Hong Kong, Thailand, Burma, Borneo, etc. What impressed us as military officers was the technical knowledge about modern warfare and modern arms that Netaji displayed.

On 4 July, Netaji held an inaugural session of the conference of the delegates of Indians living in East Asia. A meeting was held at the Cathay Building which was completely packed. At this meeting, in a historic speech, Sri Rash Behari Bose handed over the reins of the Indian Independence Movement to Netaji Subhas Chandra Bose.

Netaji accepting the great responsibility that was handed over to him said:

Friends! The time has now come for freedom-loving Indians to act. Action in war-crisis demands, above all, military discipline, as well as unflinching loyalty to the cause. I, therefore, call upon all my countrymen in East Asia to line up in one solid phalanx and prepare for the grim fight that is ahead of us. I am confident that they will do so...

I have publicly declared several times that when I left homeland in 1941, on an important mission, it was in accordance with the will of the vast majority of my countrymen. Since then, despite all the restrictions imposed by the C.I.D., I have remained in constant touch with my countrymen at home...

Patriotic Indians abroad have been working as genuine trustees of the freedom fighters at home. I can assure everybody once again that whatever we have done up till now, or may do in future, has been and will be for the freedom of India, and we shall never do anything that is either against the interests of India or will not be in accordance with the will of our people...

In order to mobilize all our forces effectively, I intend organizing a Provisional Government of Free India. By winning freedom through our own efforts and sacrifice, we shall be acquiring the strength whereby we shall preserve our liberty for all time... I warn you that though we are absolutely sure of our final victory, we can never afford to under estimate the enemy, and we should even be prepared for temporary setbacks. We have a grim fight ahead of us for the enemy is at once powerful, unscrupulous and ruthless. In this final march to freedom, you will have to face hunger, thirst, privation, forced marches and death. Only when you pass this test, will freedom be yours. I am confident that you will do so and thereby bring freedom and prosperity to your enslaved and impoverished land...

On 5 July 1943, the formation of the Azad Hind Fauj was announced to the world. That day Netaji inspected all the Azad Hind Fauj forces on a ceremonial parade held in front of the municipal buildings in Singapore. After the inspection, Netaji addressed the Fauj:

Soldiers of India's Army of Liberation!

Today is the proudest day of my life. Today, it has pleased Providence to give me the unique honour of announcing to the whole world that India's Army of Liberation has come into being. This Army has now been drawn up in military formation on the battlefield of Singapore, which was once the bulwark of the British Empire. This is the Army that will emancipate India from British yoke... Every Indian must feel proud that this Indian Army has been organized entirely under Indian leadership, and that when the historic moment arrives, under Indian leadership it will go into battle... Standing today on the graveyard of the British Empire, even a child is convinced that the almighty British Empire is already a thing of the past...

Comrades! My Soldiers! Let your battle cry be: "To Delhi, to Delhi." How many of us will individually survive this war of freedom, I do not know. But I do know this, that we shall ultimately win and our task will not end until our surviving heroes hold the victory parade on another graveyard of the British Empire the Lal Killa of ancient Delhi...

Throughout my public career, I have always felt that though India is otherwise ripe for independence in every way, she lacks one thing: any army of liberation. George Washington of America could fight and win freedom, because he had his army. Garibaldi could liberate Italy because he had his armed volunteers behind him. It is your privilege and honour to be the first to come forward and organize India's National Army… Soldiers who always remain faithful to their nation, who perform their duty under all circumstances and who are always prepared to sacrifice their lives, are invincible. Engrave these three ideals in the inmost core of your hearts.

Comrades! You are today the custodians of India's hopes and aspirations. So conduct yourselves that your countrymen may bless you and posterity may be proud of you. I assure you that I shall be with you in darkness and in sunshine, in sorrow and in joy, in suffering and in victory. For the present, I can offer you nothing except hunger, thirst, suffering, forced marches and death. It does not matter who among us will live to see India free. It is enough that India shall be free and that we shall give our all to make her free. May God now bless our Army and grant us victory in the coming fight!

On 6 July, another ceremonial parade of the Azad Hind Fauj was held in front of the Municipal Buildings in the honour of Gen. Tojo, the Premier of Japan. After taking a salute of the Fauj, Netaji and Gen. Tojo retired into a room for a brief talk in which Tojo congratulated Netaji on the formation of the Azad Hind Fauj and assured him of the full support of the Japanese nation.

On 9 July 1943, Netaji held a mass meeting of Indian civilians and the Azad Hind Fauj, and told us in a stirring speech which ran as follows:

I would like to tell you quite frankly what made me leave home and homeland, on a journey that was fraught with danger of every kind. I was lodged safely in a British prison when I silently resolved to risk everything in the attempt to escape from the clutches of the British. Having been in prison eleven times, it was much easier and much safer for me to continue there, but I felt that the cause of India's independence demanded a journey abroad, regardless of the risk that it involved.

It took me full three months of prayer and meditation to decide if I had strength enough to face death in fulfilling my duty. Before I could slip out of India, I had to get out of prison and in order to do so, I had to go on hunger strike demanding my release. I knew that neither in India nor in Ireland, had a prisoner succeeded in forcing the British Government to release him. I knew also that Terence Macswiney and Jatin Das had died in the attempt to force the government's hands. But I felt convinced that I had an historic task to fulfil. So I took the plunge, and after seven days of hunger strike, the government unexpectedly got unnerved and set me free, with the intention of taking me back to prison again after a month or two. But before they could seize me again I became a free man...

Friends! You know that I have been actively working in the Independence Movement ever since I left university in 1921. I have been through all the civil disobedience campaigns during the last two decades. In addition to this, I have been repeatedly put in prison without trial, on the suspicion of having been connected with secret revolutionary movements whether non-violent or violent. In the light of this experience I came to the conclusion that all the efforts that we could put forward inside India, would not suffice to expel the British from our country...

To put it briefly, therefore, my object in leaving India was to supplement from outside the struggle going on at home... On the other hand, the supplementary help from outside which the national struggle at home so urgently needs is in reality very small. The help that our countrymen at home needed and still need is a two-fold one; moral and material. Firstly, they have to be morally convinced that their victory is assured. Secondly, they have to be given military help from outside.

The time has come when I can openly tell the whole world including our enemies, as to how it is proposed to bring about national liberation. Indians outside India, particularly Indians in East Asia, are going to organize a fighting force which will be powerful enough to attack the British Army in India. When we do so, a revolution will break out, not among the civil population at home, but also among the Indian Army which is now standing under the British Flag. When the British Government is thus attacked from both sides – from inside India and from outside – it will collapse, and the Indian people will then regain their liberty. According to my plan, therefore, it is not even necessary to bother about the attitude of the Axis Powers towards India. If Indians outside and inside India will do their duty, it is possible for the Indian people to throw the British out of India and liberate 388 millions of their countrymen... Friends, let the slogan of the three million Indians in East Asia be: "Total mobilization for a Total War... out of this total mobilization, I expect at least three lakhs soldiers and three crores of dollars. I want also a unit of brave Indian women to form a death-defying regiment who will wield the sword which the brave Rani of Jhansi wielded in India's First War of Independence in 1857...

Our countrymen at home are now hard-pressed and they are demanding a second front. Give me total mobilization in East Asia and I promise you a second front... a real second front for the Indian struggle.

CHAPTER THIRTEEN

NETAJI TAKES OVER DIRECT COMMAND

On 25 August, Netaji formally assumed direct command of the Indian National Army and issued a special order of the day which ran as follows:

In the interest of the Indian Independence Movement and of the Azad Hind Fauj, I have taken over the direct command of our Army from this day.

This is for me a matter of joy and pride – for an Indian there can be no greater honour than to be the Commander of India's Army of Liberation...

I regard myself as the servant of 38 crores of my countrymen. I am determined to discharge my duties in such a manner that the interests of these 38 crores may be safe and that every single Indian will have reason to put complete trust in me. It is only on the basis of undiluted nationalism and of perfect justice and impartiality that India's Army of Liberation can be build up.

In the coming struggle for the emancipation of our Motherland... the Azad Hind Fauj has a vital role to play. To fulfil this role we must wield ourselves into an army that will have only one goal, Freedom of India, and only one will to do or die in the cause of India's freedom. When we stand, the Azad Hind Fauj has to be like a wall of granite; when we march the Azad Hind Fauj has to be like a steam-roller.

Our task is not an easy one; the war will be long and hard, but I have complete faith in the invincibility of our cause. Thirty-eight crores of human beings, who form about one fifth of the human race, have a right to be free, and they are now prepared to pay the price of freedom. There is consequently no power on earth that can deprive us of our birth-right of liberty any longer...

Comrades! Our work has already begun. With the slogan "Onward to Delhi" on our lips, let us continue to labour and fight till our National Flag flies over the Viceroy's House in New Delhi, and the Azad Hind Fauj holds its Victory Parade inside the ancient Red Fortress of India's Metropolis.

On 2 October 1943, the 75th birth anniversary of Mahatma Gandhi was celebrated all over East Asia. Addressing a mammoth meeting of Indians in the Farrer Park, Netaji said:

I shall devote myself to an estimation of the place of Mahatmaji in the history of India's struggle for independence. The service which Mahatma Gandhi has rendered to India and to the cause of India's freedom is so unique and unparalleled that his name will be written in letters of gold in our national history for all time to come...

When the last World War was over and Indian leaders began to demand the liberty that had been promised to them, they discovered for the first time that they had been betrayed by perfidious Albion. The reply to their demand came in the form of the Rowlatt Act in 1919 which deprived them of what little liberty they still possessed. And when they protested against that Black Act, the Jallianwalla Bagh massacre followed. For all the sacrifices made by the Indian people during the last World War, the two rewards were the Rowlatt Act and the Jallianwalla Bagh massacre...

After the tragic events of 1919, Indians were stunned and paralysed for the time being. All the attempts for achieving liberty had been ruthlessly crushed by the British and their armed forces. Constitutional agitation, boycott of British goods armed revolution, all had alike failed to bring freedom. There was not a ray of hope left and the Indian people were groping in the dark for a new method and a new weapon of struggle. Just at this psychological moment, Gandhiji appeared on the scene with his novel method of Non-cooperation or *Satyagraha* or Civil Disobedience. It appeared as if he had been sent by Providence to show the path of liberty. Immediately and spontaneously the whole nation rallied round his banner. India was saved. Every Indian's face was now lit up with hope end confidence. Ultimate victory was once assured...

For twenty years and more, Mahatma Gandhi has worked for India's salvation, and with him the Indian people have worked.

It is no exaggeration to say that if in 1920 he had not come forward with his new weapon of struggle, India today would perhaps have been still prostrate. His service to the cause of India's freedom are unique and unparalleled. No single man could have achieved more in a single lifetime under similar circumstances. The nearest historical parallel to Mahatma Gandhi is perhaps Mustapha Kamal, who saved Turkey after her defeat in the last World War, and who was then acclaimed by the Turks as the "Gazi".

Since 1920 the Indian people have learnt two things from Mahatma Gandhi, which are the indispensable preconditions for the attainment of independence. They have, first of all, learnt national self-respect and self-confidence as a result of which, revolutionary fervour is now blazing in their hearts. Secondly, they have now got a countrywide organization which reaches the remotest villages of India...

Mahatma Gandhi has firmly planted our feet on the straight road to liberty. He and other leaders are now rotting behind prison bars. The task that Mahatma Gandhi began has therefore to be accomplished by his countrymen at home and abroad ...

I would like to remind you that when Mahatma Gandhi commended his non-cooperation programme to the Indian nation at the annual session of the Congress at Nagpur in December 1920 he said, 'If India had the sword to day, she would have drawn the sword.' And proceeding further Mahatmaji said that since armed revolution was out of the question, the only other alternative before the country was that of non-cooperation or *Satyagraha*. Since then times have changed and it is now possible for the Indian people to draw the sword. We are happy and proud that India's Army of Liberation has already come into existence, and is steadily increasing in numbers...

Establishment of the prov. government of the Azad Hind
The historic conference called by the Indian Independence League was attended by delegates from all over East Asia and assembled at the Cathay Buildings, in Singapore at 10:30 hours on 21 October 1943. Sri Rash Behari Bose read the welcome

address and Col. Chatterji read the secretariat report. Then Netaji came to the rostrum and delivered a thrilling speech for an hour and half. He held a vast audience of thousands spellbound. He explained in Hindustani the significance of the establishment of the Provisional Government of Azad Hind. The speech was translated in Tamil by Sri Chidambaram, our well-known lawyer of Singapore.

Loud and prolonged cheers echoed and re-echoed in the vast hall as Netaji took the oath of allegiance to India. He was so moved that at one stage minutes passed but his voice could not triumph over the emotion which struggled in his throat. The emotion that suddenly swelled up showed how deeply each word of the oath and the sanctity of the occasion had affected him. In a now loud, now soft, but always firm voice, he read out: 'In the name of God, I take this sacred oath that to liberate India and the thirty-eight crores of my countrymen, I, Subhas Chandra Bose, will continue this sacred war of freedom till the last breath of my life.'

And here he paused. It seemed that he would break down. Each one of us had been mentally repeating each word of the oath. We were all leaning forward, physically trying to reach the granite figure of Netaji. The whole audience was merged in him. Pin-drop silence. With lips tightly closed and eyes glued, body tense, we waited for him to overcome the struggle over emotion. Presently he began in a solemn voice, like an organ in a church:

> I shall always remain a servant of India and look after the welfare of thirty-eight crores of Indian brothers and sisters. This shall be for me my highest duty.
>
> Even after winning freedom, I will always be prepared to shed the last drop of my blood for the preservation of India's freedom.

The tension was relieved. We could breathe again freely.

Then each member of the provisional government came up in front of the vast conference and individually took the oath. 'In the name of God, I take this holy oath that to liberate India and thirty-eight crores of my countrymen I will be absolutely faithful to our leader Subhas Chandra Bose and shall be always prepared to sacrifice my life and all I have for the cause.'

Proclamation

Netaji then read out the proclamation which would go down as an outstanding document in the future history of our country:

After their first defeat at the hands of the British in 1857 in Bengal, the Indian people fought an uninterrupted series of hard and bitter battles over a stretch of one hundred years. The history of this period teems with examples of unparalleled heroism and self-sacrifice. And in the pages of that history, the names of Siraj-ud-doula and Mohanlal of Bengal, Haider Ali, Tippu Sultan and Velu Thampi of South India, Appa Sahib Bhonsle and Peshwa Baji Rao of Maharastra, the Begums of Oudh, Sardar Shyam Singh Atariwala of Punjab, and last but not the least Rani Laxmibai of Jhansi, Tantia Topi, Maharaj Kunwar Singh of Dumraon and Nana Sahib are for ever engraved in letters of gold. Unfortunately for us, our forefathers did not at first realize that the British constituted a grave threat to the whole of India, and they did not therefore put up a united front against the enemy. Ultimately, when the Indian people were roused to the reality of the situation they made a concerted move and under the flag of Bahadur Shah in 1857 they fought their last war as freemen.

Forcibly disarmed by the British after 1857 and

subjected to terror and brutality, the Indian people lay prostrate for a while but with the birth of the Indian National Congress in 1885 there came a new awakening. From 1885 till the end of the last World War the Indian people, in their lost liberty tried all possible methods – namely, agitation and propaganda, boycott of British goods, terrorism and sabotage, and finally armed revolution. But all these efforts failed for a time. Ultimately, in 1920, when the Indian people, haunted by a sense of failure, were groping for a new method, Mahatma Gandhi came forward with the new weapon of non-cooperation and civil disobedience.

Thus, the Indian people not only recovered their political consciousness, but became a political entity once again. They could now speak with one voice and strive with one will for one common goal. From 1937 to 1939, through the work of the Congress ministries in eight provinces, they gave proof of their capacity to administer their own affairs. Thus, on the eve of the present World War, the stage was set for the final struggle for India's liberation.

Having goaded Indians to desperation by its hypocrisy and having driven them to starvation and death by plunder and loot, British rule in India has forfeited the goodwill of the Indian people altogether and is now living a precarious existence, It needs but a flame to destroy the last vestige of that unhappy rule. To light that flame is the task of India's Army of Liberation.

Now that the dawn of freedom is at hand, it is the duty of the Indian people to set up a Provisional Government of their own, and launch the last struggle under the banner of that government. But with all the Indian leaders in prison and the people at home totally disarmed, it is not possible to set up a Provisional Government within India or to launch an armed struggle under the aegis of that government. It is therefore the duty of the Indian Independence League in

East Asia supported by all patriotic Indians at home and abroad to undertake this task – the task of setting up a Provisional Government of the Azad Hind (Free India), and of conducting the last fight for Freedom, with the help of the Azad Hind Fauj organized by the League.

The Provisional Government is entitled to, and hereby claims the allegiance of every Indian. It guarantees religious liberty as well as equal rights and equal opportunities to all its citizens, lt declares its firm resolve to pursue the happiness and prosperity of the whole nation and of all its parts, cherishing all the children of the nation equally and transcending all the differences cunningly fostered by an alien government in the past.

In the name of God, in the name of bygone generations who have welded the Indian people into one nation, and in the name of the dead heroes who have bequeathed to us a tradition of heroism and self-sacrifice, we call upon the Indian people to rally round our banner and to strike for India's freedom. We call upon them to launch the final struggle against the British and their allies in India and to prosecute that struggle with valour and perseverance and with full faith in final Victory – until the enemy is expelled from Indian soil and the Indian people are once again a Free Nation.

This was signed on behalf of the Provisional Government of the Azad Hind by: Subhas Chandra Bose – Head of the State, Prime Minister and Minister for War and Foreign Affairs; Capt. Mrs Lakshmi, Women's Organisation; S. A. Ayer, Publicity and Propaganda; Lt. Col. A. C. Chatterji, Finance; Lt. Col. N. S. Bhagat, Lt. Col. J. K. Bhonsle, Lt. Col. Gulzara Singh, Lt. Col. M. Z. Kiani, Lt. Col. A. D. Loganadhan, Lt. Col. Ehsan Qadir, Lt. Col. Shahnawaz representatives of the Armed Forces; A. M. Sahay, Secretary with ministerial rank; Rash Behari Bose, Supreme Advisor; Karim Gani, Debnath Das, D. M. Khan, Y. Yellappa, J. Thivy, Sardar Ishar Singh – Advisors, A. N. Sarkar – Legal Advisor.

Declaration

The Declaration of War was made by the provisional government of the Azad Hind on Britain and the U.S.A. On 25 October 1943, in the presence of a huge mass rally of Indian civilians and the A.H.F. assembled in front of the Municipal Buildings, Singapore, Netaji read out the following declaration:

'The second meeting of the Council of Ministers has unanimously passed the following resolution at five minutes past midnight:

The Provisional Government of Azad Hind declares war on Britain and the U.S.A.'

As soon as this was declared, shouts and slogans rent the skies and volley after volley of frenzied cheering greeted the news. For a full quarter of an hour, the vast audience of over 50,000 was uncontrollable. The crowd broke the cordon in several places, trying to reach the platform. When Netaji asked them to stand where they were and raise their hands to express their approval, a forest of hands went up. Then the soldiers lifted their rifles and placed them on their shoulders giving their consent by a forest of bayonets. It was a scene which I shall never forget. I saw some girls of the Rani of Jhansi faint due to over enthusiasm. They were lying unconscious on the ground and with clinched fists were repeating our battle cry 'Chalo Delhi, Chalo Delhi'.

INDEX